BRIDGE OVER TURBULENT WATERS

DHARMIKA
(P. BURLEIGH)

*To Maitribandhu
With all best wishes
love Dharmila*

BRIDGE OVER TURBULENT WATERS

Copyright © 2022 Dharmachari Dharmika/P.Burleigh

First Edition, August 2023

All rights reserved.

ISBN 9798389155435

Published by *Triratna InHouse Publications*
www.*triratna-inhouse-publications.org*

Cover art & design by Dharmika

All rights reserved. No part of this publication may be reproduced or utilised in any form or by any means, electronic or mechanical, including photocopying, microfilm, recording, or by any information storage and retrieval system, or used in another book, without written permission from the author.

TRIRATNA
INHOUSE
PUBLICATIONS

Contents

Appreciation 4
Introduction: Bridge over Turbulent Waters............................... 7
Chapter One: Childhood (1949/0-15) Water under the Bridge........ 9
Chapter Two: Adolescence (16-21) 30
Chapter Three: Vision and Responsibility (21-22) 56
Chapter Four: Walk-a-bout (22-23) 74
Chapter Five: Magic Bus (23ish) 91
Chapter Six: Pundarika (23-24) 103
Chapter Seven: Old Bailey (24-25) 120
Chapter Eight: India and Australia 2nd time (25-26) 134
Chapter Nine: 'Land of the Long White Cloud' (26-30) 149
Chapter Ten: New Zealand 2nd part (31-36) 171
Chapter Eleven: NZ - Japan - Moscow - UK (age 35) 200
Chapter Twelve: Padmaloka—Aslacton—Vajrakula (37-44) 220
Chapter Thirteen: Guhyaloka (43) 245
Chapter Fourteen: Bridge Over Turbulent Waters (43-73).......... 260
Mediterranean Voyage.. 278

Appendices 295
    The Metta Sutta of Loving Kindness. 296
    Hakuin's Song of Meditation 298
    The Root Verses of the Six Bardos 299
    This Life... 295
    The Heart Sutra 301
    Practical Tips on Stopping Smoking: 302

NB Thank you to: Subhuti, Aloka, Danashura, Saddhaloka Lokabandhu, Niall and others for encouragement. Thanks to my Parents, teachers, readers, and for responses as given overleaf…

Appreciation

Dear Patrick, Re: 'Bridge over Turbulent Waters', I very much enjoyed reading this, particularly the early years--- it did recall London then very clearly, though it wasn't quite the life I was living at the time (more's the pity!) You have an engaging way of talking about yourself as if things just happen to you without any effort on your part--- but perhaps they do. I suppose it's your religious faith, but never do you seem to blame anyone for anything that has happened to you.

> Extract from a hand-written letter.
> Alan Bennett, British actor and writer.

Dear Dharmika, I am glad you are polishing your life-sketch, as I am sure it would be of general interest. You may certainly include my poem 'Meditation' in full. Perhaps you could let me have a copy of the updated draft when it is published. (Later Bhante asked, did all of that really happen? To which I responded, relatively speaking yes! And that if anything, I had played it down, and tried to keep it concise and true.)

> Sangharakshita, extracted from a post-card.

'Knowing you a little I expected to be to be amused, which I was. As an ex school-teacher childhood intrigues me, yours was an unusual one. Measured against my own life, it seemed at times appalling and at others full of freedom and adventure. The spell in Japan (especially Eeihiji) was very evocative and the trial at the Old Bailey produced a whole plethora of responses from fear, amusement, anxiety to feelings of absurdity. The illustrations set the atmosphere of the book, as a real journal, not a work of fiction.

> Nandaketu

I am very glad to have your book, which is helpful and inspiring, incredible that you survived, and the nature and quality of your later life. Many Thanks for everything.

> Caroline, Ken and Edward

I have enjoyed very much reading your 'Bridge over Turbulent Waters', Quite gripping and informative - I am very glad you have done it. Very nicely written too - It reminded me a little of 'Denton Welch' – ta very much

Aloka British Artist, Sculptor and Writer.

An amazing life! Thank you, inspiring and encouraging.

Manujsiddha

Thank you for writing 'Bridge over Turbulent Waters', which I have thoroughly enjoyed reading, many of the Centres: Christchurch NZ (71-74); Pundarika; Brighton, LBC and Auckland (5 years) are familiar to me. I found your early years a great read, and rejoice in your merits and steadiness of purpose, having come from such a disrupted early life.

Anjali, Triratnaloka

Thank you for your moving account 'Bridge over Turbulent Waters', I am full of admiration and respect for how you have dealt with life.

Vajragupta (f)

I've been reading Dharmika's autobiography which is a real eye opener, I found it inspiring and delightful - you made a glorious Saturday out of much which was obviously painful and difficult.

Sarvananda, British Writer and actor.

Thank you for showing me your autobiography, which I found gripping, the first part is particularly good, very picturesque, I certainly feel I know and understand you a lot better.

Subhuti

I read your book in Spain at Guhyaloka, I enjoyed reading it, very interesting, an excellent chuckle, it ought to be filmed, you in the full lotus posture at the Old Bailey would make a great scene. Anyhow well done!

'Vic', a photographer

INTRODUCTION
Bridge over Turbulent Waters

This is a connected account of a journey from age 0-43ish, plus a postscript and some appendices. It tries to be a concise and objective account of a sojourn, and is based on memory insofar as that is ever possible. It is a simplistic series of recollections, trying to make sense of and to share with others how life conditions us, and a reminder to be wary of various pitfalls, to somehow reduce self-clinging, and come back to one's own true nature, opening to the light of gradual or sudden awakening, as may be symbolised by the unfolding of a White Lotus…

My father Lionel Burleigh was an artist and entrepreneur whose various projects, as well as earning him a place in the Routledge & Kegan "Book of Heroic Failures", also caused a play to be written about him after his death, in which he was portrayed by the film actor Rex Harrison. While my well-meaning but domestically incompetent parents never married, they did have nine kids, the fifth, myself, born in 1949. At age 13 I found myself homeless, without formal education, and rootless on the London streets.

After various exploits which ranged from the sordid to the slightly surreal, as well as encounters with a variety of people, eventually I succeeded in reaching adulthood, having luckily survived various encounters with drugs which were never particularly sought after, though they helped in making changes and letting go of the past. Eventually I came to a sort of turning point. Thus at twenty-one I became vegetarian, stopped smoking, took up yoga and meditation and started a quest for meaning. This period up to age twenty-five is interspersed with various encounters and travels around the world and overland across Asia including Iran around the time of the Shah's demise and almost my own, after becoming unwell and near to death in Kabul.

Having barely survived, eventually I am back in London squatting, and working on the T.V. series Special Branch, before finding myself in real life inadvertently appearing at the Old Bailey on my twenty-fifth birthday, for something which I hadn't done, after having being wrongly identified by a presumably well-meaning citizen, and eventually being unanimously acquitted. Thereafter, recoiling from the combined effects of the case just passed, and not having anywhere proper to stay. I go to India, Australia and New Zealand, where I spend ten years before returning to the U.K. via a spell in Japan.

Another theme which recurs is brief accounts of interactions with varied cults and sects, from the 'The Children of God' who tried to convert me while on a train in India to the Moonies who (with some ulterior motives) offered me shelter during my first few months in NZ. Then, in due course, I became more closely involved with the F.W.B.O. (The Friends of the Western Buddhist Order), a Buddhist movement which I had first encountered at Pundarika in Archway London. Part of the story outlines some of my experiences with the F.W.B.O. and leads up to a four (though in my case five) month retreat in the Spanish Mountains, and then concludes with my arriving back in the U.K. Having now been ordained and given a Buddhist name Dharmika, which means something like one who lives or stands by the truth, which hopefully is a quality which to some degree manifests in this manuscript, provisionally entitled 'Bridge Over Turbulent Waters'.

Finally, there is a concluding chapter and epilogue which briefly cover my endeavours from 1993 to 2023, plus added appendices.

CHAPTER ONE
Childhood (1949/0-15) Water under the Bridge

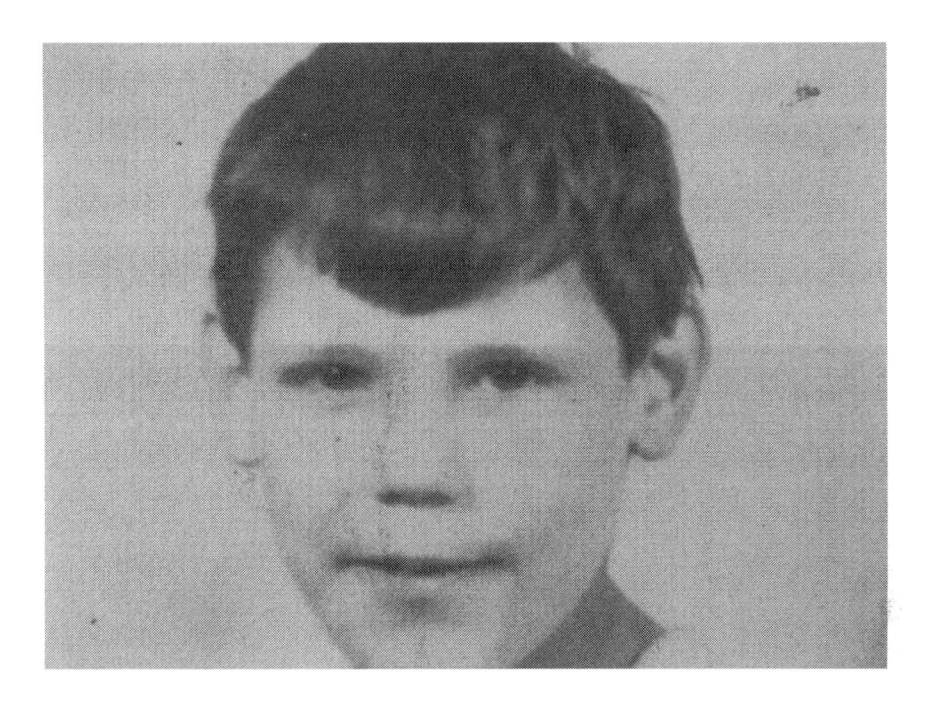

Making a start

In cosmic terms, my forty years of living is insignificant, yet that insignificance has contained much heart-beating; heart-feeling, and heart-dreams... As well as endless empty forms: Name? Age? Ethnicity? Gender? Education? Marital Status? Economic Status? Inasmuch as we are told "Life begins at forty", then my life may be just beginning; even so, I'm going to write mainly about my first four decades, which like an illusion have arisen and then faded away, like sweet sixteen, no sooner has it come, than like a dream it is going and gone.

    I was born early on an August morning in 1949. My first work experience: for which I don't remember receiving the promised ten shillings, was helping to make a commercial (for Bistro gravy) which was filmed at Pinewood Studios. I was aged thirteen and in between filming was taken for walks by a tutor to study trees and leaves. These few school days were my best, as I had a teacher's attention, and I found the days actually enjoyable. At that time I was living with my parents in a house off Tottenham Court Road, in London's West End.

My next job was in the field of education, which is to say I was delivering leaflets for Encyclopaedia Britannica. I was now fourteen and living with Jim B, a friend of my parents, in a flat near Hampstead Heath. He was a bass player in the Johnny Dankworth (jazz) Band, as well as having occasional work with the B.B.C. His interest in me was not just platonic. But being one of nine children I wasn't used to getting attention and appreciated his friendliness, as well as being taken out to see movies like "Lawrence of Arabia" and "Lord of the Flies". Eventually he decided to go off travelling, and I had to quickly find myself a live-in job which would provide me with a home. Behind Harrods in Knightsbridge was the small and rather snooty but charming Basil St Hotel, a place of tradition and good taste, catering for upper-middle-class, highbrow, conservative types. I was now fifteen and it was here that I now worked as a pageboy, dressed in a blue-twill uniform and wearing white gloves on special occasions such as society wedding receptions, when I would swan about offering cigarettes from a silver tray to elegant guests; leftover cigarettes were used to feed my own nicotine addiction established from about age thirteen.

The hours were split duties spread over twelve hours, the job had its 'ins and outs' on messages, and its 'ups and downs' driving the old-fashioned lift. There was some skill involved in getting the lift to stop evenly; then one would call out "mezzanine floor", or "going up" etc. Often mink-coated ladies young and old, dripping with diamonds would brush their assortment of firm and not so firm bosoms past my sleepy eyes and I would be revived or enchanted by expensive French perfumes that wafted into my face. I shared a small room in the service area of the hotel with another boy, whom I most remember for the way on summer nights warm enough that one didn't need any blankets; I would be woken by rhythmic movements coming from under his white sheet. I was quite able to empathise with his predicament, though personally I tended to be a bit shy about such matters and would wait till he was out of the room on a different shift. On one afternoon when I might have been caught out, but wasn't, I lay afterwards on my bed thinking about my childhood and how I had come to be a page boy, or what at times seemed to me 'a modern-day slave'.

BRIDGE OVER TURBULENT WATERS

My Parents

My father was an eccentric, nomadic, bohemian artist. Although quite colourful, he was also capable and had some achievements to his name. His slightly rebellious streak may in part be due to having had a rough not to say harrowing time, at the prep school for Harrow. Then after further education elsewhere he spent about a year as a medical student before he changed course. Later, after art school, he became a theatrical designer, and with his first partner designed all the costumes for a film called Evergreen which starred the old flame Jessie Mathews. He was unconventional for the time and my parents didn't marry in the formal sense, though they did stay together. He mostly earned his living through painting pictures and murals, though he tried to supplement his income with other projects, for one of these British Rail leased him a train, the interior of which he redesigned, and this ran between London and Brighton as the Regency Bell. His other exploits included starting his own newspaper the Commonwealth Sentinel, the money for which was put up by Lord Thompson of Fleet Street. Although my progenitor won't be found in the book of 'Who's Who', he did make it into the 1979 Routledge & Kegan Paul publication 'The book of heroic failures'. After his death a play was written about him called 'The Lionel Touch', in which he was portrayed by the actor Rex Harrison at the West End Lyric Theatre. Although it was not a particularly accurate play, the title alludes to him (Lionel Burleigh), in those days being well known around Fleet St and Chelsea for his ability to extract money from you, which he would pay back when his next job came up. His friends on Fleet Street would sometimes require him in return to provide fodder for a story. One example that springs to mind is an occasion when, for a fee from a national newspaper, my mother stuck my father's work up at the Tate Gallery, to draw attention to his latest exhibition.

That my birth began at Waverly Station in Edinburgh is not surprising to me as my parents were often on the move. At the time we were homeless, this I've gleaned from my father's manuscript "Nine kids on a paint brush". I was the fifth child, eventually there were three boys and a girl both above and below me.

My mother was a little more down to earth than my father; her grandfather was a pioneer in tropical medicine, and her maiden name 'Sydenham' is to be found recorded on the parapet of a London hospital. In the war she was in the W.R.A.F. and later among other things she worked as a dancer. On one occasion she was obliged to rescue Toby one of my brothers from a fire, which she accomplished, despite suffering burns. In recent times she worked as a reader/companion to Winston Churchill's widow, the late Clementine Churchill, who, judging from the inscribed book my mother received, seems to have very much appreciated her companionship. As a child I recall that despite often being homeless there was a brightness in my father and a positive outlook from my mother, we were occasionally a close-knit family although paradoxically not often together, mainly because of financial difficulties. My first recollection of this sort of thing starts at about age five.

***

St Christophers and Abbotsbury

We were living in a bed-sitter in Kensington when I discovered that as they were behind and unable to keep up with rent payments, to my dismay my parents were going to Jersey in the Channel Islands to live on a boat, and I was going to be left behind. So it was that I found myself first in an emotionally desolate and disturbing place 'Everil Court', closed down after a few months due to neglectful management and inappropriate staff misbehaviour, and then moved to the brighter St Christopher's for about a year, often feeling abandoned and quite confused as to what had happened. After about six months I began to forget my parents and become happier and more adjusted to the new situation. I was also starting to receive attention from a lady, who was considering fostering or adopting me, which included occasional excursions in her wooden framed Morris 1000 and a bond of friendship was developing. Then one day my now somewhat forgotten mum, suddenly reappeared on the scene and retrieved me like a piece of left luggage from a deposit office and took me to live in a small village called Abbotsbury which is near Weymouth in Dorset. I was not very keen to go and had to be coaxed with promises of a lovely drive through the New Forest, which I was told had lots of wild ponies and horses. Although my childhood was punctuated with countless broken homes, and only short spells at about fifteen schools, there were periods when we had relative stability, such as the eighteen months in Abbotsbury, where I enjoyed many hot sunny days romping about in leafy shaded country lanes, or just lazing in the garden under the myrtle bush, the warm air rich with the scents of many flowers and teeming with butterflies, dragonflies, and big buzzing bumble bees.

We were considered by the villagers to be a rather odd family, as my father could often be seen hitchhiking his way to some town or another to try and find an establishment in need of a mural on its walls. Meanwhile, we kids would all be half-starved and having exhausted whatever credit we might get, would eventually be drawn by hunger to go to various shops and ask for cardboard boxes, so that while the shopkeeper was distracted we could shove Swiss rolls up our jumpers. (I went back there recently and had a few laughs with Mrs Lexington now in her eighties who kept a shop on the corner, who by her conversation showed she could still remember us, and apparently with affection.) Though I quite liked Abbotsbury School, there were some aspects which didn't endear me to the place, such as being caned on frozen hands for arriving late, having struggled through the snow without any breakfast.

Again, there was a time when Mrs Mitchell my class teacher inspected me, to check both my testicles had descended, I was about five or six and showed a little interest in what she was doing, which caused her to explode with a display of anger at me, and of course sent me into paroxysms of guilt. She also succeeded in teaching me basic arithmetic along with reading and writing. One of the things I did like about the school week was the trip to Weymouth on Friday afternoons in a minibus, for elocution lessons, to try and cure a stutter or stammering which I had some of my time in Abbotsbury, in which I followed most statements with bbbbb...

My bluest period in Abbotsbury was during a few days when my parents were away trying to raise some money. For unknown reasons, with the help of my sister Mercedes, who would have been about ten and myself six or seven, I was partially painted with Prussian Blue oil paint, in various parts, then taken for an excursion through the village and into the mill pond, pretending to be a native. Well, the natives were not amused and nor was I when I got home, as the sun had thoroughly dried the paint which was now quite uncomfortable, and much to the surprise of my sister, we found that no matter how much we scrubbed with water the paint wouldn't budge. So I had to stay blue, till my parents got back after a few days and got to work on me with a bottle of turpentine. At about this point in my daydreaming, there was a bang on the door, it was Ian the other page boy trying to get in as he had forgotten his gloves. I let him in and he said with a small smile on his face that he knew what I had been doing. I blushed and neither confirmed nor denied. After he had gone I continued working out what had happened in my childhood.

It was in Abbotsbury that I fractured my wrist, and then wet the bed saturating the plaster cast, so that everywhere I went people kept saying pooh. Eventually we had to leave Abbotsbury, and so I said goodbye to Seaway Lane (reputed to have been a smugglers route), St Catherine's Chapel on the hill above us, Chesil Bank beach with its strong currents and of course the nearby swannery where I earned pennies swinging open the gate for tourists in the summer.

From Abbotsbury we made the long and exciting journey to London by train, where we were met at Victoria Station by press friends of my father. In those days anything unconventional seemed to be used for a story, and of course he got paid as well. The piece they ran was about an itinerant artist with a troupe of half-clothed kids, unwed mother and dog seeking somewhere to stay, complete with photo.

***

St Vincent's to St Patrick's

The fun didn't last and soon I found myself in a Morris Minor, being driven by a priest, en route to a children's home run by a convent in Mill-Hill on the outskirts of London. St Vincent's to me, aged seven or eight, was a formidable place, highly polished with long sterile corridors. To my eyes the nuns seemed like strange stern creatures, with those big white floppy headdresses (as in the film Mary Poppins). It was perhaps unfortunate and not representative; that on my very first day I found myself obliged to watch a boy about my age being forcibly made to eat the food he had just regurgitated. I don't remember having any trouble myself as long as I kept quiet and behaved. In contrast to this, I recall a Nun giving out sweets on a saint's day, which regardless of whether sinner or saint I was surprised to receive, and looked back wondering; as I gazed into my benefactor's eyes, why she didn't really seem to see me? I think she and others were perhaps as much in need of affection as I.

After about six months my parents got the lease on a house at 34 Windmill St, off Tottenham Court Road in London's West End. The couple of years I spent at Windmill Street aged about ten often seemed to be fraught with financial difficulties, though there were occasional good times when we had plenty of everything and my mother would look after us very well. My father's studio was often the brightest part of the house, with the floor and furniture polished and perhaps a big log fire, and my father painting happily as long as he had plenty of cigarettes. Often I ran chores to fetch these, or to Windsor and Newton's to buy oil paints or a sable brush which I wasn't to chew.

I mostly enjoyed my time at St Patricks primary school in Soho, with its rooftop playground, and clearly recall wending my way to school through various backstreets and alleys, before having to cross over Oxford Street and then I was nearly there. The long afternoons after school and during holidays were mostly spent trying to fill in time, much of which was spent in the Science and other museums around Exhibition Rd. When one was hungry there were various options which included going to the back of the Middlesex Hospital and tapping on the windows and asking the nurses for free ice cream, which they were generally quite generous with, or there was rummaging through what had been chucked out by various establishments, also there was the Tattler (Tottenham Court Road), and (Victoria Station) Cartoon/News Theatres, where once admission had been gained, I would be able to lose myself in Disney Land. Occasionally strange men would edge up to my seat and make offers of one sort or another, such as displaying three-pence and simultaneously resting their hand on my knee. Once, this happened from both sides of me simultaneously, so I took both three-pence's and then climbed over the seat in front and left.

***

Windmill Street

At other times my mother would send us to Hampstead Heath when she could afford the 24 bus-route fare, with a bit over for ice lollies. And enjoyed many hot summer days there, and also swimming in the Serpentine in Hyde Park.

My less happy times at Windmill Street included one winter when it was very cold, which was not helped by the electricity being cut off and my parents being on edge, as they hadn't any cigarettes, and of course we were all hungry. There had been an argument about something and I was sent to bed early, the room was dark, my bed cold, and being quite upset I climbed out of my bedroom window, which was at the top of the house and sat with legs dangling over the edge looking down at the pavement with tears streaming. I was intoxicated with disturbed emotions and feeling hopeless. Just as I was slipping my bottom over the edge, in a flash out of the dark of the night; some force outside of me, like lightning penetrating into my head, caused me to reconsider, and instantly I reflected that if I wanted sympathy, then I also wanted to be there to receive it. So with tears still flowing and heart throbbing I came back in and went to bed.

Another no less perplexing time which occurred at some point at Windmill Street, was when I was half asleep in my somewhat derelict room at top of the house, inexplicably at some point, I found myself slightly struggling and having something put over my face, the next morning I felt a bit 'drugged', then later when I went to use the loo, I felt shock and confused when I found my penis was all puffy and abnormal, in retrospect it was clear I had been taken advantage of in some way. Of course I didn't dare say anything to anyone.

***

Things got a bit better; I was now about ten and starting to feel I belonged in the area. My parents had taken to sending us to Sunday school with the local Catholic Church in Ogle St, and through them I had started attending the cubs. So I was starting to make friends and enjoy life a bit, then one day I came home from school and there was the inevitable note on the door saying we had been evicted and I was to go around to a flat in Percy Street, the dwelling place of the Waters family. Somewhat disorientated and disconsolate at this sudden disruption, and loss of my few possessions, I eventually found my way to the home of the Waters. As it turned out the few weeks spent living with them were a lot of fun and educational. I had my first go at playing with a typewriter, which was really fascinating, and also had the use of a pair of wooden stilts, which I practised on up and down Goodge St, a busy part of Central London. While staying there I appreciated the attention and kindness I received from Bobby Waters, I also recall being quite impressed, that when she got stopped by a policeman, she made a point of taking both the name and the number of the poor young man, who seemed rather taken back.

Bridge over Turbulent Waters

* * *

St Josephs, Orpington, Sevenoaks

Of course the happy interlude at Percy St with the Waters family couldn't be expected to last, as they could only afford to keep me for a short period, and so I eventually found myself transferred to an orphanage in Kent, which also looked after homeless children. St Josephs marked my transition from primary to secondary school. Having just turned eleven I felt quite alone in a strange world. The place was run by Benedictine monks in black robes, though it was the boys who tended to be the most intimidating. Their antics at various times over two years included stealing all my clothes and leaving me naked and stranded about half a mile from the school buildings, knocking me out and leaving me to come around in my own good time, and elsewhere pushing me into the deep end of a swimming pool, fortunately, another boy had secretly warned me to hold my breath and somehow hop along on the bottom towards the shallow end. Of course I tried to stand my ground. As when one boy beat me and bashed my head for about twenty minutes until he realised that even if he killed me, he wasn't going to get the number of my combination lock.

Apart from these various assaults, looking back as well as feeling abandoned, what I found just as disconcerting was the general banality of the place. Though there were some good times like cleaning and polishing the dormitory floors, which involved lots of running and sliding with cloths wrapped round one's shoes on Saturday mornings, when we were allowed to hear the radio, and I would feel moved by various popular songs which would twang my heartstrings and make me think of going home. Home was a sort of metaphor, for a place where your heart can be open, and you can feel protected, and have some sort of individual identity. Though my experience was that all homes are insecure and may fade away at any moment, even so at night in my bed I used to yearn for home, which sort of signified family or even happiness or belonging and that sort of thing, and particularly when trains could be heard going by in the distance I used to feel really homesick.

It was at St Joseph's that I caught pneumonia and shivered convulsively for three days, standing by radiators to keep warm and trying to defend myself from the rough and tumble until I was repeatedly throwing up and couldn't be overlooked, then I was dispatched to the infirmary where the matron, an old battle-axe was pretty hard going, though the women doctor who eventually came was far more sympathetic. While in the infirmary it was noted that somehow I had lost half a tooth and an abscess was forming. On rare occasions groups of boys would be taken out for excursions, on one of these occasions a group of us had been driven in a mini-bus by Brother Daniel to see the Xmas lights in Oxford Street, which for me was painfully nostalgic as we passed very close to where I had lived, had we been allowed out of the van I would have retreated.

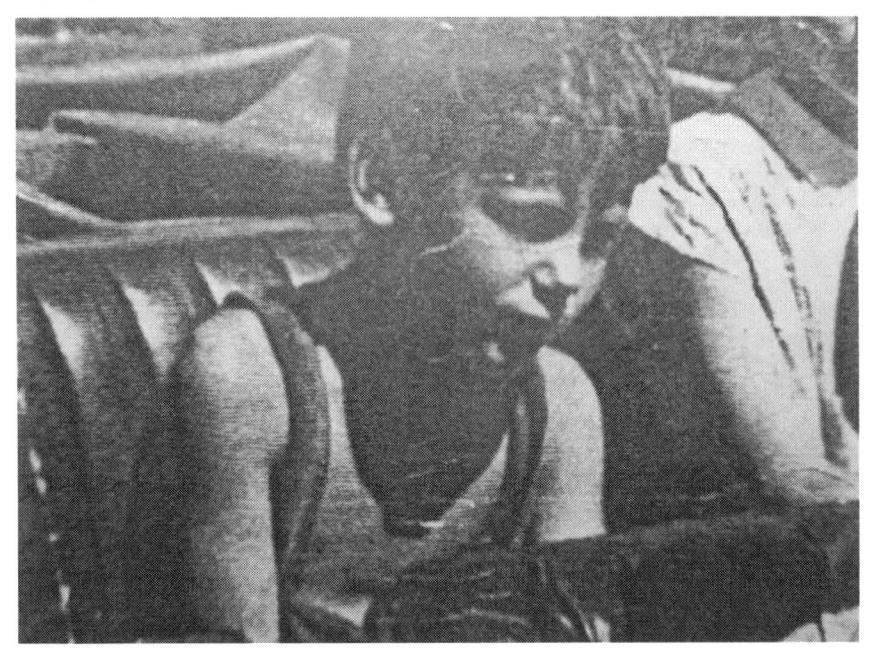

The monks were a funny bunch; they seemed to fall into three types the young and very strict, the old and cragged with fag or pipe hanging from their mouths, and the ever so big variety. It was the latter who charmed and delighted me on one memorable occasion. I had run away, I don't know where I thought I was going, but I had left the school at lunchtime and tried to take a train to London. This fell through as an astute ticket collector realised I hadn't a ticket and phoned the school. So with trepidation I made my way back, hoping to re-mingle with the lunchtime play, but they had all gone in and I was taken off by a fellow who was probably the biggest monk in the school and he seemed all the bigger for my being quite small. He took me through a weave of corridors unknown to me and started to unlock a door. I had only been shown a cane once at the school but now felt certain I was going to be thrashed, so I was very surprised and puzzled when he found me a cream bun in the storeroom and gave it to me saying I must be hungry and then sent me back to my class.

Generally the school didn't seem concerned with educating us, so much as keeping us occupied. So when we were not in classes, most of the time was either football, snooker or a mind-numbing selection of low-quality television which seemed to be endless repeats of heart-deadening programmes like wrestling and boxing or cowboys killing each other. I've also never forgotten the bathing arrangements at St Joseph's, in which about twenty boys at a time would be herded through the shower area, all naked and leaping about like maniacs trying to avoid the countless alive or squashed large black cockroaches that seemed to infest the changing areas. On one occasion a parent came to visit me, this consisted of tea and an inedible sandwich in some seedy cafe, and my begging to come back and live in their bed-sitter, followed by a few tears on my part and explanations of why that wouldn't be possible, and eventually the poignant walk back to the school. Although in due course a day did come when low and behold, I was going to be taken home which apparently was now in Reading. The battle-axe matron became friendly and told me to tell my parents that my broken tooth and abscess needed early attention, 'no chance' I thought.

* * *

The Goya affair & Scarborough

Going home usually meant a few weeks of everything being alright, and then money would run low and problems start to arise, this time it was a bit different. A friend of my father's, who had a large hairdressing saloon, was letting my father use the upper floors at a giveaway price. I enjoyed my first few weeks in Reading which I remember for its large biscuit factory and the river where I used to go and sit. I also recall being very hungry at times, and having to go to Woolworths to swipe peanuts, or again searching through the hair salon downstairs for any leftover sandwiches. We had been living in Reading for about four months and things were looking up. My father was preparing for and about to have an exhibition; to me, as a twelve-year-old, everything seemed relatively stable and happy, till they suddenly all went haywire.

One day lots of reporters started turning up, then on the second day lots of police, and by the third day my new home was fast crumbling beneath my feet. Apparently what had happened was a picture by Goya of the Duke of Wellington had been stolen, I think from the Tate gallery, and for some obscure reason some of the press were convinced my father or mother were involved in the picture's disappearance, as some sort of publicity stunt to draw attention to my father's forthcoming exhibition. In fact he didn't do things like that, but even so the police were obliged to follow up every possible avenue. Unfortunately this was the sort of publicity that our benevolent landlord did not want and we were given a few weeks' notice to leave. Eventually after about six months the newspaper most responsible for the mishap, coughed up about £500 and a written apology. But that didn't help much, and in the meantime we were homeless, which; inevitably meant my siblings and myself were again scattered all over the place.

It was now a couple of weeks before Christmas and we were staying on a floor somewhere in London, when my father explained he was going to dispatch me and my older sister to go and stay with our grandmother in Scarborough, though due to lack of finances Mercedes didn't come. I was a bit unhappy at Kings Cross Station as I was only told at the last moment that I was going on my own. I was now eleven or twelve and had never met any grandparents, and furthermore, she didn't know I was coming. To cheer me up my father brought me some chocolate and crisps and asked a ticket collector to keep an eye on me. I was glad he wasn't watching when I had an embarrassing disagreement with the chocolate and crisps, which had tasted fine at start.

After an uneventful journey apart from being sick, I arrived in Scarborough and somehow found my way to the address and rang the bell. Whoever opened the door I don't recall, but I gave them a note introducing me as their grandson and asking them to look after me over Xmas. My grandfather was quite chirpy, though it was my grandmother who seemed to rule the roost. After the initial surprise she inspected inside my pants, and then made me at home, and I was well looked after over Xmas. Though she soon informed me that I wouldn't be able to stay, and a few days after Xmas found myself en route back to London. The journey provoked some anxiety in me as I felt sort of guilty or ashamed to let anyone find out that I didn't belong, that somehow I didn't have any place in the 'puzzle' called society which surrounded me. I had been told by my grandmother to wait on the platform at Kings Cross when the train got in, and that the police would meet me. But in the event I missed them or they weren't there and I shortly found myself in the bustle of London, homeless and without any connections. To the eleven- or twelve-year-old that I was, the pound or two which I had been given seemed to represent quite a few bars of chocolate, and part of me felt briefly for a moment, excited at having the freedom to be able to go where I liked! Though this quickly wore thin, and after an hour or two of confused wandering, I made my way to a familiar cartoon/news theatre where I was able to break down and cry without being seen.

By coincidence, the friend of my parents who played the bass in the Johnny Dankworth Band who I referred to earlier was there, and this was when I had first encountered him. He was surprised to come across me, and offered to put me up, till he ran into my parents. That night in bed I felt what seemed like a small strange creature walking up my leg, but of course it turned out to be his hand. Although in conventional terms he may have abused me, his fiddling about didn't seem that drastic, and in any case I needed somewhere to stay and I was quite well looked after with cigarettes and food, though I did feel embarrassed and said nothing on the following mornings. Eventually, after a few weeks he traced, and then reconnected me with my parents, who were now living in a small, dark seedy bed-sit in Soho, and so I found myself again living at home.

* * *

Soho, Anne and Preparatory School

Peter Street in Soho was the location of my new home, the bed-sit was very small, the rain came through the roof, and we only had a single bed between us, and when late at night my parents made love, I would find myself involuntarily 'evicted' from the bed and would feel rather small! Shortly I started up at St Martins in the Fields school, which was adjacent to the church in Trafalgar Square. As with most of my schools, the teachers and children had little understanding or empathy with 'rootless' kids, and would assume your studies were not up to scratch because you were stupid or lazy, or that you just didn't want to learn.

To get to school usually meant a mixture of walking and running through the London traffic, though I would sometimes be late for the morning assembly. In the evening generally there would be no hurry to get home, so I would get exhausted playing football in our playground behind St Martins church, and then wend my way back home via Berwick Street Market. As I came closer to home and walked up Peter Street friendly women would sometimes make remarks like "you're a bit young aren't you dear?" I was now about twelve. Sometimes on getting back I would feel abject loneliness, perhaps as there were no books or radio, or anything to eat or do, and having no idea when my parents would be back. Sometimes though pre-pubescent I would try unsuccessfully to masturbate, then cooling off at sink tap, I would feel guilty and worthless.

My few months in London's red-light-district came to an abrupt halt after we got evicted one day. From there I went to live with a woman who my father had just finished an affair with. She was a voluptuous person, with red lips and big breasts. At about this time I had my thirteenth birthday and was becoming quite self-conscious and was very embarrassed at being obliged to bathe naked in the same room as her. Perhaps partly due to her Scandinavian roots, she seemed to be amused by this. Anyhow I mostly enjoyed the few weeks spent with Anne Swede, both for her large personality and her generous nature. Apart from having just finished an affair with my father, she was also having an affair with a gentleman called Tom Horsefall who was the headmaster of a prep school in Wandsworth. And one day she announced she had arranged for me to go to prep school and that I would lodge with the headmaster, as he had a spare room in his house next to the school.

Being the sort of creature that I was, I deduced that having just reached thirteen I was too old to go to prep school, but it seemed I had no choice. To prepare me for the event, my kind benefactor took me to Harrods, she knew that I could play chess quite well, which my father had taught me and said she would buy me a pocket chess-set and a set of clothes at the same time.

Thus I duly arrived at the school with Ann, and she introduced me to the headmaster Tom Horsefall, known to the boys as donkey-drop. He was quite a charming old fellow, and a bit eccentric, during the war he had been in India and couldn't bear to see crossed swords, even to the extent that when we were eating he wouldn't want knives on the table to overlap. Being the only boarder/lodger we would eat alone, with the food being served from silver platters by a servant woman who was rather timid and I recall had one or two fingers missing. On about the first night he asked me what I thought of Ann's bosoms, which just made me blush. On other occasions such as when the Canon came to tea, the conversation would be above my head and more sober.

As for the school itself, hardly surprisingly, my schoolwork was not up to date, and I didn't really fit in. Apart from learning the name of Julius Caesar the main thing I remember was being held down by a group of boys while a classmate stuck his hand into my pants and squeezed me, which quite shattered my image of what prep-school was all about. I also recall I once used inappropriate language and the headmaster was obliged to take me into his study. Where he informed me the boys would be listening at the door, and then proceeded to give two of the best to a piece of furniture. My few months at prep school finished when my parents started to rent two large rooms at the Langorf Hotel, which is Frognal spelt backwards and is situated just off the Finchley Road in North London. I was sorry to later hear that Tom Horsefall died in a traffic accident, after stepping out to get some cigarettes.

My parents were busy with some new project I can't remember which, but during this period I was charged with looking after and feeding my younger brothers and sisters, whom I hadn't seen for quite a while. It was during this period that I learned how not to cook spaghetti, eventually I stuck to simple things like baked beans. Soon it became apparent the venture wasn't making enough money to keep up with the rent and as the bills snowballed my parents kept a lower and lower profile, till one day they just didn't come back. As a result of this, one evening the proprietors phoned the police and informed them they were about to turn five kids out, I don't know where the other four were at that time. So the police told them to hang on and sent a rather foreboding black van to pick us up. The police were friendly and seemed not to know what to do with us, as it was getting late, but eventually we were dispatched to various homes where they could find vacancies. In my own case I woke up the next day to find I was in a remand home, and my bed was surrounded by boys wanting to know what I had done. I was only wearing a pyjama top which was all the night gatekeeper could find, so I didn't feel like getting out of bed, and instead just lay there protesting my innocence.

* * *

Remand school, Shelly's old home and Sussex

When the people in charge finally realised I hadn't actually done anything, or at least I hadn't been caught in any such act, they decided I should be segregated from the other kids, and stuck me in a small room. My parents had found out what had happened and been in contact, apparently they had raised some money and come back to the hotel to find us all gone. Eventually I was picked up from the remand home which was somewhere on the outskirts of London and after a few days of staying on peoples' floors, found myself in a minivan being driven by a fellow called Sandy to Sussex where my parents had found a new home. Finally we arrived at Highly Manor, a beautiful old English mansion, situated near Balcombe in eight acres of peaceful Sussex country, about eight miles from East Grinstead, apparently with a history that could be traced back to 1326, and whose past owners include Queen Elizabeth 1st and Percy Bysshe Shelley's family. The present owner was Miss Violet Gordon, she and my father had been friends for some time, and she had invited us to come and live there.

Miss Gordon was about seventy; but still a strong and hardworking lady, and from my observations of her, she seemed to live on a diet of Fru-Grain and Guinness. In her earlier years she had been a nurse, and at some stage she had converted Highly Manor from an old people's home into a hotel, which though hardly ever full seemed to do a brisk business in Sunday afternoon teas.

From time to time there would be interesting guests, like the pilot working from Gatwick, who made a point of bringing me back some oranges with their leaves still on, and who at some stage showed me over an airliner's flight deck. There was George the funny old fellow who wasn't a guest but worked in the garden, who for some reason was a ward of court in Miss Gordon's custody. As a youngster I was soon familiar with the 'secret' underground tunnels which ran below the property and of course was also familiar with the grounds overhead, which in the summer would be covered in vivid rhododendrons.

Miss Gordon took an interest in me and after it had been arranged for me to start attending a school in Cuckfield, she drove me into Hayward's Heath and brought me the necessary uniform and bits and pieces. Unfortunately she couldn't buy me the level of schoolwork and achievement; that would be necessary if I was really to reintegrate into school life!

For me Cuckfield Secondary Modern School was like I might imagine a large sausage factory, rather cold and impersonal. Where the teachers mostly only found time to point out that my work wasn't good enough, but rarely had time to consider why that might be. With the exception of the art teacher who did actually talk to me once in the grounds, which both surprised me and made me feel quite good, she also showed an interest when I mentioned my father was a painter. I appreciate if I had a more stable background, then I may have experienced school differently. Be that as it may, the fact remains that for me the panoramic bus journey from Balcombe village a mile or so from Highly Manor to Cuckfield School was a strange affair, inasmuch as I found it enjoyable, while at the same time I dreaded arriving and often hoped for the bus to crash. But invariably I would soon find the bus going over the hump bridge, which would give me that sinking feeling both literally, and in the sense of reminding me that soon I would again be in that sort of purgatory. Where I would have to muddle through another day of being shunted about and ridiculed, but mostly just overlooked.

At about this time, when about twelve, my long overlooked abscess and related distorted teeth, which had been forming in my mouth for a couple of years had now got so bad that I had to go into a hospital in East Grinstead, which I was told had a high reputation for its achievements with burns victims during the war. I was there a couple of weeks, I recall the man alongside had awful burns which gave me quite a shock, though he was very friendly. In fact they did a very good job; though it involved stitches, a blood transfusion and the loss of some teeth, thus the facial distortion which had taken place before the operation started to subside. After I got out of hospital I was feeling better and looked forward to returning to Highly Manor and was disappointed to find the bicycle which I had had access to was now gone, and worse still we were now moving and apparently shortly going to live on the South Coast.

For those that don't know, Eastbourne is supposed to have more sun than any other spot in Britain. But despite this our new home, which was not on the grand scale of Highly Manor was rather damp, and seemed to be infested with anonymous insects which at night would creep out and cover my body in bites, I was sleeping on the floor with bedding, and felt sore and disturbed; eventually a strong-smelling ointment was prescribed which had to be applied each night. To add to my problems I had to start at a new school in Bexhill-on-Sea, one of those large impersonal secondary modern schools, though one of the saving graces of Bexhill school was that despite not being able to pay, I got taken on an excursion, which involved two weeks camping at Seaford and romping about below the Seven Sisters, a stretch of magnificent white cliffs. And despite being caught smoking, which was now becoming a habit, I had a good time. Eastbourne is also known for Beachy Head, over which I enjoyed many a walk. Though I tended to feel dizzy if I went too close to the edge, from where sometimes people would throw themselves off! Not that I was that way inclined, at nearly fourteen I was now more mature. After selling Highly Manor Miss Gordon had helped us to get the lease on our place in Eastbourne, and she moved to a new hotel she had acquired in Llandovery in Wales. After a few months my parents decided we should move on to Brighton, where they eventually found a place and we duly departed from Eastbourne without even being evicted, much to my amazement!

* * *

Brighton to Knightsbridge

Brighton seemed to me a romantic and lively place; our house was in George St between a pub and a betting shop, which was not far from the Pavilion and close to the sea. I was fourteen and since I wasn't particularly keen to go to another school, my parents decided I could help out around the place, including in the shop below which we used in various ways from art gallery and cafe to novelty shop. The year was about 1965 and the summers seemed very hot, this was the time of Mods and Rockers who would overrun the seafront on long weekends, it was the period when President Kennedy was assassinated which upset me, I was washing the dishes when the news came on the radio.

In Brighton I also got to spend time with my sister Mercedes when we would have siestas on the roof with hot rolls and coffee just lazing in the sun, at other times my brother William and I would play football until we were collapsing from the heat and would then strip off and plunge into the sea and then afterwards try and get a free ride on the dodgem/bumper cars on our way back.

Although we were a family of nine kids, our life experiences were quite different and not all of us were there. My eldest brother Mervyn was brought up by my grandparents, he had a regular lifestyle and went to school and got a degree in zoology, I only met him once. Mercedes was mostly educated by my father, she married Simon an architect, worked in the film industry and has since changed partners and now lives with John in Chiswick. Ricky was next: he spent a few months in the army then bought his way out and married a Welsh girl and later unfortunately he committed suicide leaving a son. Toby, the one above me, was quite good-looking and seemed to have lots of girlfriends; he worked in films, played the guitar and composed music. William and the other younger kids had less erratic childhoods, so it's all the sadder that he seemed to have such a rough time later on, he was very much the apple of my father's eye and along with most of my younger siblings went to various stage schools, and to some degree his future seemed assured. At one stage during our spell in Brighton, my father wrote a screenplay around him called 'The Kid Brother' which was all set to be directed by Herbert Wilcox, but this later fell through. William was quite successful in his acting career especially as a youngster and at one stage constantly received fan-mail, after he had played a leading role in a film 'The boys of St Paul St'. He also at various times had parts in West End plays, including one by Alan Bennett which I enjoyed going to see (with a complimentary ticket). Later he went to America, where he started to develop problems, after his drink at a party was spiked, or in relation to L.S.D. for which he was quite unprepared and as a result was in and out of hospitals for quite a while. Since then, with stops and starts he has been in a slow process of coming to terms with his future, which so far hasn't included further work in the theatre.

After him came Samuel who has been more robust. I recently received an article which was in the Hampstead and Highgate Express, about some project he was working on, in which he describes himself (among other things) as an artist and musician, though for the last few years he has also been doing social work, and at present lives in West Hampstead. Which brings me to Mary Honey who lived with Richard her American husband, in Ash House on their large estate, in Devon, along with his collection of classic Porsche motor cars, which leaves last but not least, Andrew who has acted in various films and worked on the lighting system for the original 'Rocky Horror' theatre production and currently lives and works in London. Of course these rough appraisals of my brothers and sisters don't sum up their lives, which are still developing and changing. Coming back to Brighton, I recall at that time Toby was working at the Grand Hotel, since I remember being impressed when he told me the actress Hayley Mills was staying at the hotel. And a little later Mercedes was working as a hostess on the 'Regency Belle' which was the train my father had running between London and Brighton.

About this time I was disconcerted to find I was going to have to go to hospital again as another abscess had formed. This time it was arranged for me to go to the Middlesex in London, the same place where the nurses had been so generous with the ice creams at the back windows. My couple of weeks there were uneventful other than losing a few front teeth which resulted in having lots of stitches in my mouth and a blood transfusion; I remember the shock of accidentally seeing the state of my swollen and distorted face in a mirror. My father came to visit me, though he was not completely sober, which embarrassed me, as after the nurse went away she came back to find my dad had climbed into bed with me, but he did bring me a packet of cigarettes. I had been addicted to smoking since I was thirteen, which was about a year, so he knew I would be desperate and I smoked some of them in the loo, though I had half a pack confiscated, when they got discovered while I was being given a blanket bath and everything got exposed.

When I got back to Brighton things seemed different, various projects had fallen through and we were behind with the rent, this all peaked when the bailiffs started coming round looking for my father and on one such occasion, he had to hide outside my bedroom window while I got into bed and pretended I hadn't seen him when the bailiffs came into the room. Eventually everything collapsed and I found my only choice was to go and live with the bass-player fellow, who had been putting in quite a few appearances; one occasion he came into my bedroom and I had to fend him off, saying my sister might enter the room. Presumably he had offered to my parents to put me up at his flat in Hampstead.

So it was that I moved to London and eventually to my job as a page boy at the Basil Street Hotel in Knightsbridge, it's one thing I realised to be lying on my bed perusing my past and quite another to try and explain it, let alone put it on paper! Even so I decided there and then that one day I would try to, but for the moment I had to stop daydreaming as I only had only about twenty minutes till I was expected back on shift in the front hall. In preparation I started to get dressed and put on some 'Deep Heat' which is the name of the ointment I used, to numb the pain caused by ligaments strained by repeatedly carrying heavy luggage, which seemed to weigh more than me, and it was partly this, and that standing about twelve hours a day caused painful night cramp, which led to my deciding to give in my notice. When I did finally do this, the assistant manager, who I quite liked, rather to my consternation offered me a rise from seven up to eight pounds ten shillings a week, but though I had partly enjoyed my six months as a page boy, I decided to stand by my decision to leave and gave a months' notice.

CHAPTER TWO:

Adolescence (16-21)

R.A.C. Country Club to Bayswater

The month ran out fast and after a short interlude I found a live-in position at the Royal Automobile Country Club in Epsom, where I learned how to operate the switchboard and fulfilled other tasks when required, like helping on golf course or replenishing flowers. While I appreciated the open space, the place in general seemed dull and alienating for a fifteen-year-old, and I was a little depressed by my windowless box room and lack of friends. But as it turned out I didn't stay long as my father happened to speak to the manager by phone when he was trying to contact me, probably to borrow some money and inadvertently, and rather to my bemusement, made some inappropriate remarks to the rather uppity manager. After which I felt uncomfortable about staying on.

Back in London, after much searching, I found a very small bed-sit and it was from here that I experienced my very own 'first eviction'! The landlady had stated that no cooking was allowed. Unfortunately after about a week, I needed to heat some basic food by turning my two-bar fire on its side, but being inexperienced in surreptitious cooking, I was somehow detected, since the next day I arrived back in the rain to find my few belongings out on the steps in a box. After pleading with the landlady, I called the police who informed her I was entitled to some notice but she disagreed. I was a little cross and protested and she made some sarcastic remarks about "little prince-charming throwing a tantrum" which made me feel stupid, so I picked up my things and accepted the friendly policeman's condolences that there was nothing he could do and left. Even though I had broken the house rule of no cooking, I felt let down.

My next move was to a job at a large hotel in Bayswater, which looked impressive from the outside, but behind the facade was in some respects rather cheap and seedy; my own accommodation was a tiny room in the basement which featured rats running about on pipes above the bed. The work was tedious, and being young and naive I was surprised to find myself accosted by the apparently tipsy receptionist who was a friend of the owner, she was a rather forcible woman and actually forced her hand down my pants, after cornering me when I was trying to leave the building one day, and then playfully called me a 'dirty little wretch' when she found I had been affected by her behaviour. Bearing in mind I was about fifteen to sixteen, I recall there were also a couple of other minor incidents, one from a Spanish chambermaid and the other from a friendly male waiter about twice my age.

A few days later I was transferred to another of the group's hotels in Bayswater, which was of a slightly better grade. The manager was friendly and I wasn't worked too hard, though it soon transpired that his interest in me was not just as an employer. After a few weeks I decided to leave and go to Jersey in the Channel Islands, and try to pass my driving test, which I had been told was easier over there. This plan didn't suit my boss and he tried to persuade me in various ways to stay, then as a last resort he invited me out for a meal with his 'wife', as he had an offer he wanted me to consider. So one evening I turned up at the designated place to find my employer dressed in a smart suit and his 'wife' in a dress and wearing heavy make-up. He explained his plan in which he would teach me to drive and how I would have the job of collecting hotel guests from the airport. All the while his wife kept beaming at me, yet during the course of the evening I kept thinking she looked odd, till it eventually dawned on me, rather to my bewilderment, that she was actually a man. I decided to continue with my plan to go to leave, despite having inadequate money.

* * *

Jersey Royals

In the clouds and now about sixteen, I accepted an offer from the flight steward, and brought a brandy and ginger-ale, (my father's tipple), which gave me a short-lived high, then the plane landed and I left my case at the bus station. The afternoon was hot and I immediately got down to the task of visiting numerous hotels dotted about the island, where I introduced myself and enquired after a live-in position, but increasingly to my dismay only received endless rebuffs or exclamations of "perhaps in a few weeks"!

I ended up sleeping in a bus shelter and the next day found a job picking potatoes, 'Jersey Royals' as they are known today. The work was back-breaking and the farmer would come to the barn and awaken me out of a pile of blankets and straw on a barn floor, at about four-thirty in the morning and work would start with the sunrise and continue to sunset, except for short interludes when I could gorge myself on local produce, mainly potatoes, tomatoes and milk. Despite the hard work, I enjoyed the sunny weather and being close to the land, and would flag out exhausted at the end of the day. Also the barn where I was bedded down contained a giant wooden cask of farm cider, one cup of which; would knock me flat if the work hadn't already done so. After a few weeks the novelty of being a 'farm-boy' grew thin and my back more sore, so since I was hardly making any money I decided to quit, or at least keep my eyes open elsewhere.

While I was having a milkshake at the Rendezvous Cafe in St Heliers, I found a new position, without so much as asking, the owner Sid H a small friendly man with a slightly laughing face; asked me if I was interested in a job as a salad hand, with accommodation, which I accepted. After I had moved in and been working there a short while and become dependent on the situation, he then started bringing in other elements to the work quite unrelated to salad-making, which required very little of me and added another third to my wages, eventually he declared my accommodation was too damp and moved me into to his flat upstairs.

Meanwhile some acquaintances of my parents, who had discovered I was in Jersey, invited me to tea and on hearing where I was living very much disapproved, and offered to perhaps get me a job on a lobster/fishing boat. So not long after I was picked up early one morning on my day off and driven to what seemed a remote part of the Island. As we descended fast down a long hill through lush countryside coloured by the rising sun, my prospective employer explained we had a tide to catch. In short, the day out on the boat was both exciting and dangerous, inasmuch as I wasn't used to the pace and occasionally nearly got tangled up in the ropes much to the alarm of those about me, also I was squeamish about what happened to the lobsters and was sickened when I saw a large dogfish beheaded, and not surprisingly wasn't offered a job.

Living at the Rendezvous was a bit like 'Fagan's den', inasmuch as the owner who spent much of his time gambling on horses, seemed to have attracted a staff consisting of homeless youngsters, who tended to gather about and look up to him. During this period I was taking conventional driving lessons, as well as free lessons from my employer in his Mercedes saloon, free that is, as long as I didn't object to his being a bit free with his hands. Sid H didn't seem a bad chap; inasmuch as he showed some kindness and concern which at the time I quite appreciated. It was he who when I was inadvertently affected by alcohol, got me back to the house, though later, with help of others, pulled down some of my clothes and took various photos, I was in a haze and fell asleep. Eventually, when my 'sixteenth' birthday came I took my driving test, and to my satisfaction, but perhaps the sorrow of my instructors, I passed first time, and shortly afterwards decided to return to England.

Charles House to Ireland

On arriving back my money soon ran out, and since I didn't know where my parents were living, basically there was no one I could turn to. After a few days I began to get hungry, thus it was that I turned to 'Charles House', which isn't Buckingham Palace, but the name given to the social welfare office along Kensington High Street. This was my first puzzling encounter with bureaucracy on its more frustrating part of the spectrum, inasmuch as after waiting for hours and making an application, I was refused help as I couldn't produce any old pay-packets. The following day I returned with some 'pay-slips', but was refused help as I hadn't got a proper address, by now I was even more hungry and trudged away to return the next day with a required rent-book only to be told I wasn't old enough to claim and that I should go home even though I hadn't got one. Eventually I was given some emergency short-term help, about three pounds.

A few weeks later I applied for a selling job with an American company, whose office was at an address in Bond Street, when I got there the receptionist told me the man I had spoken to had left ten shillings for me to get some food, and I was to come back later ready to start there and then. About 4pm that afternoon I met my new employer, a bristling and breezy American salesman and shortly I found myself on the road in a mini car and heading for the north. After a period of training I was allocated to a team in Scotland, the job was selling magazine subscriptions door to door.

My new team manager was less charming than the overall manager and seemed almost fanatical in his approach to selling, in fact on one occasion I watched him almost empty the purse of a blind woman, after selling her a magazine subscription. It was his attitude that made me decide only to stay with the company till they had taken me to Ireland. In fact, my sales in Scotland were low enough that they were in two minds about whether to keep me on, but they did and a few weeks later I found myself on the ferry to Northern Ireland.

In Belfast the following morning I awoke on the floor, in our cheap guest house, to the strains of Bob Dylan's 'Hey Mister Tambourine Man!', blaring out of one of the boy's transistors, I felt entranced and I wondered what it all meant. I was quite surprised to see the police had guns and was naive enough to ask one officer whether his gun was loaded, he assured me it was. One encounter was with a highly spirited young Irish fellow, he noticed me and we seemed to spark each other off, he insisted on buying me a drink before we parted ways. After which I continued with my door-to-door sales script, which went: "Good morning are you the 'lady' of the house? ... well I'm part of a team of boys in this area on an international travelling tour/ contest, and I wonder if you would be so kind as to consider voting for me... At this point I would explain that voting took place by making a subscription to a magazine, and then I would bedazzle them with the different subjects available i.e. motoring, sailing, gardening, decorating etc. But I didn't sell enough and was glad they decided to give me my fare back to England.

* * *

Underground and funeral

The Glendower Hotel in Kensington was in need of a waiter, and I needed somewhere to stay so I applied and got the job, though they weren't happy to find I had no black trousers and also were not particularly impressed by my non-existent waiting skills. In short I was asked to leave after a few days and for good measure the manageress gave me a dressing-down for wasting their time, she looked up from the desk and said slightly provocatively "if she was my mother she would take down my pants and smack my bottom" which made me blush. This embarrassment was further exasperated, because on my last morning there I couldn't face getting up, and so locked my door and stayed in bed till about ten o clock as I was feeling anxious and fed up.

My suitcase was still at the left luggage office as I hadn't the money to get it out, and from there I drifted into a spell of walking the streets and sleeping on the Underground. I haven't forgotten sheltering from the rain in doorways in Park Lane and realising that despite my external poverty, in my heart at moments I felt waves of inexplicable happiness, and slightly bemused by my situation as I wandered drenched and hungry past the opulent frontages of Park Lane's hotels, and I even wondered whether 'they' climbing out of plush cars and wandering into exclusive hotels weren't the real poverty-stricken ones, even so I also felt embarrassed by my predicament and ashamed of my existence, and didn't know where to put myself, especially after I had walked a few miles and got exhausted.

I soon learned that for the price of an underground ticket I could at least get warm on the early morning trains, and that by slumping forward with my head over my knees, could even sleep in a fashion. Then around about eight-thirty I would wake up to the rush hour and look up to see freshly dressed people looking away as I looked up. Then I would take stock of where I was and travel to the appropriate station before emerging into daylight. At about this time I reconnected with Miss Gordon, the lady who had owned Highly Manor and who now had a smaller hotel, the Kings Head in Llandovery which is in Wales. I'm not sure how it came about, except that she invited me to come and help out for the summer season. One way or another I eventually arrived there, and as I wasn't old enough to work in the bar she employed me as a waiter in the afternoons and evenings. It was very informal and friendly like working as part of a family, and I enjoyed not having to worry too much about anything and going for long walks in the Welsh hills with 'Joy', the same Labrador Miss Gordon had kept at her previous hotel in Sussex.

During this period one of my younger brothers (Samuel) came to stay in the hotel and we got up to various pranks which included my borrowing the car, to prove to him that I could drive, this entailed pushing the car for about a hundred yards up the road in the middle of the night, before I dared to start the engine, after nearly getting stranded somewhere; we resolved not to do that again. It was during this summer that I learned my father had lung cancer and wasn't expected to live more than a few months. My parents were now living in a spacious flat in Cornwall Gardens, which is quite a lovely old London square with big leafy trees. When I could, I went to visit and took my father a bottle of cognac and tried not to be too shaken by his deteriorating state. Later when I went again just before he died, I was shocked to find he had lost every speck of hair such as eyebrows, as well as turning very pale and had withered down to very little. So it was that I bid my father farewell, and he gave me a watery smile as he called me over and said goodbye.

Later when I went down from Wales to the funeral, my mother told me that just before his death he had expressed he was quite happy and had died peacefully. The funeral was a strange affair; my mother and siblings were not much used to ritual or conventions and while saddened, were nonetheless bemused by the sight of us all trying to behave properly, but anyhow in various ways we paid our last respects and then went back to a sort of 'wake' at Cornwall Gardens. Hitch-hiking back to Wales that afternoon I took with me a small bundle of my father's clothes, (a couple of shirts and ties), which my mother had given me.

I had quite a good rapport with the person who picked me up, but after he dropped me off and I saw the car speeding into the distance; I realised I had gone and left my inheritance in his car, but I wasn't too upset as my father had always taught me not to lay too much importance on material things. His obituary appeared in some papers shortly after March 17th and later George Hume, a friend of his, wrote the play about him mentioned earlier, in which he was portrayed by Rex Harrison. To celebrate the opening of his play 'The Lionel Touch' George invited us to the first night, and later took us out to dinner. These days at the touch of a few computer keys Lionel Burleigh can be seen painting in various old news clips on the internet...

* * *

Cornwall Gardens to Alderney

Cornwall Gardens near Gloucester Road tube was to be my next home, at least for a short while since my mother had asked if I would like to come and try out living there. Since after I moved in there wasn't actually a spare room I slept in the hall which was large enough to act as one. The wall which I slept next to was adjacent to the house next door and on occasions I would wake up transfixed by an overwhelming soprano voice coming through loud and clear from next door. This turned out to be the Australian opera singer Joan Sutherland practising, and my mother subsequently introduced me to her. Being a fairly shy seventeen-year-old I didn't tell Joan Sutherland that she had inadvertently introduced me to opera, I continued to enjoy hearing her practice. Going from the sublime to the less developed, while at Cornwall Gardens I also had a part-time weekend job at London Zoo which involved cleaning out monkey houses and I developed a bit of a friendship with the late Guy, their resident gorilla who has since deceased.

My mother eventually had to move from Cornwall Gardens to a smaller flat; meanwhile Ray a friend of hers had offered me a job at a hotel he owned on a small Channel Island. To get there I made my way to Jersey, and then he flew me over to Alderney on his small private plane, which intrigued me no end, as I had to help him look out for the runway. At first I was used for labouring work renovating the hotel and then as a waiter until I accidentally dropped soup on a vicar. Life on the island was rather insular and for me revolved around long hours with little pay, I did clean out and transform an old cellar, and to recuperate I would lay in sun listening to old pop songs such as 'lazy Sunday afternoon', and occasionally Ray's wife would massage my lower back, occasionally I drank some the tax-free booze, and in turn overslept, then his wife would come and pull my bedclothes off me. Anyhow in due course it was time to depart, and she suggested that back in London I should try registering with a model agency, which surprised me, as I associated the word model with females.

* * *

Bird in Hand, to Golders Green

Back in England I found a job through Alfred Marks, which was as a live-in trainee barman, I didn't let on that I was still seventeen, and travelled to Maidenhead area where I was given the job at the 'Bird in Hand' and moved in on the spot. The boss was a tall slightly balding man with a lively wife and a plush car with electric windows. I suppose what I remember is the different ways I used to try and fill in the emptiness of my existence while I was there, which included masturbation, popping pills given to me by the other young barman who -considerate chap - did at least warn me not to drink with them, scoffing chocolates from the nearby garage shop, drinking, and gambling. Thus one afternoon the boss happened to notice me mesmerised in the hall, and losing my meagre wages in the 'fruit machine' or 'one-armed bandit', in just a few words he made me realize how stupid I was being, and I learned there and then to only invest what you don't mind losing, and not to be mis-led. Sometimes he and his wife had me play cards with them, and I was a bit sorry when they drove off in their sleek Lancia or Jaguar to be on holiday. The bar was frequented mainly by middle-class, middle-aged customers who seemed to talk mostly about their cars, their insurance policies and golf. I sometimes found the atmosphere banal and depressing, and eventually I won eighty pounds on the horses, had a couple of drinks, and ended up on the customer's side of the bar, where I had a few naive things to say about what I perceived to be their views of existence, one good-hearted regular said "if he was my father..." I felt inadequate and left.

* * *

Soon my money ran out and I was obliged to find another live-in job, this time washing dishes at a hotel near Goodwin. Here I was not treated as well as at my previous job, at some point a local council official declared my caravan to be unfit habitation; admittedly there were few facilities, and in the courtyard I encountered a large half-poisoned rat, averse as I was, I felt sorry for its suffering; so didn't tell anyone. Despite its shortcomings I liked the caravan enough to have displayed some of my doodles on the wall, but I was treated quite badly, and was expected to work long hours and compulsory overtime without notice. The new bland accommodation was a few miles, and I was given occasional impressive car rides by the owner's son, who drove his sports car like he was on Goodwin racetrack. On another occasion I was kicked by a chef, though later he insisted on giving me a harmonica. After I had been there about a month, one Saturday afternoon, when I had already had more than enough dishes for one day, I was given my pay packet and informed I would have to do an extra shift and was left to get on with more pots and pans. But I decided to leave there and then, so rather than argue with my unfriendly employer I just climbed out of the kitchen window, walked up the road into the sunset and didn't look back.

The following evening I found myself in Earl's Court trying to find somewhere to stay, when I bumped into an acquaintance from Jersey who offered to put me up for the night. I hadn't yet smoked marijuana, but this changed when the boy insisted I try some. The Afghanistan hashish soon caused me to flop out on the bed for a few hours. When I came to wondering what had overcome me, I noticed one of the girls preparing a syringe to 'shoot up' heroin, which being averse to injections wasn't my cup of tea, and so despite their persuasions and then disapproval, I resisted the further enticement and left, rather to the disgust of my friend. Still in Earl's Court I became quite unwell for a few weeks, after having stupidly being under someone's sunlamp for an excessive period, which wasn't helped by being on the streets and having nowhere to stay.

During this period I passed a few hours in an all-night cafe feeling both sick and dejected, and reflected on the words of an elderly woman in a shop who had commented that I looked in need of help. Not long after this I found a sleazy bed-sit in the area and was briefly entertained by a bunch of 'rogues'. They were more worldly-wise than myself and having received standard educations didn't suffer from my predicament of being 'well-spoken' and yet 'semi-illiterate' and generally lacking in self-confidence. One of these chaps was an ex-boxer, yet he was very softly spoken and seemed to take an almost protective attitude towards me, another of them was a tall wheeling and dealing gambler, he was quite a good chess player, though so was I and on one occasion he enticed me to put up ten pounds against his Honda moped, I won and to my surprise he gave me the moped which I used for a number of months until a hire purchase company re-possessed it, thus it became clear he hadn't completed the payments.

Around this time my previously neutral attitude to the police became slightly jaundiced. Previously I'd been stopped by two female officers near Piccadilly on my moped, they asked a couple of questions then looked at each other and were almost motherly towards me. Now I got pulled up one evening by a couple of detectives who jumped out of a squad car. It was clear one was aggressive, and as he twisted my arm I noticed his breath reeked of alcohol, but I also noted that the other man wasn't impressed by his colleague's behaviour and discreetly made him stop, and told me to go, thus I escaped, feeling ruffled and wondering what that had all been about. This of course was the era when there was a lot of polarisation between young people and the police, caused by the rebellious atmosphere of the late sixties and early seventies, when many police, and young people, were stereotyped into different camps whether they liked it or not, and treated as one of 'them', just because one happened to be in uniform, or young and homeless. In fact I did nearly get into trouble about this time, as I had a spell without money which went on for so long that I was forced to go into a Chinese restaurant and have a meal, after which I was apologetic and offered my name and any address. They got quite angry and threatened me with various sharp utensils, before taking the only bit of warm clothing I had worth more than the couple of pounds owed.

I had to leave Earl's Court and was obliged to take the first job I could find, thus shortly I found myself working at the Wimpy bar in Golders Green. The manager was a friendly and sympathetic bloke and seemed to have a soft spot for me, and when he realised I hadn't actually got anywhere to live, perhaps partly because I was quite a good worker he started letting me sleep in the store room, and I soon learned that by placing two large cardboard trays of wimpy buns on the floor and then covering them with clean tea-towels; I could sleep quite comfortably for about four hours knowing the boss had the key to the storeroom and wasn't going to let anyone in during that time. So it was that I became quite accustomed to sleeping on Wimpy Buns and then doing my shift of work, and sometimes selling the very buns I had slept on, the customers still enjoyed their buns, and I was actually quite generous and tended to give extra to anyone who looked hungry.

* * *

Paris to Marble Arch

About this time an Australian girl, twenty-three and about five years my senior, started to take an interest in me, and eventually we went off hitch-hiking. On our first night we shared a bed in Paris, though as agreed our friendship remained platonic. The following day we were trying to hitch to Spain, though by the middle of the night we got so cold we were forced to take any lift we could get and ended up with an overnight ride going not South but to the North of France. And from there she 'hitched' us a ride on a yacht to Jersey where we were put up in a hotel for the night, and later flew back to London. After which, she went back to flat-sharing with a bunch of girls, and resumed office temping, before returning to Australia.

For myself I accessed a high turn-over rooming house and slept in the bathroom, later I found a small room in Marble Arch, the little money I was able to squeeze out of the social security never covered much more than the rent, and there didn't seem to be much work about.

This was a bit of a difficult time, the room I was living in was pretty dire and being uncultured and without friends or enemies, life seemed lonely and meaningless, it also seemed bizarre to be hungry in the midst of plenty. Being eighteen I naturally used masturbation as a way to distract myself from my feelings of inadequacy, though when I overdid this I invariably felt worse rather than better. Life also seemed a little sordid as I had resorted to picking cigarette butts off the street, which I then rerolled in thin paper which is usually readily available to the 'needy' in any version of the Bible, or the works of Shakespeare. Not that any disrespect was intended, I just needed to smoke and didn't really mind whether it was 'holy smoke' or 'smoked sonnets', so long as I smoked. During this phase I occasionally resorted to picking the bathroom gas meter to get a few coins, with which to buy some chocolate from the vending machine so as to stave off hunger. None of this made me feel particularly good or happy, so I decided to try and break out of the world I seemed to be locked into.

After much searching, I found a non-residential position as a night porter at a block of flats in Marble Arch, and though the estate agents were a bit dubious about my young age I was eventually given the job. I had vacated the bed-sitter, and so now had to make do with a few short naps during the small hours. My work mostly entailed letting residents in, up to about midnight and then a bit of cleaning and delivering papers and mail at about six in the morning. So the time in between was my own to some extent, or so I thought. Consequently I devised a plan to save some money, which was to find another job to do in the day, in the event I found two. In the mornings I worked for a fruit and veg. shop making deliveries on a trolley to local businesses and in the afternoons I worked as a kitchen hand. For a while this all went very well except I was starting to get very tired and realised I would have to get some proper sleep, so I decided to take a chance and bed down properly at nights, thus I not only brought an air bed but also some sleeping shorts and an alarm clock. The block of flats I was working in were quite plush, the reception area had a chandelier overhead and a large counter behind which I sat. So it was on the carpet behind my counter that I concealed my practice of going to sleep, between about two and six in the morning. Until the inevitable happened and one night I woke up to find the estate agent staring down at me in disbelief, I climbed out of my airbed a bit sheepish in my shorts and t-shirt and received formal notice to leave.

Central Casting to Spain

For one reason or another I swallowed my pride and contacted my older brother Toby and his girlfriend whose phone number I had, and they agreed to put me up for a few days. While staying there a couple of his friends called over. One of them, Mandy, was about twenty-five, quite good-looking with fine round features, an art graduate; well-spoken, assertive and cynical about what she called 'the system'. Anyhow she took a fancy to me and suggested I came and spent the following night at her place in Belsize Park. She was quite forward and I was quite backward which made things quite simple. I didn't let on that I was still a 'virgin' and was quite surprised by some of the activities she included in the short meeting, though I didn't say anything and just laid back and enjoyed it. Later the other person who had been with her called round. His name was Ken and he was about thirty and spoke with a soft northern accent, he moved like a dancer and his interests in terms of sexual orientation seemed to be both male and female.

He pointed out that since I couldn't actually stay at Mandy's place, if I wanted I could come and stay at his place in Hampstead (off Finchley Rd) which had a settee which turned into a bed. So it was that I moved into Ken's room in Greencroft Gardens. Ken seemed an interesting fellow and had many colourful friends, from New York 'Time Life' reporters to black musicians. His own life revolved around what I called 'Ken's holy trinity' namely: marijuana (only for personal use), the whole spectrum of jazz music especially Miles Davis, and old Rover motor cars, of which he owned about three, and his pattern of existence (except when working on movies, or mending his motor cars) was almost invariably to spend half the night smoking and listening to jazz, and then to get up till well after midday. Ken's room was totally bohemian with brown paper bags over the lights, loads of car parts stuffed under the sink, which occasionally doubled as a pee receptacle, the cupboards and floor were overflowing and unkempt. There was a good collection of books which ranged from Jean-Paul Sartre and Sigmund Freud to Aldous Huxley and George Orwell. And when I eventually tired of the mess and refurbished the room, I also had to erect three twelve-foot shelves to carry all the books, some of which I had started to read.

Despite occasional arguments we got on quite well and though our lifestyles were quite different I was quite happy to have somewhere to stay and he didn't seem to be in any hurry for me to leave, and so I became a sort of official 'phantom lodger' sleeping on the fold-down bed and keeping my things in a single draw. The housekeeper Maureen, a hardworking and cheerful Irish lady, seemed to quite like me, and turned a blind eye to my staying there, even though his room was only meant to be a single. But in any case the owner of the house, who was a doctor, kept a very low profile and left her very much in charge.

Ken mooted the idea that I should start doing film work like himself i.e. extra work (crowd scenes), doubling (where one is used for long shots) and stand-ins (in which you look after your 'star' and improvise his part while they set up the lights and camera angles). But this meant I had to get into the F.A.A. (The Film Artistes Association) which was the union one had to join to do that sort of work within a fifty-mile radius of London, which also covered all the main studios. So the help of my brother Toby was enlisted as he was on friendly terms with a senior shop steward Tony C, and thus I duly joined the F.A.A. After which it was just a matter of registering with Central Casting, a large agency in Soho which allocated that sort of work to the few thousand people on their books, who each evening between about four and six o clock, faithfully 'checked in' then waited for the more often than not reply "not at the moment".

My first job was on location in Carnaby Street on a film 'The Man with the largest brain in the world' which featured either Terry Thomas or David Niven I can't remember which. But I do recall I made about forty pounds and feeling a little indebted to my brother for his help, I agreed to his suggestion that we take a holiday and hitch to Spain for a couple of weeks, and so after a few hasty preliminaries I found myself on the road to Spain via the South of France. The first hiccup along the way was with a French girl at a Youth Hostel in Paris, who cornered me on the stairs and insisted on giving me a 'French Kiss' by pushing her tongue in my mouth, which felt like I had been invaded by an unwanted intruder, and it was just as the surly warden came by, who blamed me and nearly had us both chucked out.

Toby and I eventually via Marseille, continued over the Pyrenees to Spain and Barcelona and made ourselves at home on a campsite, which after a few days we could no longer afford and so we had to resort to climbing over the back wall. While I didn't really have the inclination or confidence to actively enter into relationships of any sort, Toby, who was about three years older than me, previously had various female friends as well as a dalliance with Clement Freud, and was soon preoccupied with a Spanish girl and went his own way. The weather was very hot so sleeping rough was easy, though before long I was only living on bottles of chocolate milk and money dwindled faster than expected. About this time a fellow of my own age introduced me to some pills which he claimed would stave off hunger. This wasn't a good development and resulted in my nearly being hit by an on-coming train, but I was saved by a kind Spanish man who urgently incited me to vacate the track, then I later slept in a public car park, where I had an encounter with a car, perhaps driven by a Franco type, and came to the next day to find myself covered in blood. I was quite embarrassed and didn't know what to do with myself.

Over the next few days three of my fingers which had been damaged became septic and swelled up, meanwhile I was again becoming hungry and unkempt. I went back to a cafe near the old campsite and the owner kindly gave me a free breakfast, though I had only asked for a drink of water, which as well as refreshing me, made me feel good that some people are capable of acts of kindness, without judging about whether or not you deserve help. Later that same day I ran into the youth who had given me the pills in the first place, and his more responsible side must have come to the fore, as he asked how I was, and seeing my fingers needed attention he told me he knew of a place where I could get some free treatment. So that evening he led me on walk high up into a remote area till we came to a convent, where he rang the bell and then spoke to a nun and left me with her.

The nun, who was probably fed up with the likes of me turning up on their doorstep, wasted no time. She took my hand and after a quick examination of my fingers got some hot water and 'bleach' and proceeded to scrub the infected parts and then put my hand in a bucket of salt which formed a cake around the damaged parts, and then led me to the door. This seemed to do the trick as my fingers eventually cleared up and in due course, I was again able to twang on the Spanish guitar which I had later acquired.

My next task was to try to get myself repatriated; this basically involved hanging about the British Consul for a few days until they were convinced I was desperate and that I had had enough, and that I wouldn't be back in a hurry. When eventually they agreed to consider my case, another day was spent grilling me as to whether I had any relatives who could financially help me out. Then finally they announced they were going to take my passport as security and pay my fare 'home' by train, the loan did not include enough money to buy a cup of tea.

* * *

'Performance' to 'Ann of the Thousand Days'

Within days of arriving back in England my financial situation took an 'about turn', after I 'checked in' to Central Casting and was given a job as Mick Jagger's 'stand-in' on the film Performance. This didn't mean I had to look exactly like him, just as long as I was similar height and size, so they could use me to set up the lights etc. Funnily enough Mick Jagger was then at his peak as a rebellious rock star and pop idol and yet I have to admit I was only partially aware of him and wasn't particularly interested so long as I got paid. I was introduced to Mr. Jagger by the very friendly director Donald Cammell (a lovely person), who was working alongside his co-director Nick Roeg. The rest of the crew were a busy yet amicable bunch, but it was Donald Cammell (whom I recently learned was born in Edinburgh), who most impressed me for putting himself out to make me feel of some worth. The film set was in a large house in Lowndes Square just off Knightsbridge and I worked there for about two months, though I must admit it may have been longer, but I was living in less than helpful circumstances, and once or twice slept through the alarm.

While I was interested to see famous people appear before my eyes, (such as James Fox who was one of the cast) and able to observe them at work, it has to be said a large part of me just wasn't interested in all the hype connected with film-work, though I did like the colourful sets and some of the people, I had only just turned nineteen and since my development as a young adult had been quite inadequate, I was naturally plagued with feelings of inadequacy, as well as being introverted and self-conscious. My most awkward moment on that job, was after I caught a lice infestation in my pubic area (one of the perils of living in cheap accommodation), I was told I would need to dust myself with D.D.T. Unfortunately I used too much or the wrong sort of powder, and the result was my 'Thomas Henry' got very sore and in the healing process some scabs formed and had started to fall off.

It so happened that at around this time, filming was due to take place of Mick Jagger and Anita Pallenberg inside a large octagonal-shaped bath, which in preparation for shooting had been filled with clean water; which was then slowly heated with an element, so after much preparation everything was ready for filming. This was going to be a close-in shot and for my part I was required to climb into the water in shorts, with Anita Pallenberg, a buxom and friendly lady whose own stand-in seemed to be absent on that occasion. So although I was playfully whistled at by some of the crew as I climbed into the bath, the upshot of all this was that all eyes, lights and cameras were focused on the bath, when suddenly little unidentified objects started floating to the surface, as a result of which shooting got held up for about half an hour, much to the consternation of the directors and crew, and I joined in the general show of bafflement, as I was too mortified to suggest what might have been the cause. Incidentally, the D.D.T. certainly got rid of the lice and nearly a little more than I had bargained for.

Not long after this I moved back to Ken's room, and to supplement film work, which was sporadic, I joined up with Lee Allen's 'cleaning agency' for which one was paid a standard rate for a four-hour session. Often the work involved little or no cleaning; instead I would find myself having tea with little lonely Jewish ladies in Golders Green who didn't really want cleaning done so much as someone to talk to, which suited me fine. One old dear used to spend much of the time showing me her wedding photographs and also occasionally asked for and gave me haircuts. At other times I encountered odd situations, from the slightly intimidating lady who required that I scrub her kitchen on my hands and knees and complained if I overlooked a spot, to the concert pianist and his friend who, much to my surprise, kept all sorts of bizarre equipment in their cleaning cupboard which I had to sort through in order to find the vacuum cleaner. Then there was the very strict Colonel's wife who always gave me a cup of tea dead on eleven o clock, not to mention the woman who was some sort of theatrical agent, and had the most amazingly husky voice like something out of a movie. So domestic cleaning could be hard work as well as unpredictable and quite amusing at times.

Over the next couple of years, up to the age of twenty-one, I had countless jobs on films such as Stanley Kubrick's Clockwork Orange, and was self-conscious at having to wear a toga or short kilt, which to my embarrassment I had hitched up by the wardrobe mistress, while others looked on. I don't think that scene was used, and until later I had no idea what that film was going to be so horrible. Then there was a film with Roger Moore and Tony Curtis, the latter seemed very warm hearted and no less exuberant in real life than on celluloid, and I recall one day he just walked over to me and introduced himself while shaking hands, perhaps I looked in need of attention, all eyes had turned on us, it didn't take much for me to feel chuffed. I also did some doubling work on 'Sunday Bloody Sunday' on behalf of Murray Head who had hurt his leg coming off a motorbike and they needed someone to run down a hill at Greenwich carrying a kite. It was on that film, when I had to stand opposite Glenda Jackson for a few minutes, and while used to being in such situations, I couldn't help but note how down to earth and straightforward she seemed, inasmuch as we looked into each other's eyes close up for a few minutes and she didn't seem in the least bit concerned but if anything a little amused. I also recall the director John Slazenger being kind to me one morning.

I never quite knew what to expect when checking in. Would I be rubbing shoulders with John Wayne or Donald Pleasance, Charlton Heston or Betty Davis, or would it be a less glamorous call for the B.B.C.? The ladies who answered the phones at Central Casting (Peggy and Doreen at that time) often seemed to speak through their noses, and would either say "not at the moment" or something like "Patrick we need a 'deluxe' or 'filthy' hippy" (as the case may be) "at Shepperton Studios 6am sharp" or "can you go for a fitting or an audition?" or the like.

On one such occasion I turned up for an evening job on location outside Camden Town police station (for which I had previously auditioned with a German film company) to find a small group had gathered to watch the filming, then was quite self-conscious to find that the only scene they were going to be filming was a long shot of myself. It turned out I was doubling for a German youth who in the film gets released by the police, then walks down the street and reunites with his father. It was quite a useful evening as on top of quite a good chit (wage), they bought the jacket I was wearing for about twenty pounds, which had only cost me a couple of pounds second-hand, and because it was a cold night also stood me a taxi home. Working on films, while colourful and sometimes interesting, was also not really what I needed; constantly changing from one role to another wasn't helping me to find my own identity although it was sometimes fun. In other respects, I observed that even the 'successful' and famous are not always entirely' satisfied, and sadly haven't necessarily found fulfilment or happiness. (I was shocked and sorry to learn years later learn that the film Director Donald Cammell had committed suicide).

These simple reflections on what actually constitutes real success or happiness continued to preoccupy me while I worked on another film 'Ann of a Thousand Days'. This was a large 'call', and the work was hot and a bit tedious hanging about in costume for hours on end. Partly to fill in the time I succumbed to an offer of a 'smoke', and was soon a bit 'high' and was just about to 'crash out' (lay back) in some quiet corner on the set where I wouldn't be noticed, when I suddenly found a hand on my shoulder. It was an assistant director, apparently they were going to film a scene where Richard Burton, who was playing Henry VIII, would make a long speech and they needed a pageboy on either side of him, and since I was about nineteen or twenty, I apparently looked the part and of course would earn a lot more money. So after having my clothes removed, two wardrobe chaps assisted me into a rather strange-looking costume, then I found myself to one side of 'Henry VIII', who had apparently had a drink or two and wasn't too hot with his lines which was upsetting the director. Meanwhile I was trying to keep a straight face; though I was a bit stoned and could just manage to stand straight. By the next day the 'Henry VIII and his page', were both a little more 'sober' and we also had developed a little bit of a rapport, to the extent that in the afternoon while the rather uptight crew were getting things sorted out, Richard Burton came over and innocently put a hand on my waist and made a friendly comment. The filming continued and I had a small 'walk-on' where I had to bow to the king, and then take some papers over to the bishop, though I don't remember how much was in the final version. But I do recall that after checking the 'rushes'(early preview of filming), an assistant director remarked that I had looked a bit spaced-out.

***

Peculiar incidents

Coming back from the theatrical, to some no less peculiar incidents, which took place in my more mundane day to day life; it was around this period that my older brother Toby invited me to stay overnight with him and his new English girlfriend Sally. As it turned out there was only one double bed, but they said I didn't need to be shy and there was no reason why they couldn't fit me into the bed, I hadn't imagined it would go any further than that, but still I was a bit self-conscious about being in bed with them, and all the more astonished when at some point Sally rolled over from my brother, climbed on top, and made love to me in a slightly wild and Dionysian fashion. My surprise did not altogether diminish my enjoyment, though I was lost for words. Also, around that time there was an occasional friendship with Susan from New Jersey was generous, she had a crush on me, and we had some modest contact. Perhaps partly because she was from the USA, Sue was a very lively and energetic person and when she did visit, she was often doing things like making me hash cookies.

* * *

It so happened that on my twenty-first birthday, a few months after Sue had returned to New York, I couldn't help noticing she, or someone else, had left behind a bottle of pills. I was on my own and even though I hadn't got any money; I felt, one way or another I should perhaps celebrate my twenty-first birthday. In retrospect I don't know why I was so silly, but the fact is I put on Paul Mc-Cartney's lively song 'It's your birthday' and took a few pills thinking I would dance a little bit, but after taking some of the pills I just got speeded up and kept dancing with the music, till eventually I didn't know what was happening. After a while I half collapsed down the stairs and headed up to Finchley Road where the evening rush hour was just getting under way. My own 'rush hour' now nearly came to a sudden halt as I stumbled into the traffic. Fortunately there was a friendly traffic policeman on the scene, and all I recall is his helping me to his motorbike and perching me on its side while he called for an ambulance, I just collapsed down the other side of his bike.

When I regained consciousness; I found myself in a white hospital room, where I was about to be given a stomach pump. The duty doctor who had probably been on call about twenty hours and would perhaps have liked some sleep himself, seemed a little inconvenienced by my having come round. I then went and made matters worse by asking for a cigarette, for which he gave me a bit of a dirty look and said smoking wasn't allowed. I asked to leave and was able to do so after filling in some forms, as well as a few questions from the police about where I had got the drugs, and I explained the 'Mandrex' were legally prescribed pills inadvertently left behind, by a girlfriend who had returned to America.

Some weeks later back in Ken's bedsit I flicked through a book 'Sense and Sensuality' which is a play on 'Sense and Sensibility' and was written not by Jane Austen, but one Rodger Bowdler, from whose great grandfather comes the term to 'Bowdlerise'. He was older than Ken and lived in a flat in Kensington High Street, where on his classical guitar he played Elizabethan music, and bred Siamese cats. Rodger and Ken were friends via the film industry. My interest in his novel (published in the U.K. by Sphere 1971, and then by Dell in USA), was that it was a novel based partly around Ken, and I am also briefly alluded to in the second chapter. In which he refers to me when he has just come into Kens bed-sitter, "I came into the room to find a long-haired youth of about twenty stretched out on a bed, he didn't seem arrogant like most (with which I agree) and asked for an opinion on his rather naive cubist art, which covered much of one of the walls". (The novel uses different names) Sadly by the time I was mature enough to have a sensible conversation with Rodger he had died, he was always telling me that he thought I was too much under the influence of Ken and that I should try and find a place I could call my own, and periodically I would take up his advice and try moving to a new place.

* * *

Alcohol, British Gas and Enterprise

To finance moving into a new room, I found work driving a van and cleaning during the nights in central London, with 'Independent Cleaning Services', I wasn't qualified to do much else. In this respect, while I'm grateful for a few months here and there, when I was taught basic reading and writing, by a few occasionally caring and helpful teachers, even if I had been able to access the so-called 'education system', would it have prepared me for the trials and tribulations of existence and engendered in me some sense of values and vision for the future, rather than just mechanically stuffing me with fragmented information, which far from making me a healthy person, or a useful cog in the system; just left me completely unprepared? I don't doubt our society would benefit if school-leavers learned not just how to be useful, but also how to lead meaningful lives, how to relate to one's whole being in a healthy way, how to be aware of the danger inherent in drug and alcohol misuse, and again how to cope with the loneliness and alienation which may come to most at some time or another. In retrospect, while I appreciated my parents' bohemian attitudes to life, in practice they were able to enjoy that, partly on the basis of both having themselves had quite good educations, and were helped in having had at least some degree of stable home life. Ignorance is not really bliss, and I would have found it helpful to have had an education which encouraged both learning and the development of a positive, healthy and creative approach to life and knowing how to access any help or advice available.

* * *

As it was, I'm afraid at this time in my life, apart from occasional 'creative outbursts' I seemed very much to be scraping the bottom of the barrel, and this really came to a head, after I moved into a small room in Camden Town. In short late one night feeling exhausted, and then finding the sordid room was overrun with bed bugs, I went out and sat on the stairs and had a general sense of hopelessness, I resorted to a bottle of lager which heightened my sentimental indulgence and then in a confused and hazy state I nearly succumbed to the same sad 'fate' as my older brother Ricky who had committed suicide a few years earlier. After making a few preliminaries I turned on all the gas appliances and resigned myself to an 'early departure' but as luck may have it, after a while the gas stopped hissing and I realised the money had run out, feeling inconvenienced I went out to get some change for the meter but the fresh air brought me to my senses, and instead of wasting money in the gas, I decided to take a taxi over to Ken's place.

When I got there I was glad to find he was in and he immediately realised something was up as he said I looked white as a ghost, I also had quite a headache, but the next day I seemed to be none the worse, for my experience with British Gas. A few days later at Ken's suggestion I moved back into his place, which although it was only a single bedsitter, was still a lot better than the place where I had been. From here my twenty-first year started to take an upward turn, due to various factors, one was that my mother through a friend of hers had managed to secure me a small corner of floor space in a Kensington High Street, (in-doors) 'flea-market' which I had asked her to do if she got the chance. And so, for the next few months I was engaged with building a useable stall, a triangle about four or five feet to each side and about seven or eight feet high. Thus, I absorbed myself in creating and running a small business which involved everything from building my kiosk with a good display space, I could serve from the inside on a seat or, out on the market floor. As a comment on the self-obsessed 1970s I named it: 'Me Me Me', it was painted yellow and decorated with a few fleeting bubbles, and above that was a cross-legged meditating figure. So I became busy making wristbands, chokers and belts, to add to the rings, incense and other stock I had acquired. As it turned out the stall did quite well when I opened, which was during late summer and this led up to a busy Xmas, when I found I was selling almost all I could produce, though naturally this tapered off after the new year and to some degree for various reasons, my interest in being a stallholder, eventually became less sustainable.

* * *

'The Road to Damascus' via Oxford Street

Some months later, probably early spring as the pear tree which could be seen from Ken's window was starting to blossom into a great mass of fluffy whiteness, Mandy the art student, who had first made love with me, told to me one day; that she knew of this substance (L.S.D.) which she explained if taken in the right conditions would give me an experience of 'the truth, the whole truth, and nothing but the truth'. She explained that if I took it, then I would go on a 'long trip' and to some extent I would 'die'! But that it would help me to have a perspective on my place in the universe. Of course I was intrigued, and wasn't sure whether she was kidding or what, but I agreed that perhaps I should try it. When Ken found out what was 'in the air', rather to my surprise he was less keen, and he explained that, taking 'acid' as it was called could have devastating consequences and one really couldn't know what to expect as it affected different people in different ways, so the idea got pushed aside. But by mid-summer I accepted the offer and in due course I found myself in possession of two yellow tablets, which were procured for me from Ian a Glaswegian artist who was living in the area, in a large squat/ mansion, where subsequently for a while I was to live. (I am sorry to add, he later committed suicide.)

A few days later on a sunny morning I was with my brother Toby in West Hampstead. He had found out about the tablets and I agreed to let him have one of them. We were seated on a wall, having earlier 'dropped the tabs' i.e. taken them, but nothing seemed to be happening. So eventually we thought I had been duped and we gave up on anything happening, meanwhile my brother wanted to take his car into the London's West End, to do some shopping. So it was that by about midday we found ourselves in a traffic- jam in Oxford St, when needless to say strange things started happening to us, I can't really speak for my brother but we seemed to be sharing similar experiences, we found ourselves breaking down with nervous laughter as our physical bodies seemed to be slightly melting away. So we decided to get out of the car, which we did but then remembered we were in a traffic-jam and couldn't really leave the car there, so we got back in.

Fortunately the first slight wave of 'psychedelic experience' which was about to engulf us, didn't seem in a hurry and even slightly subsided, meanwhile we realised at least to some extent, that it was important for us to find a 'natural and harmonious setting' before the 'trip' came on full, so we pulled all the stops out and headed for Hampstead Heath as directly as we could, though we did actually stop and pick up a couple of people on the way whom we dropped off just before we arrived at the heath. As we walked from the heath car park we met a bunch of frizzle-haired Californians, either we told them or they picked up on our forthcoming 'voyage' and they wished us good luck.

By now the 'trip' was coming on stronger and stronger! fortunately we had managed to get ourselves into a fairly secluded part of the heath, by which time we both 'lost' ordinary consciousness and didn't really start to re-contact each other again for about seven or eight hours, during which much of the time, I was 'anchored' to an old tree, rather like a child hugging to his teddy bear when feeling insecure or uncertain about some new experience.

In short, what followed over the next seven or eight hours was first a complete 'blank out', mind and body just seemed to disappear and 'me' with it. I suspect this was because the experience was just too much for me to handle, so I just fell into a sort of swoon. When 'I' came to normal 'consensus reality' as we experience it day to day, had completely broken down, my physical body was gone, and 'I' was just a speck of consciousness in a vast sea of waves of light, just energy flowing in energy, the sort of thing the Beatles alluded to when they sang "Strawberry fields, nothing is real, nothing to be upset about". It was rather like I was experiencing myself and the objective world, via a very strong microscopic and yet expansive experience, which caused not only all boundaries to break down, but also reduced everything to atoms and molecules, which in turn also broke down ad infinitum, but of course things do relatively exist, and after a few hours that relative reality started very slowly to come back into some sort of focus. So gradually I became aware of the heath and the trees whose leaves shimmered, glittered and sparkled like trillions of fascinating jewels with dazzling rainbow light shining through them.

To the extent that my first trip was a really good one, I've also had very horrible trips. This was caused partly by unhelpful settings, (in one case a bed-sitter with someone's television blaring), combined with having taken the stuff because I wasn't in a particularly happy state, thus I learned the hard way that L.S.D. is not to be used for solving difficulties, as it only tends to highlight whatever is there. Fortunately, as my first trip had been very positive, I was able to remember, as I was being accosted by various apparitions and unpleasant experiences, that basically this was 'all in my mind' and I had faith that if I relaxed as best I could, they would eventually pass, which they did.

While I was astonished and inspired by my good trips, I was no less shattered and at times terrified by the bad ones, and decided that psychedelics are not something to be played about with. But I was grateful for what I had experienced, as the total breaking down of my 'consensus reality' or normal waking state, at least to some extent brought home to me, that I should let go of the past and shouldn't blame my parents, or society, or myself, for past shortcomings, but instead should try and bring a little light and positivity into existence.

CHAPTER THREE

Vision and Responsibility (21-22)

Letting go of the past.

Coming back from Hampstead heath that evening there was a funny taste in my mouth and my body felt worn out, I also suffered a slight paranoia as I stepped back into the hustle and bustle of traffic and people, lots of people with all sorts of faces some friendly some less so. When I got back to my bed-sit where I lived I was only able to utter the proverbial 'wow'! The contrast between what I had gone through and that which I had come back to seemed peculiar. Initially I found myself reacting to the sordidness and cramped conditions of my material situation and general psychological outlook. Gradually it sunk into me that though I had experienced an intense and prolonged altered state, even so I hadn't really changed nor had the world to which I was returning.

Even so my 'consensus reality' had been shattered, my model of the past was completely broken down, my view of existence was shaken up and I very definitely felt motivated to let go of the past and try to take charge of my future, in fact I felt quite deeply in my bones that henceforth I was basically responsible for whatever I did, even though I wasn't sure about the way forward.

I was now twenty-one and had come of age. Over the next few months, I effected various changes in my life, which included stopping using drugs, stopping eating meat, or other creatures, and stopping cigarette smoking. The latter was partly brought about as the result of a subsequent L.S.D. trip during which, while trying to smoke a cigarette, I experienced my physical organism and in particular my nervous system as if it were a sensitive bright plant shimmering and reaching up and out to the sun, and then I puffed a cigarette and felt a black cloud of poison come into my lungs, and watched as it choked my nervous system, causing it to shrink back. Thus, it became clear to me that much as I was totally dependent on smoking (I was a heavy smoker from age thirteen to twenty-one), my self-respect and common-sense required that one way or another, I would have to phase out my nicotine addiction. So, I decided I would need to find a way to block the siren song of craving for tobacco. How I successfully did this shall be detailed in an appendix to this book.

I realized the idea of returning to being clean and green, wouldn't be enough to curtail my ingrained addiction to tobacco. Giving up, needed to be sustained, by taking up helpful and satisfying practices, like walking, swimming, or jogging. Also learning meditation, and ways to calm and fulfil one's heart and mind. Also, I did feel that by clearing the ground of poisonous, and unsatisfactory addictions, I would be motivated to take up a more fruitful and creative way of life, than could be expected from just filling my emptiness with smoke. Of course implementing these changes would come neither quickly nor easily and had to be developed and nurtured, even in the face of occasional setbacks. Naturally I tried to share my enthusiasm for my new way of life with my friends, but not surprisingly they were not particularly interested, though to some degree they tolerated my newfound values, perhaps expecting them to be a passing phase.

* * *

Starting afresh

With the arrival of the end of the year I accepted an offer to spend Xmas at Ken's parent's house in Blackpool. After eventually getting his Rover-90 car up to scratch, we piled into his poor-mans 'Rolls Royce' and enjoyed a sedate drive to Blackpool. Unfortunately on arrival Ken very soon managed to lose his lump of hash, which for him was a major catastrophe, and most of Xmas and Boxing Day was spent looking for it. The significance of this spell for me, apart from enjoying having a proper bedroom and a comfortable bed, was that I discovered a book on Hatha Yoga, "Yoga and Health" by Selvarijan Yesudian and Elizabeth Haich, a copy of which I later acquired back in London: Simple practices such as Yoga; Tai Chi; as well as swimming and walking; can all be very helpful in improving well-being and creating a good state and basis for meditation. Thus, when back in London, over the next few months I started practicing yoga and meditation as well as regularly swimming and using the springboard at the Swiss Cottage Swimming Pool which in mornings was often empty, and later in after in afternoons studying in the adjacent Library. Also, I enjoyed making good use of the natural pools on Hampstead Heath the effects of all this, along with choosing to become vegetarian and stopping smoking, was that I felt better and continued to feel more confident and motivated in various ways.

The house where I lived had shared bathrooms on the landings, and this was the only place where I could find some quiet and relatively uninterrupted space, I figured I could bath briefly and then do periods of Yoga and Meditation, with more extended periods if no one had been tapping at the door. So it was that I became quite used to sitting in the full lotus in the bathroom, and giving appropriate mumbles if anyone knocked on the door. These combined periods with yoga and breathing exercises, seemed to help me a lot in my efforts to stop smoking, and soon I was not just swimming but actually enjoying it and also started to become more proficient with the spring board, and delighted in rising up into the air, then reaching to my toes as my legs flipped up behind me, and I slid gracefully into the pool feeling like a care free dolphin.

At this time the I.L.E.A. (the Inner London Education Authority) were less financially constrained than they became, and I soon discovered there was a whole array of day and evening classes that I could attend, as well as the Camden Arts Centre which was just up the road from where I lived.

Over the following months, as my yoga practice deepened, my states of mind clarified and my heart felt happier and more confident, I started to feel that to be a happy healthy human being is a good start, but also that I needed to heighten and deepen my levels of consciousness, and somehow come to terms with the nature of existence, also I wanted to improve my communication skills with other people and to be more in touch and open to learning. Meanwhile in order to shake off old habits; and not be drawn back into them, I needed some positive alternatives. So for starters I put the following advert in the local paper: "Penniless student offers partner for instruction, for driving, swimming, hatha yoga, and chess etc. Can also work in the garden, paint the kitchen, or walk the dog". As a result of which I landed a very good job and a developing friendship with a family in Hampstead. The fact that they paid me well was secondary to the help I received from just being in contact with healthy, straightforward and unexploitative employers. Michael and Pat Floyd who were themselves kept busy with an architectural practice, continued to employ me on and off for the next few years. Along with film work, this gave me a sort of tethering post and I enjoyed walking their dog the late Mitsey, as well as watering the plants and sometimes house minding while they were away.

Alongside part-time work and occasional film jobs, I had started regular life-drawing and colour technique morning classes at the nearby Camden Arts Centre, as well as evening classes at various Adult Education Classes in subjects which included: psychology, philosophy, hatha yoga, photography, guitar, English and judo, most of which I found quite interesting and enjoyable. Generally I was quite keen to go into things perhaps a bit more fully, than was really the scope of the evening class situation. In fact, my most fruitful studies were to come not so much from the class situation, as from reading a book on comparative religion and philosophy in the seclusion of a quiet part of Swiss Cottage library. The book in question was called "The Bible of the World" and contained writings from all sorts of traditions and had quite an effect on me over the next few months, as shall become clear later.

My general routine when possible was art classes in the morning, into which I would get quite involved, and then in the late morning quite a solid period of swimming and spring-board diving, in the air I would touch my toes, and then glide into the water, in what was often an empty pool. after which I would usually feel excellent and then after an inexpensive lunch at the nearby vegetarian community café, I would relax by listening to some music in one of the booths that were available in the library.

Thus it was that I would then approach my period of study often feeling already quite fulfilled, emotionally positive and very much alive. Perhaps because of this I often found while reading, all of my energies would be quite focused and concentrated and my experience of reading was totally absorbing and often very inspiring, so much so that I sometimes felt quite amazed that I was enjoying myself so much, almost irrespective of what I was actually reading.

* * *

Beginners luck

This charmed way of life, as should be quite clear, hadn't just fallen into my lap, in fact I did have to discipline myself and make an effort to keep the momentum going, and at times I did wonder where in fact I was going. Ken, whose sofa I was living on was pleased I had stopped smoking and had encouraged me to reconnect with bicycling which was a helpful move. He and his friends while usually friendly and well-meaning, generally resisted my efforts to interest them in what I was up to, and sometimes distracted or inadvertently impeded efforts, to cultivate a simpler and drug-free lifestyle and find meaning and purpose to existence. By now I had for about the last nine months completely stopped smoking or using any sorts of drugs and was quite happily leading an almost semi-monastic life, though I would masturbate when I felt I needed to.

Generally I was leading quite a self-contained and directed way of life, though I wasn't indifferent to the various sufferings of people in the world, and it was partly the fact of so much strife and turmoil which drove me to stay with the process of trying to sort out what is really of value in life. After coming home from the library and attending various chores or whatever needed doing, I would wait for a quiet period in the evening when most people were out and the bathroom on the landing was free, and then I would go and start up what was usually the highlight of my day. This consisted of first a quick bath to loosen me up, then some pranayama breathing exercises and asanas. While young and without forcing, I slowly became accustomed to sitting in the full lotus posture, which with gentle, modest and careful practice, had become gradually more accessible and comfortable over a few months, of course one can also sit in other postures or on a chair. Anyhow having established a good posture, I would meditate opposite the bathroom door, and focus on my breathing or a spot on the door in front of me and gradually become very calm, serene and concentrated. As far as it went this practice was very good, and I generally felt quite satisfied from doing it. But it just so happened, that after a few months a Buddhist meditation practice per chance was presented to me at what seemed just the right moment.

One day during my studies of "The Bible of the World" at Swiss Cottage library, I came across a preparatory meditation practice in the section on Buddhism and felt it would be a good idea to try it towards the completion of my usual practice. So after writing down some notes on what was a slightly more 'complicated' meditation practice than I was used to, and then having memorized the relevant details, one evening after my preliminary practice I then continued into what was a quite new and surprising experience. In a way the technique was irrelevant, the reason for its effectiveness was more likely that some groundwork and preparation had already been done, and so I was at least a little ready. Also there was an element of what is sometimes referred to as 'beginners' luck' inasmuch as I was quite fresh and new to what I was doing, and had few if any expectations or preconceptions. Anyhow for whatever reason the practice just worked much to my surprise, and gave me access to an 'experience' more satisfying than anything which I had encountered before.

Trying to explain this may be like trying to communicate the taste of sweetness, the colour of light or a beautiful fragrance, what I can do is to try and describe some of my own observations. In short my mind and body would dissolve into light, and simultaneously my breathing, which had by now become a tiny subtle point; would just dissolve with a sort of 'ping', and appear to completely stop. While on the first occasion this slightly awed me, as I wasn't used to such happenings, even so I wasn't too disconcerted, as the experience as a whole was so utterly delightful and felt totally natural. So I trusted the experience and happily let myself dissolve into it. And so I would abide in some form of 'Samadhi' or total absorption, for about forty-five minutes. Yet my body would stay erect and my mind, though apparently empty, was actually richer and more fulfilled than I could recall. It did not feel like a mere trance, but more like my self-consciousness had been dissolved or absorbed into an ocean of light. This experience was not a 'one off' and I was able to continue with the practice for a number of months. And am quite happy to admit, that at times this 'experience' of meditation was ecstatically blissful! And at times left me almost wonderstruck, and feeling that I had really almost inadvertently, stumbled across "The peace which passes all understanding". One thing which became undoubtedly clear to me after the first of these sessions, was that this experience, which seemed to come from gradually training and transforming mind and heart, is the 'philosophers stone', 'the drink to quench all thirsts' and to continue the clichés, 'the fountain of inspiration' which can uplift even the most troubled heart. Furthermore this experience, which wasn't obtained through artificially getting high, but was a natural and organic process of spiritual unfoldment, which seemed to transcend at least temporarily the difficulties and problems of existence. And more often than not, would leave me in a much better state for appreciating and coping with the wonder as well as the turmoil and tribulations of ordinary day-to-day existence.

In Buddhist terminology there is a parable in "The White Lotus Sutra" which alludes to a blind man who finds a precious jewel in the midst of a dung heap, so on my own level the experience felt a little like this. But after a while I became aware how easily this 'peak experience' could slip through my fingers, and felt it was my responsibility to live up to it, and even if it was just a 'flash in the pan', it was for me to capitalize on the experience and to try to transform my life accordingly.

* * *

Going forth

Incomprehension, indifference or slight interest was what I mostly seemed to find when I tried to share my thoughts and aspirations with other people about me, including teachers at some of the classes I went to. I mention this because as time went on, I reached a point where I felt it wasn't enough to just have blissful experiences and that meditation shouldn't just be an end in itself, and I didn't feel I could find the answer just in books. After a while for various reasons, I felt I couldn't continue living where I was, also I wanted to find some clearer understanding about meditation practice, so that I could give some expression to my experience and share it with others in an appropriate context, and not feel concerned at being ridiculed. Gradually I became aware that often, not only did people not want to change themselves, but they seemed to want me to stay as I was. But despite this I felt I needed to pursue the course I was on, and that 'standing by' what I believed in, was the best way I could be of help to others. In this respect there's an Indian adage that 'in order to grow, a small plant needs to be protected, then after it has grown stronger, is less easily trampled on, and in due course may be of benefit to others. Naturally I tried to share my values with other people but felt very much out on a limb and not very able to communicate. To try and get some perspective on things, occasionally I went on sojourns: I hitch-hiked to Snowdonia and stayed at Youth Hostels, another time I hitched to Cornwall, where the mass of vivid yellow and mauve wild flowers on the cliff-tops seemed particularly wonderful to my city worn eyes, and also I enjoyed meditating in a hut on the beach. Another area I spent time hiking was under the vast white 'Seven Sisters' cliffs near Seaford. I appreciate it can be inappropriate to enthuse about one's 'spiritual encounters', yet by comparison to me it seems odd, that we find it normal in society to be bombarded with an endless flow of half-truths via advertising and various forms of media, some of which may be entertaining and other parts clearly downright harmful. So, in this respect I was surprised having just returned from a spell out of London, to see on a Hampstead high street billboard a non-commercial advert, in the form of a picture of the South Indian Guru/teacher Sri Chinmoy, and below this in large letters one of his aphorisms which ran "When the power of Love, replaces the love of power, man will have a new name, God". Up till then I had not thought of meeting any external teachers. Now partly due to my circumstances and partly because I was intrigued, I took down the details of his forthcoming event.

Angels seemed to be hovering around the entrance, when one evening I duly arrived at Friends Meeting House in Euston Road. As I drew closer I was able to see that in fact they were young men and women dressed in white dhotis and sarongs and to some extent looking fairly radiant and happy. I was a bit taken back and didn't know what to say, but I went in and found a seat. While I waited in a seat, I was half expecting to hear some sort of talk, but to my surprise when Sri Chinmoy came on the stage, he communicated himself mainly through silence. His 'Darshan' or presence didn't seem to contradict another of his aphorisms, which ran "Purity is my body's name, clarity my mind's name, sincerity my heart's name and spontaneity my soul's name", and his presence did seem both potent and to affect the atmosphere. To add to this after a while he gave a recital of some quite haunting flute music.

At the end of the evening's proceedings he invited those interested in the audience to come up on to the stage and have some closer contact with him, by standing in a line on the stage, while he in turn walked along, thus meeting people's faces individually. I decided not to go up at first, but then went up, as I thought perhaps, I was avoiding something. It was about this time in my life that despite my semi-literate state, I tried to express myself in a piece of prose, which crude as it may be, was along these lines:

People move in different states,
Human, 'sub-human', and trans-human,
People move about with 'purpose',
Doing things because they always have
Do they act in vain?
We tentatively communicate,
But rarely take 'it' very far
Lest we should find out!

People suffer because they fear the truth.
Yet truth is compassionate.
Deviation from it causes pain.

The sentiments in these verses partly express why I felt compelled to accept that invitation to have some closer communication. Also, my mind-heart was now interested in meeting and learning about other people's points of view. Being naive and impulsive, I felt I should act first and ask questions as I went along, when and where appropriate. Later, there was a small banquet for Sri Chinmoy at a meditation centre in Cromwell Rd, to which I was invited, while there I wasn't interested in eating, as I was preoccupied with coming to terms with what it was that I was getting involved in, or at least 'checking out'! After the meal, just minutes before Sri Chinmoy left by taxi for the airport, I tried asking a few questions. His disposition towards me seemed quite friendly and some of the questions were answered, but I hadn't chosen a very good time, and others were not resolved, and were sort of left hanging in the air.

Meanwhile I let myself become provisionally involved in what seemed quite a positive and friendly group of people and started going along to some of their shared meditations. It had been suggested to me by Sri Chinmoy that I should cut off my long hair, which I was quite attached to. At first I exclaimed what! But later, on consideration, I felt that since I was so attached to my self-image perhaps he had a point. So, a few days later, I went from having long hair to short hair.

After a few months I still wasn't sure which way I wanted to go, and it was suggested that I go for a spell in New York, to Sri Chinmoy's birthday celebrations, and so it was that I sold my much-loved Praktica Camera and with some savings went to New York. Almost as soon as the plane took off I found myself wondering what the heck I was doing, and whether it was the right thing. I sort of felt like I had lost contact with the ground and that the way of life which I had nurtured was fast receding, and that I was stepping from one steppingstone to another, which was not very clearly in focus.

* * *

New York

The sun was setting as I emerged from Kennedy airport, I was amazed at the size of some of the policemen, and thought it was a good thing I had short hair. On arrival at the place were Sri Chinmoy lived, along with others I was received by Alo Devi a senior women friend-disciple of Sri Chinmoy, she gave us the 'once over' with her deep gaze. By now I was feeling pretty exhausted, but my communication with her seemed quite good, the following day there was a similar process, which this time involved her and Sri Chinmoy.

The event seemed larger than I had imagined, and people were allocated different places to stay in various houses dotted about. The fellow who put me up in Queens District, seemed busy but friendly, he kindly introduced me to his 'Mickey Mouse' snack, cheese on toast with two large eyes made from sliced tomato. The weather was very hot and quite a few local kids seemed to be selling lemonade from their front gardens to anyone who looked thirsty.

After the main events were over, I stayed on for a few weeks, occasionally I was taken along to various venues, where public talks and meditation meetings were being held, a few were at universities including one which was at Harvard. On one occasion at a sort of large garden party, a New York television crew came to interview Sri Chinmoy, and when he was asked to describe his teaching, he stated quite simply that his was the path of 'Love, devotion and surrender' Another of his aphorisms was 'Wisdom borrowed debt repaid'…

By now I myself, at least in appearance, had become a 'New York Angel', as an English devotee had kindly given me one of his white dhotis a few days after my arrival on the scene, which he had said I should wear on various occasions, while at other time white trousers would be alright, I was quite happy to try it out and didn't mind floating about New York in a dhoti. One thing which I wasn't really ready for, was that I was supposed to try and observe strict chastity, which was something I really wasn't used to, and to add to this there was the heat, the mosquitoes and all the general hustle and bustle which I also wasn't used to, so that after a few weeks It all just seemed too much, and one hot afternoon I succumbed to masturbating, about which I felt a bit ashamed, though I got over that after a few days.

After a while I was given various jobs. One of Sri Chinmoy's devotees at that time was Maha Vishnu John McLaughlin, an accomplished and popular guitarist; in London he had given a bunch of us an impressive guitar recital. In New York he drove some of us to the coast where we played beach ball. Also he owned or ran a vegetarian restaurant called 'Annam Brahma' (which interprets as 'food is god'), so for a while I worked there, and also for a while I worked in a sort of new age book shop. His wife was also helpful and kind.

After about a month of living in New York, my general consensus was that while I had partly enjoyed myself and found the time interesting, I actually felt a bit of a mess, and that I needed some space in which to recuperate. Part of my conclusion was that while previously I had perhaps been too self-orientated and relied purely on my own efforts, now the situation seemed to be a bit too much the other way. I also felt that there were other faculties which I had previously started to make use of, and which now felt they had been put 'on hold'. So I decided to draw back from things and review the situation. Basically I felt I needed to balance devotion with understanding.

It so happened that Ken whom I had stayed with in London and his friend Rodger Bowdler (whose great grandfather had 'bowdlerised' books) were due to be in America in the next few weeks, Rodger was promoting the American edition of his book "Sense and sensuality" and had offered me a free lift from New York to San Francisco if I wanted it. So after some heart-searching I passed on a message to Sri Chinmoy that I was considering going to San Francisco, and his response was in the affirmative, at least from what I was told, and so I went ahead and made the various arrangements. Some of his San Francisco disciples came and talked with me and gave me their address to contact them when I reached the West Coast. Something I haven't mentioned is that every week or so, Sri Chinmoy conducted meditation sessions for World Peace, in a chapel at the United Nations building, these particular sessions were open to diplomats and the like, though not to the general public. I had already been to some of these sessions, and was invited to come to one, which would be taking place on the morning that I would be leaving.

So it was that on my last morning in New York, a few hours before I was due to be meeting Ken and Rodger with the car and the start of a long drive west. I found myself for the last time at the United Nations chapel still dressed white shirt and dhoti as Sri Chinmoy moved around the few people that were there sharing his darshan or spiritual presence. This turned out to be perhaps my most potent interaction I had with Sri Chinmoy, presumably he recalled I was leaving, since when he came round to me, our eye contact and communication seemed to go deeper and longer than previously. Sri Chinmoy himself at these times appeared to be absorbed in a deep meditative state, which he seemed to be able to radiate to those about him; perhaps the degree to which this happened would be affected by whether one was in a receptive state. Anyhow, one way or another I found myself drawn into a very pure, blissful and buoyant state! Later that morning after leaving the United Nations Building, now in normal clothes and heading with my backpack to meet up with Ken and Rodger, I noticed that I was still feeling very light and seemed to be almost floating as I walked along the pavements. And I felt that our last meeting as well resolving and clarifying some things, had also been a good reminder, which I took to heart and resolved not to just let slip away.

***

Overland (three humans in a car)

After much messing about, Rodger settled on buying a car, and later that afternoon he, Ken and myself found ourselves in a fancy-looking second-hand Malibu saloon. Although all three of us were in the same car and heading west, it soon became clear that in other respects we didn't seem to be heading in the same direction at all, in fact at times we seemed to be going in quite different directions. But despite our various ways we decided not to magnify our differences and instead to do what we could to get on with each other and to appreciate our journey across America. Our long drive once underway was uneventful, other than the novelty of just being in the States and becoming accustomed to American sights and sounds and ways of doing things. Very soon we had passed through Washington and made our way to the South via New Orleans, doing a bit of sightseeing and occasionally staying at motels along the way, we planned to camp once we were in the warmer South.

We were warned by police to look out for snakes under our tents, and though on one occasion in South Carolina I was very nearly bitten by a very large spider, I was lucky and apart from a bee sting had few problems. In Florida we visited the Kennedy Space Centre, where I have to admit that due to financial constraints, I was passed off as eighteen, though I was twenty-three and went in for half price.

The space centre seemed like something out of a James Bond movie, as the weather was very hot and the place was quite large and dotted about the grounds were security notices which if contravened could result in being shot or bitten by snakes. Inside the actual buildings was the surreal sight of astronauts in training for one of the Apollo flights. A few days later when we were camping on the beach of the Florida coast, I found myself wondering whether I was going to be blown into space myself, after we had just bedded down for the night, and then later woke up to find ourselves in the middle of a tropical storm in which our tents were not just blown down but almost blown away.

Americans while sometimes brash could also be quite helpful, as was the case when a bunch of Texans sauntered up to us on one occasion, put down their beer cans, and then pushed our car out from a beach where it had got stuck, after which they heartily introduced themselves and shook hands with us before leaving to return to a rodeo event which was taking place nearby. So it was that one way and another we eventually succeeded in making our way on to the Californian coast, through Big Sur where we stopped to look at the waves and eventually on to San Francisco, by which time we were all pretty exhausted and were all pleased to have arrived, though this now entailed making decisions and finding places to stay.

* * *

San Francisco

Most American cities didn't seem to have the density or size of London, even so they could be quite impressive and downtown San Francisco seemed to be no exception. In some ways it all seemed a bit like a dream just watching this large city materialize before my eyes. Though I soon realized I needed to put my feet firmly on the ground and find somewhere to stay before nightfall.

Rodger had decided to find a place and live on his own for a while, before later continuing to Mexico. Meanwhile Ken and I mainly for financial reasons decided to find a cheap apartment which we could share, and soon found ourselves in the Haight Ashbury area of San Francisco which had now seemed a bit of a ghost-town, as we searched around run down areas for a half decent and low priced flat.

Eventually we moved into an unfurnished apartment in Page Street, which wasn't too expensive as it had a flyover/highway running quite near to the property which seemed slightly bizarre and to underline that this was very much the land of the automobile. And on sunny days when I went and sun-bathed or did yoga on the flat roof, I would watch a little bemused at the endless stream of Cadillacs zooming past. Various incidents occurred which brought home to me that I was actually in America, one night while out a couple of plainclothes police with guns in hand briefly accosted me in their search for someone, and on another occasion a couple of black guys came along each side of me, I didn't know what they were up to, so instead of waiting to find out I put my arms partially around them and said hello fellas which seemed to make them laugh and after a while they went on their way.

Though I didn't visit the place, apparently there was a Zen centre, near Page Street where we were residents, and on one occasion I observed a Zen monk on the street whose general composure made quite an impression on me. Another incident which also made an impression on me was having a rapport with a girl. We actually came to meet as a result of her cat which one day I noticed, had a third eye inked in between its other two eyes, while I was observing this Sue (in this case from Dallas) came to the door and we soon got to know each other. She was about nineteen and yet within a few days asked me to sleep with her, in fact at the time she put it rather more bluntly than that. I pointed out that she was still living with Tom her boyfriend, so she made me come down to her flat to receive his freely given consent. But despite this, I felt she was asking me to treat her more like a sexual object than a person and much to her exasperation I declined to get immediately involved. Though I was attracted to her, I somehow felt our communication would not be helped by immediately jumping into bed with each other, and perhaps due to past experience, also felt that in some respects we would just be selling ourselves short. Despite my being a little backwards in being forwards, we continued to enjoy each other's company and went on excursions to the large redwoods and stopped off at a museum where we both sat in the half lotus posture and gazed into each other's eyes for long periods, to the bemusement of some of the passers-by, since we were seated in a gallery surrounded by lots of other seated Buddha figures.

Later it transpired that Sue was a bit perplexed, as her friend Tom was to some degree pre-occupied with the local Zen Centre, and then there was myself no less caught up with meditation. Even so we continued to get on well, though I found it hard to explain, that in the first place due to my confused background and lack of qualifications or skills I felt inadequate and lacked confidence, and in fact felt I was barely able to take responsibility for sorting out my own mixed up state of being, let alone at that stage to be able to sort out someone else's life. And secondly, I felt I had gradually lost contact with meditation practice of any depth, and I felt impelled not to be distracted from my main concern which was to have contact with people mainly a basis of shared ideals and values, and not just based on mutual infatuation.

Anyhow it wasn't long before lack of money became a problem and it became clear I would have to find a job quickly, and so I started working at the Golden Gate cinema as an usher, though I had to pretend I had a work permit. This went alright until one day the manageress suddenly announced the immigration were about to turn up, so my job had to be cut short and I left in a hurry, to the loud strains of "if I was a rich man" which was one of the main songs in 'Fiddler on the roof', the current film showing. I realized that the manageress or owner, may have fiddled me out of my wages, although she may have been correct in her assertion.

* * *

After a while both Ken and I started working for a fellow who had the franchise on an up-market ice-cream parlour called Blums. Ted, who was Irish-American, employed us mainly as we were English and he knew he wouldn't have to pay the full going rate, though we were expected to try and speak with American accents. As employers go he wasn't bad and we did have a few laughs, though we had to work six days a week and ten hours a day and sometimes longer. I enjoyed the work as it got me away from the derelict atmosphere of the place where I was living, I was now saving up to probably return to England, while Ken had plans to possibly continue with Rodger to Mexico which is what he eventually did. I didn't always find the work easy as some of the customers could be quite demanding like the man who would always complain if his knicker-blocker-glory with its ten or so layers; happened to have one of the flavours placed at the wrong level in the tall glass. My staff uniform candy-striped shirt and white trousers, matched the walls so well, that if I leaned on the wall I could hardly be spotted, but if I really needed a break I would go and sit in the storeroom and dream about leaving. The floor above Blums contained the offices of a number of psychiatrists and so both they and their clients also frequented the place and some of the conversations of both clients and the doctors could be amusing at times.

To get away from Blums, on my days off I did various things like visit Angel Island; a local beauty spot, reached by a ferry whose route went past a smaller island which had housed the prison Alcatraz. On other days I went for long walks sometimes over the large bay bridge and from time to time I saw Sue. On one of my days off, when I had been working about six months in San Francisco I went to see the (as it turned out) appalling film 'Clockwork Orange', which I had done some crowd scenes on, I don't recall enjoying the movie, but there was another movie also shown as part of the program which had been directed by Nick Roeg, and this was the film 'Walk-A-Bout' which struck a chord with me partly because of its theme, but mainly because of the spacious and timeless way in which it portrayed the Australian bush or 'out-back', anyhow I left the cinema with a strong inclination to go somewhere with wide open spaces.

In the next few days I phoned the Canadian and Australian consulates and asked about emigration prospects and found that for Canada I would have to apply from England, but Australia were prepared to accept me there and then, as long as I had a chest x-ray and passed various basic criteria. And so I announced to Ken and later to Sue my plan to leave for Australia in the next week or so pending flight bookings, I had already worked out I had just about enough money to get there. I explained to Sue that I would use the time and space to sort myself out a bit and that I was happy to stay in contact and that we could perhaps meet up in England at a later date, if that turned out to be what she really wanted to do. She felt I was being too impulsive and part of me was sorry to be leaving, but all along I had made it clear that at least for the moment I was pre-occupied by prior commitments which I couldn't really explain. Ken was also surprised, but eventually all the preliminaries were sorted out and Tom, Sue, and Ken came with me to the airport. After we had bade each other farewell, I made my way through the departure lounge and then through a corridor where a couple of large black security guards also bade me farewell and informed me my Qantas flight had already boarded, and that I should get a move on, and so it was that I left American soil, the land of Buffalos and The American Dream…

During the flight almost to my own disbelief, it started to sink in that I was now bound, not back to the United Kingdom but for the Australian continent. I can recommend flying with Qantas originally 'Queensland And Northern Territories Aerial Service', at least so far as that flight was concerned, the plane was not packed and the crew were very friendly which helped as I needed a bit of cheering up, and on the practical side, they provided very good vegetarian food. Well into the flight after we had stopped over at Hawaii and were back on course, one of the stewards told me there was some room in the first-class section where I could stretch out and get some proper sleep if I wanted to. After I came round from my sleep, I looked out the porthole and saw that the sky was a brilliant blue and I shortly learned that we were not just above Australia but also quite close to Sydney.

To my surprise the steward brought me a copy of the Sydney Herald which had been picked up somewhere along the way and gave me a few hints about where to find reasonably priced places to stay and what the current prospects would be for employment. I was glad to arrive safely in Sydney, in good spirits and not feeling too stressed;

procedures through customs didn't take long and were cordial. Before long I found myself on the streets of Sydney and it was still only about mid-afternoon, so I had a few hours in which to find a place to stay. After a few enquiries and a bit of trekking about, I made for Kings Cross which I was told had cheap hotels that were also quite central, and before long I had found a slightly run-down but adequate place, to have some rest before looking for a job and another place.

CHAPTER FOUR

Walk-a-bout (22-23)

Sydney

    Standing in an old bathtub which doubled as a shower, I moved about to get the trickle of water to cover all of my body, the afternoon was hot and sticky and though the water was not completely cold, it was still very refreshing. I got a small fright when suddenly something shot from under the bath and across the floor, at first I thought it was a mouse but then realized it was a rather oversized reddish-brown cockroach. Meditating while on the bathroom floor didn't appeal to me much on that occasion, and in any case I felt a bit oppressed by the heat. Back in my room, without thinking too much I got out my wooden flute and played a few ditties, when the bloke managing the place burst into the room. He seemed oblivious to my being only in my underpants and proceeded to demand to know if I was nuts, and whether I realized the possible consequences of disturbing his other clientele (who worked night shifts). His urgency suggested he was informing me as much for my sake, so looking a bit sheepish, I pulled on some shorts and told him, no I hadn't realized, and he calmed down.

Not feeling too comfortable, I went out for an early evening stroll and a look about, soon I was button-holed by a fellow who asked if I would come to a small gospel meeting about to take place nearby, I asked him what they did and he replied they would sing a few songs. Not having much in mind I agreed to come for half an hour. Standing there singing old hymns, seemed a bit like I had entered a time warp, I actually enjoyed just singing, as I had enjoyed singing Xmas carols when I was a kid. As I left a lady smiled and gave me a leaflet, the heading of which asked me "ARE YOU CON-FUSED?", and I reflected with some irony that in some respects this was quite a pertinent question.

Being somewhat rootless and uneducated and of a single disposition, along with my beneficial experience of yoga and meditation practice, and being vegetarian all made me an outsider (in the 1970s), as did having a clear affinity with ancient Buddhist teachings on matters such as karma, and rebirth or 're-becoming'. Just as a candle burns out and a new candle may be lit from the former, so too life ends, and in accordance with our thoughts and actions our karma, may lead to a new conception, which is a completely different life, but still may carry some subtle influence or karmic seeds from the past. Also, my believing in the potential for mundane human evolution to be superseded by spiritual evolution and even transcendental awakening may be frowned upon by some sections of society.

Thus, basically I am aware that some Christian groups wouldn't have much time for the likes of myself, unless I was to compromise and abandon what I believe most likely to be true. That said I don't really care whether we call 'it' or reality, Christ, Krishna or Buddha. In Buddhist terms the main thing for me is that people try to live ethical, spiritual and compassionate lives. Or in other words people should try to stop fighting; polarizing and causing problems, and instead create solutions. As the Dhammapada (a Buddhist text) puts it: 'Hatred is not ended by hatred, but by love, this is the law eternal, many do not realize that we are all heading for death, those who do realize this, do not fight one another, but compose their quarrels'. To me it seemed that since the church is not likely to modify its own basic tenets and practices; the only options open to them seemed to be to convert or condemn me, even so I enjoyed the friendliness and singing, and wish them and all forms of life, human goodness, spiritual beauty and divine truth.

The next day I found a job working in Sydney's Hyde Park as a garden labourer, though this entailed first passing a medical exam performed by a slightly odd doctor, but it seemed sensible to drop my shorts as requested, while he assessed whether I had any existing health issues, or I might not have got the job. I had a few days before commencing work, which gave me time to unwind and find a better room. I visited the botanical gardens and was surprised at the lushness and size of the plants and loved the birds of paradise (Strelitzias). I was also intrigued that some of the local beaches for swimming had shark nets to prevent lunchtime swimmers from becoming midday snacks. While the city itself was not that large, the Sydney suburbs seemed to sprawl out in all directions, after a bit of searching I settled on a room just a boomerang's throw from Bondi Beach. The landlord who lived on the premises was Danish and had a friendly disposition towards his tenants, even to the extent of informing me I could borrow his old-fashioned wooden surfboard, which he now rarely used.

I was quick to take up his offer, though I soon realized learning to surf wasn't going to happen overnight, even so I enjoyed splashing about in the water, and sometimes felt I must have looked a bit of a pale and comical sight to the local surfers, but I also had some reflections about them, which also tries capture something of my initial recollections of Bondi beach:

Surfers. (Sydney, Bondi beach).

I touched the beach with borrowed surfboard
My small efforts, at odds with its excessive size
Still, I enjoyed blue sky, and the soft warm breeze
Rolling white surf, and dazzling sands.

Boys and youths in shorts, glance my way
Blonde hair, bronzed bodies, white sun painted faces
With surfboards tucked under arm, entering the sea
Running too the ocean; too light; too freedom.

Soon confidently riding blue and white water,
Silhouetted by the shimmering sun,
Gliding in on rolling and crashing waves.
The day is done, they huddle in groups,
And then guzzle fruit-juice or pepsi-cola,

Smoking and joking, nibbling and nattering,
Then heading for the take-a-ways!
And in no time, we are all gone…

Soon my own skin started to get bronzed and in the evenings I covered myself in coconut oil, having usually had too much sun, and then drank cold orange juice or ate tropical fruits. After finding a large spider in my under-pants, I took to mostly sleeping under my mosquito net, much to the bewilderment of the landlord since there weren't many mosquitoes. I tried to re-establish the sort of meditation practices I had done in England but found that my state of being wasn't the same, and slowly came to appreciate I would just have to start again. Despite the heat and various distractions, I continued to meditate each day, even if this only involved contemplating a sprig of the blossoms which grew in profusion by the front door. My beginners luck now seemed to have run low, so while I tried to emulate meditation practice, also I tried to let go of any expectations. At this stage I had little appreciation of the various approaches to meditation, such as 'just sitting', 'developing/contemplating' or 'imagining', life had got more complicated and less happy, even so I still tried to be open to 'it'.

* * *

Hyde and Centennial parks

Working fulltime I soon discovered the cheapest and simplest way to shop was a place known as Paddy's market, which was run rather like a coal merchant's yard, except their merchandise was a vast array of exotice fruit and vegetables, which were on display in great big wooden crates. So the whole yard was a mass of colour, and for a few dollars I would come away loaded up with more than enough to see me through the week. My job in Hyde Park was pretty easy going, though I had to get used to a bit of teasing about being a 'Pommy' almost fresh from England. For a few days I was put with another young fellow, and while watering and attending to various tasks we talked. He was a proper trainee gardener; he showed me his butterfly collection and told me about a course he had recently finished. At tea breaks I was exposed to various fun and games from the various characters that made up the parks quota of workers and was soon accepted as one of the boys, though one older bloke took exception when he saw me eating a yogurt one lunchtime, and declared 'this was what you would expect from a prissy pom', and that 'I'd only been here a few days and already I was lowering the depot's standards, by eating yogurt, which was office girls food, and by implication only for wimps! He was about sixty, six feet tall, weather-beaten and I couldn't help being amused and laughed.

    Generally they were quite a friendly bunch and I got on well, though I could still expect the occasional prank like when they asked me to go to the shop at a particular time, and I came back absolutely drenched from a downpour, the like of which I had rarely seen and realized they had foreseen this. I didn't mind as I had actually been amazed by the sheer volume of the rain which was quite warm and my shorts and tee-shirt soon dried. On the far side of the park was a road where lots of office girls and other commuters disembarked from their bus rides into the city, and at peak periods I would be sent over to sweep up their discarded bus tickets, which I sometimes did in a slightly exaggerated fashion, dancing about and chasing after offending tickets, with my rather oversized broom, which succeeded in amusing some of the office girls. After a while at the suggestion of my landlord, I managed to arrange a transfer to work in Centennial Park, which was closer to my lodgings near Bondi Beach, and he assured me this park was a very beautiful place, with rose gardens, duck ponds and great big Eucalyptus trees and lots of cockatoos, and he was right.

    The only drawback was that, while I got on alright with the workers, the regime running Centennial Park was much stricter, and I had to dig and toil to the point of exhaustion on most days, which in itself wasn't so bad as to some degree I adjusted to the workload, but the atmosphere was less happy, and more akin to forced labour. At lunchtimes I did relaxation exercises and even headstands inside the toilet cubicles, as the floors were clean and large enough, and late in the afternoon I sometimes meditated in the bushes in the full lotus. Centennial park was indeed very beautiful, as well as being unkempt and rugged in parts. We were assigned our own areas and for my part I worked mostly in the rose garden, and I spent many a week turning over flower beds often reciting odd bits of poetry, or mantras, or verses from pop songs. There was one from 'The Incredible String Band' : "May the long-time sun shine upon you, all love surround you, and the pure light within you, guide you all the way on". But despite using various methods to make the work more satisfying, after a few months the days dragged, and I started to feel like I was just marking time.

On one occasion I had to pull out hundreds of marigolds prematurely, because Prince Philip was going to be visiting in a few months and it was decided the beds should be re-planted so as to blossom just as he arrived. I couldn't help thinking the poor chap must find it a bit odd if everywhere he goes the flowers are just coming into blossom. For a few months I enjoyed working in Centennial Park, the trees, plants, flowers, birdlife, and scents were all new to my eyes and ears, and at the end of the day I often felt happily worn out as I trudged up to the depot with my wheelbarrow. Then after putting tools away and rolling up hoses, I would unwind under a cold shower listening to the banter of my workmates. Then I would go and find a big warm rock and watch the sun starting to descend, before making my way home. Yet as time went on, I started to feel all I had done was move from a sordid loneliness in London bed-sitters, to a dry alienating loneliness in Australia. I just didn't seem to have any real depth of communication or contact with other human beings.

Whether young or old; aloneness within the context of spiritual solitude and practice, may be beautiful, meaningful and worthwhile, though alienating loneliness without much meaning, may become painful and difficult. In this respect, it would be good if our education system prepared us to engage creatively with all life's ups and downs. It would be helpful to learn how to be with others, but also how to be alone and at peace with ourselves. In a healthy society people could work fewer hours, and continue with learning and sharing in various ways, not just with a view to passing exams, but also to appreciate and enjoy of all that is worthy in our culture. Instead of treating education as a giant production line for making money, we could put more emphasis on producing 'happy, healthy human beings'. And revalue subjects like art, music, literature and non-competitive physical education with options such as hatha yoga, tai chi, meditation, dancing, and singing as added options.

Our society needs relationships between people, based not just on short-lived mutual infatuation, but also lasting and meaningful values. By mutual infatuation, imagine two trees leaning on each other at an angle so both trees have their own roots pulled out of the ground, so they have virtually stopped growing. And these trees are repeating to each other "I can't live without you", well of course this is true, if one of them moves away the other falls flat on its face, and they both constantly feel the weight of each other desperately clinging.

We may be better off enjoying more rounded relationships, with a balanced and healthy emotional independence, and a general sense of well-being, we may then have some basis through which to see what is really happening, and thereby be able to be real friends, rather than addicts leaning on each other. "To thine own self be true, and it follows as the day the night, that thou shalt not be false to any person"! It's said that only beasts or angels can endure sustained loneliness, and this may well be so. But I believe that at least for short periods, any well-rounded human being should be capable of appreciating his or her own company. A central Buddhist meditation practice is the cultivation of universal loving kindness, which starts with one-self, and then overflows and extends to include: friends; strangers and difficult people, feeling that love equally for all, it then extends to include all sentient beings and all forms of life, as beautifully expressed in the Buddhist Metta Sutra on loving-kindness (Included in the appendix). The Beatles pop group are right all we need is love, although that love needs to be True love.

The material world is unreliable. William Shakespeare reminds us we need a higher purpose in life, when in his play The Tempest he states: "Be cheerful sir, thou revels now are ended… These our actors, as I foretold you, were all spirits, and are melted into air, into thin air, And like the baseless fabric of this vision, the cloud-capped towers, the gorgeous palaces, The solemn temples, the great globe itself, yea all which it inherit, shall dissolve, And, like this insubstantial pageant faded, Leave not a rack behind: we are such stuff As dreams are made on; and our little life, Is rounded with a sleep". (Wordsworth Classics).

Reconnecting with my situation in Sydney, at this stage in my life I felt driven by various impulses and aspirations though I couldn't articulate them very well. At that time, I hadn't learned the difference between circumstantial loneliness, and positive enjoyable aloneness, which is quite a different matter. If there's no music in one's life, one can hardly expect to enjoy the pauses, of course the reverse of this also holds true. Gradually it was dawning on me that for effective meditation I needed to recreate a way of life which was not just hard work, but which was in human terms at least moderately happy and fulfilling. There didn't seem to be a lot open to me, but I kept my eyes open and tried whatever worthwhile options presented themselves. Initially I started helping collect money for a charity which also afforded me some friendly contact with other human beings, and not long after I started visiting a yoga centre situated in a warehouse in central Sydney, which was run by a young (Asian) Indian with long hair, who on the back of his Volkswagen sported the word -RELAX- in large bold letters.

* * *

Blue Mountains and Outback

As a result of my contact with the Yoga Centre, with some reticence I eventually succumbed to going on an organized weekend retreat in the Blue Mountains, which was to be conducted partly in silence and also consisted of a semi-fast, made up of a diet of a variety of tropical juices and fruit like bananas if one really needed to eat, which was easy to adapt to since the weather was very hot, and of course I enjoyed trying the variety of juices.

The bluish hue of the mountains and the deep valley surrounded us did inspire a feeling of wide-open space and expansiveness, I was also intrigued by the odd-looking ants and all sorts of other insects which I hadn't encountered before. It was enjoyable having good company and yet maintaining silence. The silence wasn't dull or oppressive, but light and happy, and seemed to add to our delight as we stripped off and plunged into deep rock pools to cool off during the hot afternoons. In a way this little retreat felt like the first holiday that I had ever had, although at times I became aware of underlying currents of confusion and uncertainty, which I didn't express, other than to acknowledge they were there. This was partly tied up with feelings of being rootless and having no sense of achievement or belonging.

When people asked me what I had done at school and other complicated questions, I could never find satisfactory answers and tended to feel worthless. As a youngster it didn't occur to me to reverse the question and perhaps ask "What did school do to me?" With hindsight it is easier to appreciate that in those days teachers' situations were limited by the demands of the situation in which they worked, such as having oversized classes and minimal time, training, or resources for responding to or dealing with the needs of children with inadequate or repeatedly disrupted home-lives.

Since most of the retreat was in silence, I just observed my various thoughts and feelings arising and eventually passing away like clouds in the sky. For two consecutive evenings I was able to meditate or just lie on my sleeping bag and experience myself as I was, without having recourse to distractions, apart from glancing around at the other participants in the church or scout hall we were using as a dormitory or eating bananas and sipping fruit juice. In due course Sunday afternoon arrived and it was time to emerge from the Blue Mountains back into the hustle and bustle of Sydney. After being back at work for a few weeks, I couldn't wait to get away again. There was a long weekend coming up and on this occasion I decided to go into the bush. I didn't prepare for my excursion very carefully; in fact I went (for the most part) barefoot, in a pair of shorts and t-shirt, with a sunhat, a sleeping bag, insect repellent and a water bottle.

My idea was to fast and thereby travel light on my mini 'walk-a-bout'. To reach the National Park I travelled by train, and then after collecting a few leaflets from an information office, I headed into the bush. That evening as I read the leaflets, I was a little startled to realize the area I was in was noted for funnel-web spiders and various snakes that could prove fatal. Though I slept alright, I might have preferred to have had a tent and other gear.

Because the weather was very hot I didn't find the prospect of going without food for two or three days too hard, even so when I came across a family picnicking and camping in style, I was starting to feel hungry and perhaps also looked so, since they offered me a piece of toasted Vogel's (a popular bread in Australia) with margarine and Vegemite, though I kindly declined their offer, I later on realized that I had been affected by their friendly disposition, and even that I was feeling a bit lonely and sort of emotionally alienated from the rest of the human race, and I acknowledged that there was a part of me that wanted to be in contact with other human beings.

Over the next couple of days, I started to realize in this instance I wasn't particularly on retreat in the sense of opening to higher levels of consciousness. But it was more that I needed to find space in which to experience various hurts and pains, which I felt could be exorcised by spending time on my own. And in a sense it did help. I enjoyed being away from civilization and in a relatively wild and primitive environment, where I could dance and sing and laugh and reflect as well as meditate and chant and briefly sunbathe naked under the vast blue sky, and at nights listen to the silence and be mesmerized by the myriad stars.

After three days a train was due, though this would have entailed finding my way back to where I had disembarked, and I decided it would be easier to try to get to a road and then hitch back to Sydney. I was lucky not to get lost. By the following day I had managed to do this and even got a good lift quite quickly with a youngish man who during our conversation told me he was a trainee naval architect, and he of course wanted to know what I had done at school and that sort of thing. So I told him something to the effect that my father had believed that most education systems tended to hinder as much as to help in the development of young people, and so he hadn't made much effort to keep me at school, though he had taught me to play chess and imbued me with the values and principles he considered important. Though I admitted on a practical level, my alternative education hadn't really equipped me to participate in modern society.

After showing some genuine interest in his vocation, I proceeded to enquire to what degree he felt his career would give his life meaning and satisfaction, and was it not possible that his life might just be swallowed up by mediocre living, and that his place in society might if he wasn't careful, just act as a 'siren song' to undermine his incentive to look much further than enjoying his lot and hoping it lasted for ever. Of course I admitted in other ways the same might happen to me. In fact our conversation was quite light-hearted and we laughed at the development of our discussion. We also enjoyed quiet interludes and appreciated the changing scenery which eventually started to give way to built-up areas and before long I was back in the city where we bade each other farewell and I made my way back to my bedsit at Bondi Beach.

My days working in Centennial Park were soon to come to an end, to make the time less tedious I was in the habit of sometimes meditating in the bushes during tea-breaks which didn't endear me to my bosses who wondered where I was during the breaks, but what really upset matters was my other odd habit of during the lunch break of doing odd yoga exercises. I found that by completely relaxing flat out on the ground for a few minutes before lunch, I would start to feel quite rejuvenated from the morning's exertions; eventually this habit of mine became accepted. I never let on about my even greater sin, which was that during the afternoon tea-breaks I sometimes did headstands on the toilet floor behind the locked door where I couldn't be seen, as this made me feel less tired after having been on my feet most of the day. The toilet cubicles were quite clean and large enough; it was just a matter of putting a jumper on the floor.

I was quite able to go up on my head for five minutes and to descend smoothly without anyone being any the wiser, until the inevitable happened. One afternoon the over-all boss was having a pee, after which he must have been checking some money, some of which fell on to the floor. So he bent down to stop a coin rolling under my door and noticing there was something there he looked under the door and straight into my face, which was of course upside down. Our eyes met and he looked totally puzzled and I myself was speechless, and my face broke into a smile, as the thought flitted across my mind how bizarre it must appear to this strait-laced elderly Aussie to see this whipper-snapper pom peering at him apparently the wrong way up.

As my mind searched for a plausible excuse, I thought of saying I was homesick but decided not to send the situation up, and to just explain what I was doing. But in the event he said nothing and asked no questions. In fact the other staff also had their idiosyncrasies. For instance there was the part German fellow who always wore leather shorts and wellingtons no matter how hot it was and often gave me funny looks in the showers. Then there was the boss's assistant who was quite friendly towards me and asked to take a photo of me, and always seemed quite caring. The top boss (with the exception of when he saw me under the door) usually exuded an air of being confidently in charge, and seemed to run the park somewhat like a military establishment. There was also my own section foreman Bill, who was quite unassuming and a very hard worker, and it surprised me to discover that he was a Seventh-Day Adventist and thus a vegetarian, and yet he seemed to have more stamina than anyone. Though I am also vegetarian; I usually couldn't keep up with his pace. He was also quite tolerant and didn't mind me chanting mantras or singing verses while I worked. Bill told me he was fond of music and that he played an electric guitar, which surprised me as he was about fifty. Eventually my job at Centennial Park came to a sort of natural conclusion, by mutual consent. After serving a few weeks' notice, I completed my quite long spell of tending rose-beds and lawns in the endlessly shining sun, often to the chorus of untamed cockatoos flying overhead or the melodious sounds of the red-beaked black swans and various sorts of ducks on the nearby lake.

BRIDGE OVER TURBULENT WATERS

* * *

The Pacific/India Express

The journey from Sydney to Perth across the Nullarbor Plain takes about three days by train. I've really no idea why I decided to go to Perth, it may be that I had itchy feet, but it's more likely I just fancied a long train ride. I felt quite excited at the prospect of riding right across Australia and had no qualms about doing it in the comfort of a modern train; though I would rather it had been on a steam train with windows that actually opened.

The preparation for leaving Sydney hadn't taken long and my belongings easily fitted into a rucksack. I found I had been allocated a two-berthed cabin with a young man of about my age, he was from New Zealand and it soon transpired, to use the common parlance that he was gay. In general matters we got on quite well and he let me choose the top bunk, but I was a bit nonplussed when on the first night he asked if he could come up to my bunk and masturbate me, this wasn't what I had in mind, but though I firmly declined his offer, he was quite persistent till eventually we reached a compromise in which he would hold my (by then aroused) member briefly, after which he would return down to his own bunk and make do with his own devices. Basically, in as friendly a fashion as I could, I had made it clear I didn't feel like having my energy splattered all over the place. I was also a little embarrassed as we hardly knew each other and even if I did have bisexual awareness, I felt quite contented just to keep things simple.

Not to say that now and then I wasn't quite happy and able to acknowledge my sexuality and to masturbate if, as and when I felt I needed to let off steam. My tendency towards chastity wasn't for self-righteous reasons, but more because I found this actually afforded me longer spells of feeling quite happy and contented, though it's also true that I was perhaps having a bit of a reaction to the phase in my teens when I had got into the habit of using masturbation as an escape clause, brought into action when I was feeling down or dejected. At that time it hadn't really occurred to me that masturbating wouldn't really be able to satisfy me or give what I really needed. The same holds true for some sexual relationships when they are neurotically motivated, in the sense of trying to get out of one's sexual experience, more than sexual experience can actually give one.

In the mornings I was able to meditate on my bunk before putting it up for the day. The train had a sort of streamlined look, though the atmosphere was a bit sterile, but I enjoyed making use of the various facilities especially the hot shower which actually worked and of course didn't have any cockroaches. One of the rail-car conductors seemed to have funny ideas about how to serve the public inasmuch as he sort of cracked up when I pointed out that I was vegetarian and told me he didn't have any kangaroo food on board. In fact I had only asked to be given whatever was available less the non-vegetarian bits. But it seemed he wanted to have a debate over the issue so I gave him a few things to think about and reminded him that kangaroos and vegetarians ate their food fresh and that his main source of protein was actually second hand-food. He seemed to appreciate that I hadn't just taken his jibes sitting down.

I had come well prepared with lots of fruit and nuts, though when we crossed the inter-state boundaries I had to hide my bananas in the lamp shades to prevent them being confiscated, the reason being to prevent the spread of fruit fly or crop-related diseases. But in that respect I did make a point of consuming what I had brought and didn't take any fruit off the train. Though this did mean after the first state boundary I had to eat the foodstuffs in question within my cabin or the stroppy conductor may have started asking questions. That said at one of the station stops, I got some exercise and returned to see the train inexplicably departing five minutes early, and had to run about fifty yards and jump onto the side of the receding train, I somehow gained entry, then to my relief was reunited with my backpack and essential documents, then to calm myself I pulled out a large carrot and sat there munching, clearly to the bemusement some more elderly passengers.

The land itself was of course quite dry and barren and the Nullabor Plain was the longest uninhabited stretch, Nullabor apparently means treeless. After we had crossed the plain we came to the old gold mining town of Kalgoolie where we had a spell off the train. The atmosphere of the place seemed to me like an old ghost-town, or a set for a western movie. At one of the street junctions there was a statue of some old cobbler with a large chunk of gold which he had either mined or discovered in the area, or if I remember rightly it may be that he found his chunk of gold on the ground one day after some heavy rains. For myself the most dazzling sights I came across in Kalgoorlie weren't any lumps of gold, but the unusual faces and especially the eyes of some of the aborigines, who had a sort of bright and childlike quality, the first fellow to walk past me on the sidewalk almost stopped me in my tracks by the way he looked straight at me and didn't avert his gaze as he went by. I daresay he may have been on his way to do a modern job, but that didn't undermine the open freshness of our communication, which almost felt like I was drawn back into the roots of indigenous Australia and Aboriginal dreamtime and song-lines.

* * *

Perth to Singapore

I now allowed a large margin for error, so this time didn't have to do a hundred metre sprint to board train. The remainder of the journey was soon over and before I knew it, I was wandering about Perth trying to find my bearings. The city seemed quite busy with lots of cars and new buildings. Eventually I found a room in a cheap part of the city in a slightly run-down house owned by a Greek man who didn't live on the property. Next to my room on one side lived a Yugoslavian man who always seemed to be either in a slightly sour and at other times slightly intimidating mood. The room on the other side of me was occupied by a young fellow who was very friendly, so I was sorry that he was due to be leaving after a few days, and I appreciated that before he left he gave me his old record player.

My room was medium-sized and pretty basic so far as the decor went. One surprising feature was it included a resident 'lounge lizard', which as I lay -partially collapsed from the heat- on my sagging bed, would slowly start to appear from a crack above the window near the ceiling on its search for flies. The creature was about eight to twelve inches long and slightly worried me at first, but we learned to live together. The fellow next door was less easy to live with, even though I tried to keep a low profile. After a few days I applied for an advertised position for a store porter, the manager found it odd that I didn't seem to have any proper school records, he said something about what he considered to be my hobo lifestyle, and that he didn't want to go to all the bother of taking me on if I wasn't going to stay for at least a year, but he relented after I suggested that I may settle down.

The job was fairly tedious stuck in a airless warehouse shoving boxes about and wasn't helped by the atmosphere of the place where I was living. My only enjoyment or emotional solace seemed to come from listening and sometimes dancing to Beatles music and other records which came with the small portable record player I had been given by the fellow who had left earlier. One evening for a bit of company as much as for the content, I went to a free public talk at a nearby community centre about auras and healing and that sort of thing, which for some reason or another set me thinking and affirmed my general feeling of malaise about my situation in Perth, and I decided after a while to return to England.

I was a bit embarrassed about giving in my notice at work but didn't receive too much flak and after a few days had managed to make the necessary arrangements to 'ship-n-fly' back to England. The large and old cargo ship from Fremantle to Singapore was expected to take about eight days and the prospect of spending a whole week at sea seemed to me even more romantic and exciting than my previous train ride. Much to my surprise, with the ship's departure from the port, there was a bagpipes and coloured streamers, and lots of people waving goodbye to loved ones; the crew of the ship was Indonesian and Filipino, the crew in marked contrast to the conductor on the train, were invariably friendly and as helpful as they could be. They seemed to have a sunny disposition by nature, which didn't seem to switch off behind the scenes. The only fly in the ointment of this balmy voyage at least at the start, was the reckless behaviour of some drunken Scots whom I had the inconvenience of sharing a cabin with. They resented anyone not sharing their state of being just about perpetually drunk. Eventually their abusive behaviour indicated it would be better to get transferred before things got worse. So, I communicated with a friendly lady bursar, and shortly found myself in another cabin, which was again inhabited mostly by Scots, but they were much more friendly, and able to respect and tolerate other people.

As the days passed, the experience of being at sea seemed for me to develop a sort of magical quality, I daresay this was helped by the warm weather and calm seas as well as the flying fish and dolphins which followed the boat. After we had made our way up through the Indian Ocean, we sailed past Jakarta and the tail end of Sumatra, the sea was very still and occasionally we came across locals sailing in small canoe-like boats. From here onwards we passed various coastlines sometimes covered in what looked like dense jungle or forests. Towards the end of the voyage I started to feel almost tangibly that the world and all life's experience really is quite ephemeral and dreamlike. I especially felt this on the last morning of the voyage, while I was sitting in the half lotus (meditation posture) on one of the upper decks in the cool of the morning, and watched the massive shimmering orb of the tropical sun, starting to rise over Singapore, as our ship quietly slid unnoticed into the harbour.

The serene atmosphere was soon shattered by the reality of having arrived and the general excitement and furore, as people prepared to disembark and milled about with their luggage. At this point a couple of fellows that I had developed a friendship with on the boat, who were going to be travelling from Singapore overland to India to see their guru, made a last-ditch effort to try and persuade me to go with them. But I reiterated that though it might be appropriate for me to go to India at some time, for the moment I felt I should just return to England and review my situation from there.

The ticket I had purchased in Perth; was a cheap package which included a night's stop-over in a hotel, half a day's free sight-seeing excursions and then the flight back to London. Later that day as I wandered about Singapore trying to keep out of the extremely hot sun, I found myself being willingly enticed into a number of shops where I was given cold coca-cola and sales talk, but had no inclination to buy any of the hi-tech on offer. In all that heat the only thing which managed to arouse any interest out of me, was a diplomat's daughter who struck up a conversation with me on a bus. She was rather well-spoken and made me feel a bit like I was being interviewed by a member of the royal family. Although our acquaintance was brief I actually enjoyed our uncomplicated and easy communication which ended as swiftly as it began, when we alighted at our respective stops.

Back at the hotel I met the fellow allotted to the other half of our double room. He introduced himself and told me, and then showed me that he had just bought himself a duty-free Yamaha flute which made quite an impression on me both for the simple beauty of the instrument and its pure and melodic tone. After a good night's sleep, I spent a slightly bizarre morning mainly at the 'Tiger Balm Gardens' which was where my free excursion ended up. At the entrance to the place was a man showing off some very large snakes. Before reaching the gardens themselves, one encountered an exhibition area with countless miniature models showing unfortunate victims being put through all sorts of grizzly tortures. Perhaps this was Singapore's equivalent to something like the dungeons in the tower of London, but they didn't much appeal to me. And so I opted to stroll about in the garden area and was amused by the antics of the bands of monkeys, but also noted the written signs that one could contract rabies if bitten, so I decided to stay shy and unbitten.

Eventually the coach took us to the airport, by which time it was early evening, which gave about an hour before the flight departed. I very nearly didn't depart at all, since having completed various formalities I decided to change some money into sterling and in the process, perhaps due to tiredness and heat, was silly enough to go and leave my small document pouch on a counter. Ten minutes later, I suddenly found myself thinking oh dear I've just managed to maroon myself in Singapore, since my air-ticket, money and passport were all in that pouch. I just about collapsed with relief, when I went back and saw my pouch still sitting where I had left it. I felt no less relieved when the flight to London eventually departed and was quite excited at the prospect of arriving back in England. The flight was to afford me another dose of butterflies in my stomach, as after a few hours flying, the night sky began to flash with lightning.

My assessment of the plane's state of repair had already been undermined by noticing the stewardess having to plug drips of water or condensation falling from the roof. So when the plane hit patches of turbulence I found my confidence in getting back home, at times plummeting at about the same rate as the plane. But to cut what seemed like a long flight short, the storm passed and eventually the plane arrived safe and sound, and before long I had disembarked. As I made my way to catch a train into London I felt almost as if I had been to the moon and back, and in some respects, it felt like magic, just to have arrived back from what had for me been quite a long sojourn.

***

CHAPTER FIVE
Magic Bus (23ish)

Home-coming

I arrived back in England on a warm summer's day, I had a few savings and was generally feeling quite buoyant as I made my way to my mother's flat in central London, yet somehow at this time; I didn't seem to connect with friends or family particularly satisfactorily. This was partly my own fault as I had turned up out of the blue and people were basically preoccupied with their own lives. People were cordial and friendly and didn't mind putting me up for a few days here and there, but I didn't really belong and experienced a sort of anti-climax. Though I was now twenty-three, it seemed in some respects I wasn't as independent as I had thought I was, as I still seemed to need some sort of interest and response from people, which just wasn't there. My contacts seemed to fall into two groups those preoccupied by domesticity and television, and those preoccupied with smoking marijuana. My efforts to be in communication with people seemed ineffective, I suppose I needed a place of my own, to relax and be myself. As well as disillusion, my 'home-coming' brought home to me that I was still homeless, in the sense of not having anywhere proper to live and of course this situation now re-presented itself, and eventually I was obliged to move into a semi-squat in North London.

Soon I realised the room, which I had free use of, was infested with fleas and the place in general was a bit of a dope den. I had only been back a month when I decided I had had enough of London. A few days later I saw an advert offering Overland passage to India for £40 by a small company called "Magic Bus". And so it was that the following week I found myself in a clinic with a nurse saying "I'm afraid sir you'll have to lower your pants a bit, as the injection has to go into your backside". She was referring to a vaccine against hepatitis B, which I had come for, although popularly it was referred to as hippy-titus. Not that I ever considered myself to be a hippy, on the contrary I was just an ordinary young person wanting to lead a simple and meaningful life, but to some degree found myself kept on the hop by lack of anywhere half-decent i.e. clean; quiet and secure in which to live, and also little prospect of any worthwhile employment. And so I was to some degree driven by circumstances, and needing to respond as best I could, sometimes without much time or space to really reflect on my impulses. I had obtained my 'ticket' from a middle-class and conservative-looking lady, from an address in North London. The house she was working from looked well-kept and made one feel the company she was part of was reliable enough. I was soon to learn that one shouldn't be quick to judge a travel company merely by the appearance of its agent, but by that stage it was a bit late to turn back, and there was little choice but to sit back and hope for the best.

* * *

Magic bus

A friend gave me a lift to the pickup point in London and I was surprised to find the coach was of a higher quality than I had expected. It wasn't until halfway to Dover that myself and the other passengers were informed that our "Magic Bus" would be meeting us at Dover. When we got there people couldn't believe their eyes. It was Cinderella in reverse, and like magic our fairy-coach which had brought us so far was about to be transformed into a right old pumpkin. In fact it looked like an old school bus which had been called back into service after being on a scrap heap for about ten years.

While a bit disappointed, I couldn't help but laugh a little bit as the driver, a wild-eyed looking man, whom I later learned was apparently half Indian and half Welsh, proceeded to reassure us that he had driven the overland trip many a time and there would be no problems. At which point he introduced his mate, a Welsh fellow about twenty-odd, dressed in full hippy regalia, whom he told us was an excellent mechanic and co-driver. A few people opted out while the remainder of us started the task of transferring our luggage from the boot of the modern coach, via a ladder on to the roof of our old heap, where it was strapped down under canvas. Then it was mentioned rather casually that there was a little snag with the starting motor which could be sorted out in Belgium; and would we mind push-starting the coach till then. After further messing about, and some wrangling with port officials, our coach, perhaps aptly named 'Magic Bus' finally made its way on to the ferry. The light of day was just beginning to dawn as we left Ostend and started our journey across Belgium and into Germany. At first, despite the starting motor, which had become a bit of a joke, we seemed to be making good progress and it wasn't until we were halfway through Germany, somewhere between Frankfurt and

Stuttgart that we had our first major breakdown. This hadn't come as a complete surprise, as our co-driver/mechanic had already been expressing some concern about odd knocking noises. So it was that we ended up camping in a German forest for three days, while the engine was pulled apart, and the starting motor was also fixed or replaced. During this period people lived mainly on supplies of food they were carrying with them and in some cases supplemented by scrumping in nearby fields. At one stage the German press came and asked questions and took photographs, probably so they could run a story about being invaded by British hippies. I happened to have a large bag of sprouted mung beans with me, which was what I lived on for a few days, there was also a shop at a service station which sold supplies. During these few days I managed to incur a small injury to one of my feet, at the time I was wearing flip-flops, as a change from my plimsoles and somehow managed to scuff my foot on the road surface. The trouble with this was the resultant cut was on the base of my foot and was to prove quite difficult to heal.

Eventually we hit the road again, and continued as far as the Austrian Alps where we again broke down. I quite enjoyed spending a night under an almost full moon by a mountain stream, though it was quite cold. From Austria we made our way through Yugoslavia, where various sights made impressions on me, including the image of cows with their heads roped down to one of their feet (perhaps to keep them eating), there were also the half-empty shops; as well as some pretty drab looking tenement blocks. I dare say there are more picturesque spots in Yugoslavia. Be that as it may, Greece, where we shortly arrived in, by contrast, seemed wonderful with its brightly whitewashed and attractive architecture, I was also impressed by the friendliness of the inhabitants, though I was slightly puzzled by the sight of the orthodox clergy in their black robes and long beards whom I didn't quite know what to make of. I just recall in the midst of a crowd, a priest fully observing me, and our eyes met in a silent communion, and just briefly, time and space seemed to stand still.

My geographical knowledge and understanding of different cultures was limited, though I had read a little of Plato's Republic and a book about Socrates. In fact my reading, which had influenced me in varying degrees, only amounted to a handful of books, such as 'Yoga and Health' (Selvarajan Yesudian, Unwin Books). 'The Tibetan book of the Dead' (W.Y. Evans Wentz, Oxford University Press), and the

Penguin Books concise version 'The Psychedelic Experience' Tim Leary, Ralph Metzner & Richard Alpert). An Anthology of World Scriptures which included Buddhist and Taoist writings, the 'Bhagavad Gita', Aldous Huxley's 'The Perennial philosophy', some of Herman Hesse's books as well as a book by Swami 'Pravananda' and Christopher Isherwood called 'Vedanta for the Western World'. While in Greece I also appreciated the easily available freshly roasted hazel nuts, which were delicious, and enjoying a refreshing swim in the Aegean Sea near Thessaloniki, but though the sea water helped, I still had a problem with the base of my foot which hadn't yet healed.

* * *

Turkey

Istanbul right away seemed to have a real mystique for me as I'm sure it does for many visitors. I hadn't been there long before I took the opportunity to visit the Blue Mosque. In my already stated cultural ignorance as well as my general naïveté I thought it would be alright if I sat on the floor in the half lotus and meditated for a short while. But to my surprise I was quickly advised by various gestures not to continue sitting there, so I had to make do with further walking about, which wasn't so easy as my foot hadn't improved and had become infected. We were to spend a few days in Istanbul while the bus received repairs to its chassis which was starting to crack and needed welding. To keep costs to a minimum I accepted the option of sleeping on my hotel's flat roof for which I only had to pay half price. Sleeping on a warm roof, though hard was quite comfortable, except that when I awoke the next morning I found one of my eyes had been stung or bitten, and was shut fast and swollen to the size of a plum.

After getting over the initial shock, I tried to carry on with things as best I could and spent most of the day trying to find a doctor, as I had yet to get another required vaccination against typhoid. Eventually after arriving at some address, I got taken by some fellow through a maze of lanes and then into some premises where I was introduced to a half-shaven man having a drink with another man. He assured me that he was a doctor and that yes, he could give me a typhus injection (which I thought was Turkish for typhoid). When I asked how much he just waved his hands and said no charge, so I sort of felt obliged to accept his kind offer. And even after he produced an over-sized and rusty-looking syringe together with half a jar of some yellow-looking liquid, I couldn't bring myself to say no, never having done an assertiveness training course. And so I let him inject me and hoped he was trustworthy. In the event he probably did give me a typhus vaccine and I didn't catch any infection.

But the next day I woke up and found I had lost the use of the injected arm, which had become painful and very stiff. On top of this my eye was still closed and the infection in my foot was now such, that I had to sort of hobble about, being careful to look where I was going with my good eye, so as not to bump my arm. That day as I stumbled about in the heat of Istanbul trying to get lotion for my eye and a bandage for my foot I couldn't help but laugh at my situation. But as I looked at the heavy loads of fine carpets, that some quite elderly people about me; were having to carry on their backs, I felt quite sorry for them and reflected that at least my present discomforts might heal in a few days, which in fact they did in due course. In the next few days realizing that my various complaints were showing signs of mending themselves, I was more confident and decided to visit a few places. First, I went to the Pudding shop for lunch, where the manager insisted on buying my second-hand Omega watch even though I pointed out to him that it was broken, so I left him to look at it while I ate some Turkish halva after I'd managed to remove the ants. To my surprise, on my way out the manager stood by his offer and bought my watch. This was to be my last full day in Istanbul, so I wanted to make the most of it.

In the afternoon I managed to make my way to the Topkapi Museum; but on the way felt appalled at the sight of a boy leading a bear by a chain attached to a ring through its nose which was slightly bleeding. After some time in the museum I bought a corn on the cob from a vendor whose cooking pot was a large metal dustbin on wheels, though not silver-service it tasted pretty good. On my way back to the hotel I had to pass what was either a prison or a police station, whatever the case the place gave me the shudders. There were two big guards outside with white hats and I got the impression that anyone taken in there could find it quite hard to get back out. But as with earlier occasions, I managed to pass without finding myself grabbed off the street and was soon back at the hotel. Years later I saw the film 'Midnight Express', which may have been partly based on that type of establishment, which hopefully has moved on.

The following morning due to further delay there was time to go to a Turkish bath. The facilities seemed really old with the interior, floor, walls, seats, and baths being mainly constructed from great slabs of highly worn marble, and I couldn't help but feel I was on a film set. But I couldn't hear any voices calling "quiet please, action", or "thank-you boys and girls, it's a wrap"! So I stripped off, left my things in safe custody, and then relaxed in the steamy atmosphere while I observed the other patrons and studied the marble pillars and curving architecture of the place. As I was leaving a massive masseur with an oil covered body with rippling muscles, had one last go at getting me to submit to a massage, which probably would have been cheap at the price. He grabbed my shoulder and his fingers immediately seemed to find their way into every nook and cranny as they squeezed and manipulated my body. But while I showed appreciation for the impressive free demonstration, I declined his offer as I felt my other arm was still too sore; to risk letting him loose on me.

Later that day we finally got our coach back and made the trip across the Bosporus and before long we were into Asia proper. As we pulled away from Europe I had the distinct feeling, I was also moving back in time, into a less technocratic world in which time moved less fast, and as we moved deeper into rural Turkey, those times when our coach stopped, we found ourselves overwhelmed by friendly groups of villagers and children curious to take a closer look at us. Though the pace of life here was slower, our own pace seemed to be gathering momentum as our driver was concerned about lost time, and henceforth he endeavoured to keep our 'Magic-Bus' on the move about sixteen hours a day.

* * *

Iran

The border crossing involved a certain amount of bartering and haggling between our driver and various officials, which gave me lots of time to look at the picture of the Shah which was hanging on one of the walls. I had no idea of any of the political unrest which was fermenting at the time and just assumed the Shah of Iran was their much loved 'King'. After a while we were given permission to enter and were on our way again. The atmosphere in Iran felt a bit edgy and our driver announced his intention that we should try to keep going almost non-stop, apart from a night or two in Teheran, until we got to Afghanistan, after which we would be able to slow down and recuperate a bit. This was to involve some arduous driving, and in the event, we broke down about halfway between Tabriz and Teheran in the middle of what seemed nowhere, but to the locals was somewhere, and perhaps even the centre of the known universe.

Realising that we were stuck for the night, those that had tents started erecting them, while others potted about doing various chores. People started to arrive and gradually their numbers increased. To my surprise these locals started to intimidate us. At first subtly and then not so subtly; but most of us seemed to appreciate that the only thing to do was to keep cool and not retaliate. In my own case I was in the process of washing, when I had my towel snatched from my hand, which was then chucked about between a few people. Since I refused to be drawn, one of them picked up a lump of rock which he held menacingly in his hand. By now I was starting to feel a bit hassled so I pulled back and walked away, I didn't quite know what to expect but they didn't do anything. That night we didn't sleep too much and fortunately by early next morning, the engine had been fixed at least temporarily. So with a sigh of relief we were able to get moving again.

Having covered quite a lot of ground, around late afternoon we stopped to replenish our water supplies and do some shopping. Soon it became clear that despite the high temperatures some people reacted to our wearing shorts, or at least this was used as a pretext for various gestures and remarks from across the street. So we made a point of not hanging about too long. To my surprise when we did later get to Teheran, people there didn't seem to bother us too much, - perhaps they were more used to foreigners. After a couple of days of keeping low profiles in Teheran, the bus was ready for the long journey across Iran and into Afghanistan. It was during this leg of the journey that I made the mistake of succumbing to a piece of pomegranate. We had been driving for many hundreds of kilometres through all sorts of rough terrain, and it looked like we would be continuing overnight, when I developed a real shocker of a headache and alongside this became horribly sick. The driver really didn't like to stop, and it wasn't till he realised there was no alternative that he ground the bus to a halt. After throwing up and out at both ends, I stumbled back and climbed aboard the bus feeling like maybe it would have really been a much better idea to have stayed at home, if I had had one.

Over the next day or two we traversed some very dusty and at times high altitude terrain. There were now growing problems with the chassis which was falling apart. And because the floor was starting to crack up, at times the coach was filled with thick dust, so we had to cover our faces with bits of cloth in our efforts to keep breathing. So, it was with a certain amount of longing that we continued to push on towards the Afghan border, stopping only occasionally to buy food, which in my case being vegetarian, usually amounted to bags of dried yellow peas which were quite crumbly and could be eaten raw, occasionally one could also get bags of fresh green raisins. The only other stops were for the toilet, and with desert stretching left and right and not a bush in sight, this often meant balancing one's modesty with how far out one could be bothered to walk. By the time we started to approach the border; most of the passengers as well as the two drivers were exhausted and starting to feel almost at the end of their tethers.

***

Afghanistan

After more bartering and goings on and some doubts about whether we would gain entry, we were allowed at last into Afghanistan. Almost right away the atmosphere felt far less tense. Although materially the country was no better off than Iran, the difference was the attitude of the people who were un-hostile, relaxed and even at times friendly.

We still had a fairly long drive to Herat. Either during this leg of the journey or a bit earlier we encountered some nomads travelling by camel, which struck me not only as being rather exotic but also as quite likely more comfortable than our own mode of transport. Iranian and Afghanistan forms of transport; be they camels, lorries, or buses were often highly decorated, making our own old school bus, for which it has to be admitted I had developed some fondness, look rather dilapidated and uncared for. The altitude in Herat as with Kabul seemed to give the air a cool crispness, though the weather was still warm and sunny. We stayed at a hotel for a couple of days while the bus was being repaired and in the mornings I was enchanted by the sight and sound of tinkling bells as horse-drawn carriages passed to and fro outside my ground floor bedroom window.

While enchanted by some sights I was sorry and could hardly believe my eyes when I noticed a down-and-out person in some way handicapped, and with bits of rubber tyres tied to his limbs as buffers so he could drag himself along on the ground. Generally seeing the plight of poor and the sick in so-called less developed countries seemed more shocking and sorrowful, than in situations where help may be available. Having rested and freshened up, in due course we again boarded our old banger and made our way at a comfortable pace to Kabul. This part of our journey went quite smoothly and was unproblematic apart from the usual flat tyres, misfiring cylinders and the on-going problem of the cracking chassis. One bright morning we arrived in Kabul; after finding lodging in various cheap hotels; which were more akin to run down youth hostels; and without much in way of facilities, we were taken for a short drive about to get our bearings of the city. An escort who had insisted on coming showed, us the new road, built by the Russians, and various other sights which he thought we would like to see. Then we were all dropped off at our respective abodes and the escort went off with the driver to help find a buyer for what was left of the coach which had brought us so far.

* * *

Please die outside

The following morning I woke up feeling most peculiar and quickly made my way to the toilet which consisted of a large mound of decaying excretion, with an intolerable stench and no shortage of flies. I soon realised I had dysentery. I was staying at Greens Hotel which included in its price various perks, but there hadn't been any mention of dysentery on their menu, though they did a good line in green salads, which had been hard to resist after so many weeks of dried peas and raisins.

By midday I felt ghastly and by evening dreadful, and over the next couple of days I got worse. The driver let me know they were leaving the next day (by public transport) and he didn't think I would be fit to travel. So I had to make my decision the next morning, by which time my intestines felt like they were on fire and I couldn't even stand up, so I didn't have any choice and had to stay put, and didn't see any of the people I travelled with or the drivers again. By now it was becoming clear that I hadn't just got a case of the runs and rather like our coach was starting to feel I may have reached the end of the road.

To make matters worse Ramadan had started and though I was dehydrating much of the time I was unable to get anything to drink, which along with a rope bed which sunk about a foot in the middle didn't help my dilemma. The next day in the afternoon, I dragged myself out of bed and managed to plonk myself down on the floor in the so-called lounge, which was a bit more colourful than the dorm, and where I could hear music coming through a couple of speakers and thus try to forget myself.

At sunset I was able to get mint tea and also derived some comfort just from seeing other people. That evening a young American gave me the address of a doctor and the next day I managed to get a prescription for which I was advised to go to a particular chemist, but that wasn't possible as I was collapsing on my feet, so I had to opt for whatever chemist I could find en-route back to the hotel. The following day I had a turn for the worse and it became clear the capsules were having no effect. To add to my troubles I occasionally woke up night and day, to find hotel staff apparently dusting my clothes. But they didn't have much luck as I had taken the precaution of keeping my nylon pouch, which contained my passport and money inside my underpants. This had become doubly necessary as I now found myself for long periods lost in fever and delirium and only occasionally having periods where I was conscious. It was while swimming around in that feverish state that the thought occurred to me that I might actually die, and was surprised to note that I didn't seem to have any reaction. This was partly as I didn't really feel I had any unfinished business; in that I had already recently managed to get back to England and had been able to spend at least some time with my mother and brothers and sisters and friends. And as for the present and future, well basically I didn't really feel I had anywhere to go and I didn't really feel very concerned one way or the other.

Whatever the illness I had it seemed to get even worse and the hotel manager came and informed me in one of my semi-conscious moments, that he was of the opinion that I was quite close to death and that while he didn't want to offend me the fact of the matter was that it would be very bad for his hotel and would involve a lot of red tape if I died there and in short would I leave. I was somewhat bemused by his attitude, and told him he had got it wrong and that I wasn't going to die, at least not on that occasion, and I had to reiterate that I wasn't going to die, until he accepted that I might not and went away.

Almost to prove my point, during a more lucid spell I pulled myself together as best I could, and this time went by taxi back to the doctor. He looked me over and asked how long it was since I had eaten anything, I told him seven days and he said that apart from taking more fluids I should try to make myself start eating again even if not much, and to emphasis his point he said that I couldn't expect to go on living if I didn't make some effort to eat and drink more.

He also pointed out after questioning me, that I had gone to the wrong chemist and gave me another prescription for something like 'intestopan' and warned me this time to be careful to go to the prescribed chemist, if I didn't want to end up with capsules full of chalk. This time I picked up the capsules by taxi and when I got back with these and a few supplies, I made myself eat a few crumbs and took some medicine before collapsing on to my bed. And needless to say woke up the next day to find I had picked up a bit.

With the combination of continued medicine and progressing from crumbs to whole slices of bread I continued to perk up and though I was still quite weak, after a while I was able to go out and have a meal and realised I was now well enough to start considering what my next move should be. I didn't really feel like continuing on to India and on the other hand I didn't think I had enough money to get back to England. Shortly afterwards I located and made enquiries at the British Consulate about the possibility of being repatriated, since I reckoned I was about ten pounds short of the airfare. To my surprise the person who saw me was very friendly, and asked me about myself, as well as how I came to be there, and made me feel a bit human. Apart from his sympathetic attitude he implied that, since I had no one in the UK to obtain money from, if need be, they could take my passport as security and lend me the balance. In the event there were few options. And so, after a few days, thanks to consulate I had a flight booked back to England, and even had enough left over to buy some presents and a pair of Afghan socks from one of the little boys selling on the street.

* * *

Homestretch

Being on the Russian Aeroflot airplane was like a mixture of technology and magic. Suddenly my environment seemed transformed everything about me was clean, tidy and comfortable and as if that wasn't enough, I was then served cold orange juice in a glass which really tasted like nectar of the gods. I hadn't participated in such delights since leaving Europe, and now was reminded just how much there is in our affluent society which can so easily be taken for granted. My decadent self now started coming to the fore and I found myself fantasizing about having hot baths, clean sheets and even baked beans on toast. I was also aware that I only had a few pounds and that in all likelihood I would have to find somewhere to squat, since I would effectively be homeless when I got back. Though I probably could get friends to put me up for the first few days, I decided to waste no time in sorting out my life as best I could and not to let myself be too upset by whatever circumstances I had to deal with.

As well as trying to sort out somewhere reasonable to live, also I needed to build up my health as I was still feeling quite run down. But to do all this I would need money, so I decided to start checking in to Central Casting for film work as soon as I got back, and if need be, sign on, once I had got an address. Also, I planned to contact the Magic bus operators and ask for a partial refund and an apology for just going off and leaving me without bothering to offer any advice or help of any sort. So having at least in my mind sorted out my various options, I tried to let go of what had passed, not to feel anxious about the future and just to appreciate the present.

CHAPTER SIX
Pundarika (23-24)

Goldhurst Terrace

Ironically, this time I arrived back with no illusions or expectations, only to find family and friends were quite pleased to see me and we seemed to be able to engage better than when I had previously returned. With the help of my brother Toby I found a place in an already established squat in a previously unused house in London (N.W.6.). The other few people living there included Richard (he and his brother Don were good friends), the place had a relaxed atmosphere, and I can recall enjoying the open plan bathroom on a lovely morning with sun streaming through the window whilst music played and breakfast was about to be served. I had only been back a couple of days when I landed a small job through Central Casting working on a television series called 'Special Branch', though I never got to see any episodes, I gather it was a popular T.V. series, about the work of some of London's police force.

Coincidentally I was to have an even closer look at police work sometime later when like a bolt out of the blue, an incident occurred in which I found myself being given the central part. The way it came about was that one morning I decided to go swimming and to call on my brother William who was living in a squat which I would pass on my way to Swiss Cottage baths, but much as I tried to persuade him William didn't want to go swimming, so I left after about twenty minutes. Much to my astonishment I had only been back on the pavement a couple of minutes when about five policemen appeared on the scene and proceeded to apprehend and search me, the situation for me was all the more confusing as they were sticking their hands up my shirt, down my pants and all over the place. When it became apparent that the only thing I was reacting to was their intrusive and unexplained manner, they decided to share with me why they were showing such interest, by now they had put their hands everywhere and I was feeling ruffled and bewildered.

So what transpired from all this flurry of activity was that I was being arrested on suspicion of having stolen some antiques, and the reason for this suspicion was one elderly lady who had just spotted me going into the house to see my brother whom I had just visited, and had immediately phoned the police to tell them that she thought I looked similar to the young person; she had previously seen coming out of some other house a few days earlier. Later at the police station, it was explained to me that the witness would have to come to the station and after taking a closer look, would then formally make her decision. They stated I could have an identity parade but that this might take six hours or longer to set up. I pointed out that I had a completely clean record, without even a driving offence against me, and that since I hadn't actually done anything, the likelihood was that once she saw me closer-up she would realise her mistake. They seemed to agree with this and reiterated that it would take quite a while to set up an identity parade and that if I was sure of my position, then they could have the woman there in half an hour, and I could be back on the street within the hour. Thus, it was that shortly a meeting was arranged, and I just couldn't believe my ears when after I had been told to stand up, she walked into the room and within seconds 'claimed me' as the person she had noticed some days earlier. I think I protested my innocence; and spluttered how she had made a wrong identification and that she hadn't got the right person, but her mind was set, and I was taken back to the cell.

 This whole experience had a surreal quality to it, and I could hardly believe it was happening. By about now I had been expecting to be at Swiss Cottage swimming baths, diving off the springboard and experiencing that sense of freedom as my body skimmed through the water like a dolphin in the blue sea. But now I felt almost stunned as I sat locked in a cell deprived of my freedom and still not believing what had happened. Eventually two plain-clothed police came in and told me I was to be formally charged, by now I was a bit more adjusted and asked them to clarify what it was I was being charged with, they were not very precise but alluded to some antique furniture which had been stolen. I felt some relief that the charge wasn't anything worse, and asked them what would happen next, and was informed I would appear at Hampstead magistrates court the following morning. So I asked them to contact my mother, which they agreed to do after which they left.

 I had told my captors that I was vegetarian and after a while was given some baked beans and then left in the cell for the rest of the day and night. The man, who locked the door in reply to a question by me, said if the place burned down it would be my hard luck. I soon found myself pacing up and down and starting to feel the sort of panic animals might feel at suddenly finding themselves locked in a cage. But being now twenty-four I was able to handle it, but I felt glad that this had not happened to me at any earlier age.

After a while I sat down and realised it was only my external freedom which was being interfered with and that there was no reason why I shouldn't choose to feel good. Then I started to feel better and I practiced meditation and relaxed. Eventually to my relief and gratitude my mother turned up and signed a bail document or something to that effect, and I emerged from my cell like a butterfly which had been trapped in a net, flapping my wings and eager to get out into open space. Later that day I appeared before a very prim and uppity-looking lady magistrate, who on hearing my plea was not guilty, set the ball rolling for me to eventually appear at, of all places, the Old Bailey. This meeting with the scales of justice wasn't due to occur for quite a number of months, meanwhile a condition of my having bail granted was that I had to agree to move out of my squat, and there and then had to provide an alternative and legally acceptable address. Apart from my mother, also present at the hearing was my old friend Ken who was also acting as chauffeur with one of his rovers, and another friend Rosemary had come along. To my surprise Rosemary told the magistrates that she had a spare room in which I could stay with her if I wanted and so that was settled.

*　*　*

Prince of Wales Crescent N.W.1

Rosemary, who was in her thirties, was separated or divorced from her husband and had a couple of children. She was a bright and cheerful sort of person and I enjoyed her company. I suppose in a way she sort of mothered me a bit, yet at the same time she didn't think too much of my actually staying in the spare room, and before long I found myself feeling slightly obliged to be friendly with my new landlady somewhat more than I had ever intended. And it seemed slightly ironic that I had in a way been pushed into this situation by the magistrates who had forced me to leave the place where I had been living. I did have some influence on Rosemary's life as she did on mine. Among other things we went for long walks with the kids, ate vegetarian meals and I introduced her to yoga and meditation practice inasmuch as I could. It was Rosemary who introduced me to 'writing letters to the press', she showed letters that she had got published on various social issues and I was quite impressed, as at that stage in my life it had never occurred to me to do such a thing. It was at Rosemary's suggestion that I brought a Yamaha flute on hire purchase, which was a good move, and gave me something positive to engage with and take my mind off the court case which was starting to hang over me like a millstone.

Much as we were good friends our relationship on the physical level didn't really work, i.e. it wasn't what I wanted, also I felt I was letting her down by not letting things go further, and I started to feel in the long term it would be less complicated for us both if I moved. About this time, I got offered a legal short-term 'squat' in a semi-derelict house in Prince of Wales crescent NW3ish, which was later pulled down and redeveloped. And so with the help of Ken and one of his Rover cars, I moved into my very own room, where I hoped to try and sort out my thoughts and feelings, which were a bit in turmoil. It soon became clear that this new home wasn't going to be as ideal as I had hoped, as it turned out to be over-run with big rats and I had only been there a few days when two of them jumped out from the grill as I was about to make a piece of toast and quite put me off using the kitchen again. But if that wasn't bad enough, what really added to the general sordidness of the place was the rather unneighbourly behaviour of some of the people living next door, who were in the habit of chucking used syringes with blood in them, so that they stuck like darts on the door of the outside toilet.

To get away from my place I sometimes visited friends, such as Ken at his NW6 bedsitter, which in turn lead to my reconnecting with his friends. On one such occasion a hashish-smoking exile from South Africa, who also happened to be an Anglican priest, whom I knew through Ken, told me after he learned I was 'pencilled in' to appear at the Old Bailey, that in his work as a parish priest in West London he at times had to appear in court, and had observed just how many people got stage-fright or became tongue-tied. He also said that when my case came up he would be glad to appear as a character reference. As a result of this conversation I decided to occasionally visit the public galleries in law courts, and thereby familiarise myself with the atmosphere and tactics used in such places, since I was determined to be neither stage-struck nor tongue-tied. Quite irrespective of the fact that I was totally innocent of the charge laid against me, the prospect of possibly going to prison horrified me and I had doubts about entrusting my fate to lawyers, and decided that I should defend myself. But my solicitor at Camden Law Centre assured me I would have every chance to speak on my own behalf, so I then started to appreciate I didn't have to leave my entire defence to a lawyer, and having one could act as an extra line of defence.

While I tried to improve my living environment there wasn't a lot I could really do, without pulling down the entire neighbourhood and rebuilding it, which is what was to eventually happen, but meanwhile I had to live there so I did the best I could. One Sunday I went to hear a short talk at the Theravada Buddhist Vihara (temple) on Haverstock Hill. At the end I asked a question about the compatibility of hatha yoga and Buddhist teaching and was told that hatha yoga was an unorthodox practice, which I didn't find a particularly relevant or satisfactory answer. So even though I put a few coins in their collection box on the way out, I didn't go back. Not long after my visit to the Buddhist Vihara, I visited the Ramakrishna Mission, (not to be confused with the Hari Krishna movement) at their large house in Holland Park, and joined in one of their services, but didn't get further involved, though I was impressed by a friendly visitor, who was a less uppity and older fellow, whom I met in the corridor on my way out, who looked almost as radiant as the picture of Ramakrishna, I had seen in a little book, some months previously on his life and teachings.

* * *

Pundarika (White Lotus) / Balmore St, N.19.

About this time, I got a letter from a young old friend in San Francisco, and we started corresponding a bit. In her letter she mentioned that she had discovered that fasting could at times be helpful, which reminded me of the fast I had done in the Blue Mountains in Australia. So I decided to have a seven-day fast on grape juice, but it wasn't quite the same as before and just made me more aware of my present environment which seemed to depress rather than uplift me. Even so I enjoyed the grape juice, but after seven days I found it hard not to go from starving to stuffing myself and learned the hard way, the meaning of an adage which says that 'Any fool can fast, but it takes a wise person to come off his fast carefully'. One of the things Prince of Wales Crescent did have to its credit was Community Supplies, a whole-food business, with a retail shop on the corner, which is where I brought my bottles of grape juice and other provisions. John, one of the people running the shop, always inspired me with his friendly and happy attitude, which was as much a tonic as the wholefoods which were sold there. It was while shopping at Community Supplies that I noticed a small hand-written notice in the window about the activities of The Friends of The Western Buddhist Order. What intrigued me about this notice was the word Friends, and I decided almost immediately that I should go along and see what they were like. Within a couple of days I was there at Pundarika, the centre of 'The Friends of the Western Buddhist Order' (F.W.B.O.)

I was quite surprised to notice the front door had obviously been painted carefully and looked quite aesthetic, despite the generally run-down tone of the area. I think I first encountered Kamalashila, who to me seemed bright, radiant and friendly, then inside I encountered another young man of about my own age, he also seemed lively; cheerful and to the point, "how could he help me"? Later I found out his name was Devamitra (Friend of the Gods). I told him I was interested to find out what they taught, and he told me about evenings I could come to; and directed me to a notice board where I could take down fuller details.

A few days later I returned in the early evening to find the place packed with people talking with one another. In the midst of all this I was almost right away, struck by the magnetic presence of a fellow not much older than myself, but whose stature made an immediate positive impression on me. I didn't talk with him straight away since he was already engaged with someone, but afterwards I went up and introduced myself, he also turned out to also have an unusual name, which in this case was Subhuti. I don't recall exactly what I asked him, but I do remember that I didn't get any unsatisfactory answers and I stayed for the evening to hear a tape-recorded lecture by Subhuti's teacher, the founder of the F.W.B.O. the Venerable Sangharakshita (Sangha meaning 'spiritual community' and rakshita 'protector'.)

While I had already been positively influenced by the atmosphere and the various faces floating about, I was even more deeply affected by Sangharakshita's lecture, both for the manner in which he spoke and what he had to say! The lecture was on the subject of Spiritual Evolution, and in it he stressed that nature, or the lower evolutionary process, only brings us so far, beyond which there is the option of a higher evolutionary process, but which requires individual spiritual endeavour. After a few more days I was back again, and found Subhuti's friendliness no less intense than before. By asking a few questions I learned that the white things hanging round his and some other people's necks were sort of abbreviated robes, and signified that the person in question was an ordained member of the Western Buddhist Order. Which meant they had committed their lives or 'Gone for Refuge' to 'The Three Jewels' these being: the Buddha or Ideal of Enlightenment (towards which human consciousness can evolve), the Dharma or way to Enlightenment as expressed in the various teachings, and the Sangha or spiritual fellowship both with one's peers and with those more developed than oneself.

In the previous week I had been introduced to the 'Mindfulness of Breathing', which cultivates calmness, clarity and concentration, with the help of four simple stages of deepening awareness of one's natural breath process, through which one becomes concentrated and yet deeply relaxed. During the present evening I was introduced to the 'Metta Bhavana'. 'Metta' is friendliness, or Universal Loving Kindness, while 'Bhavana' means to cultivate or develop. So this practice consciously makes time to cultivate positive emotions. The object of this practice is that, instead of being at the mercy of our various moods, we may choose to develop a reservoir of positive emotion, even in the midst of life's difficulties, just by sitting in meditation posture and actively cultivating states of universal loving-kindness. Bearing in mind that charity starts at home, we begin by cultivating platonic (i.e. non-sexual) positive emotions towards ourselves, and then towards a friend, then a stranger and then an enemy or difficult person, and in this way we eventually imagine the entire planet and all forms of life, bathed in Universal loving-kindness; Compassion; Sympathetic joy and Peace or Even-mindedness (Translations from Pali: Metta; Karuna; Mudita and Upekkha). After this meditation practice, I was also introduced to a Buddhist Puja which is a sort of devotional service in which we recited various verses, in this instance taken from the 'Bodhicharyavatara' (a Buddhist classic by Shantideva).

The seven verses included:

1/ Worship: Acknowledging the worth of higher states of consciousness, and that there are people more developed than our selves.

2/ Reverence and salutation: Expressing our appreciation that there are people and states of being, more developed than we are, as this implies, we too can continue to spiritually unfold.

3/ Going for Refuge: In which we recited the Refuges and Precepts. The Refuges being the Buddha, (Awakened Mind), the Dharma (The Teaching) and the Sangha (The Spiritual Community), and the precepts are ethical principles, or rules of training (such as refraining from harming life). Then came

4/ Confession (reminiscent of 'contrition, repentance and reconciliation'),

5/ Rejoicing in Merits,

6/ Entreaty and Supplication i.e. Asking to be taught and

7/ Transference of Merit and Self-Surrender.

I found performing Puja (worship) with others, in which we gave expression to our highest aspirations above and beyond ourselves, inspiring, and also appreciated that in so doing, we were creating the conditions in which higher states of consciousness could arise or descend. Apart from finding this practice uplifting, I was also very deeply moved by the sixth verse, in which we recited the Heart Sutra in English (see appendix), which seemed to indicate the highest metaphysical truths and express them in simple English, the combination of reciting the puja, with the Heart Sutra, seemed to give expression to universal and timeless principles.

***

Getting to Pundarika entailed pushing my bike up Dartmouth Hill, when returning, I tended to make my way back home via a quiet route which went past Highgate cemetery and over Hampstead Heath during which I could reflect upon that evening's talk or puja. My contact with the Friends (F.W.B.O.) continued to develop, even to the extent that I started to go on residential retreats and to have more contact with order members at least on retreats. Just the fact they were in existence inspired me, and in most cases their personal qualities seemed to exude a confidence and friendliness which influenced me no less than the teachings which they were heir to.

Among their numbers at that time to name a few there was Nagabodhi, a tall, and charming young man, who was undoubtedly a great loss to the B.B.C. where he had worked before getting more involved with the Friends. There was Chintamani (Wish-Fulfilling Jewel) a bright-eyed and softly-spoken young artist, sculptor, writer and guitarist, who seemed to embody many skills and was always a delight to have contact with. Again there was the mysterious Vessantara, the ever-kindly Devaraja, good-looking Sona, and beautiful Ratnaguna, and quite a number of women order members such as Dhammadinna and others, who all in their own ways seemed to radiate good qualities.

Having eulogised in this way perhaps I should add, that while my head may at times have been up in the clouds, almost invariably those I've been writing about had their feet planted firmly on the earth. And there was certainly no room for projecting or putting people up on pedestals, or anything like that.

Perhaps this was particularly brought home to me one evening when I met Bhante, (Bhante is a sort of affectionate term and simply means teacher, and is often used in less formal situations, when referring to Ven. Sangharakshita.)

At the time just about everybody had gone home and I was the last one to come down from the shrine room, and as I descended the stairs I saw the back of a person who seemed to have a vivid sort of presence even though all I could see was the back of his tweed jacket. There was only Subhuti about and he introduced me, saying 'Bhante this is Patrick', I didn't really know what to say, even so I did mention that I had been very impressed by his lectures, though when he asked which lecture I had listened to that night, I felt somewhat foolish as I couldn't recall the title so Subhuti had to intercede and tell him. At this time, in contrast to a number of years later, Bhante seemed slightly odd and unfathomable, and yet simultaneously I seemed to see within him a radiant youthful figure; even though externally Bhante was then about forty-eight. Unfortunately at that time I wasn't in a particularly receptive state, I hadn't had one of my better days and while I felt quite affected by Bhante's presence, I just seemed not quite ready so I sat down, which made it feel a bit like I had missed an opportunity. I didn't feel there was anything else I could do at that time, I just commented something like that I felt in agreement with what he was about; and looking back at me, he chuckled and left, with Subhuti showing him out.

My year of attendance at Pundarika wasn't all a bed of lotuses; I didn't always feel inspired and at times some of the Order Members seemed a little reserved and reticent in their attitude to me. But the fact is I was at times a bit odd and sometimes asked silly or irrelevant questions. At worst I sometimes saw the Order as being a bit elite, and with entry easier for those educated, or well-qualified or well-endowed in one way or another. But in reality people were so open, honest and friendly that I couldn't keep that attitude up.

Thanks to Subhuti's presence, I was drawn to return a few times and listened to Sangharakshita's impressive lectures including 'Evolution: Lower and Higher' as well as others. Also my perception of the Order was to some extent modified by my opening to a friendship with another 'newcomer' called Colin Fergusson, who later was ordained and became Aloka. He actually invited me back to the place where he lived with Annie Leigh for cups of tea, and I came to realize, that even with their friendliness, still I felt inadequate and that really it was my own shortcomings which I needed to pay attention to. It was because of Aloka (later an accomplished sculptor and artist), that I stayed a few months, and apparently it seems I played a significant part in his continuing contact, then before long he had strong connections with Subhuti and others. Anyone who comes along to any F.W.B.O. activity is treated as a friend, and no pressure is put on one to be involved more than one wants, but if a friend chooses, he or she may in due course become a 'Mitra' (a more committed friend). In which case one has chosen to grow and develop specifically within the context of the F.W.B.O., and this in turn may eventually lead to one's asking to be ordained. Since I hadn't yet become a Mitra, I was still at liberty (so to speak), to 'shop around' and I continued to dabble and experiment with various other circles.

* * *

Haverstock Hill and Soto Zen Centre

Concurrent to my contact at Pundarika, mainly for practical reasons I was having contact with a Zen Centre not far from where I lived, especially as this afforded me somewhere decent to meditate in the mornings (although this did require getting up at about 5am). I appreciated my contact with the Zen Centre and its participants, for the simple and uncluttered approach they had to Buddhism. I had first gone along in response to an advert, and soon became a frequent participant at their morning sits; this involved sitting opposite a wall for longish periods; and then chanting the Heart Sutra in Japanese. The chanting would start off slowly, and then gradually build up to a very fast speed which would include sound effects from wooden clappers.

In due course I was asked to help out with the decorating of their shrine-room, and it emerged that they were preparing for a residential visit from a Roshi (Zen Master) called Doshi, who apart from being in residence for a while, would also be leading an intensive meditation retreat in the countryside (which they called a 'sesshin'). Roshi Doshi eventually arrived from Israel where he was living; though he was actually 'made in Japan' (i.e. he was Japanese). On the first morning that I saw him I realised that there was nothing airy-fairy or wishy-washy about him, and so I was careful not to put a foot wrong. While at the 'Friends' I felt free to ask questions such as "If we don't exist, what are we doing here?" and they in turn, may have pointed out that relatively we do exist, but that our conditioned existence is ultimately unsatisfactory, impermanence and illusory, but that relative level can open up to higher and deeper insights. At the Zen centre things were rather stricter and more formal, though I did on one occasion venture to ask the Roshi Doshi "What should we do when we die?" and he retorted in his deep bass voice "When it's time to die, then just die!"

A few weeks later I found myself in a picturesque cottage, which was spacious and by my standards very plush and luxurious. This was the venue for the forthcoming Zen retreat. I soon had my first 'dressing down', which occurred while I was helping no less a person than the Roshi himself to move a chest of drawers. During this exercise the drawers started to slide out, so I smiled as I struggled to push them back, but Roshi wasn't amused and reminded me that we were handling someone else's property. The retreat got underway and every activity had to be performed with precision and was highly formalised and ritualised. Participants slept, ate and meditated in the same spot. In practice this wasn't too difficult, and I soon adjusted as the general atmosphere while quite intense was also light, friendly and positive. Even so, my own emotions tended to be elsewhere so my practice wasn't very concentrated. I again got into trouble with the Roshi during an exercise session when we were walking in a circle in the garden. The previous day I had asked the Roshi if I could leave my shoes off and he had said yes, but now when he noticed I was barefoot he let out a roar in my direction, which embarrassed me and I could feel had caused me to blush, while the rest of the participants seemed to be slightly amused. During the retreat we had personal interviews with Roshi Doshi, at which time we were expected to communicate how we were getting on with our meditation practice. When my turn came I entered the little interview room with a mixture of excitement and trepidation. When I looked at the Roshi I could hardly believe my eyes as his head was 'ablaze', and seemed to be a mass of energy, emanating out in all directions, and in a state of wonder I just looked, like I was seeing William Blake in an altered state of being. Soon he said, "Concrete language only" and "interview over", my practice was a bit blocked, even so the unexpected interview, had a strong impact.

At the end of the retreat, after we had packed up, I suddenly recalled how squalid my environment was going to seem when I got back to my rat-infested short-term housing, and so I picked a sprig off a bush and got myself into further trouble. I got a lift back to London in a van, and felt a bit awkward that Roshi sat in the back and said I was to sit in the front seat. Back at the centre, the Roshi and his students to my surprise had a bit of a 'party'. My involvement dropped off, till after a while I didn't go back, even so I appreciated quite a few aspects of my contact with the Zen Centre and with Roshi Doshi.

* * *

A summer afternoon

About this time, I entered a phase of retracing my footsteps, trying to work out how I had become a bit confused, and wondering which way to go next. One afternoon I went to visit my friend Ken. He was preoccupied with his car repairs but told me to let myself in and that Linda a friend of his who was an art graduate from New York was due to be calling shortly. Well after she arrived, I can only suppose that Ken must have told her I was upstairs and she must have just happened to be 'in the mood'. Since what followed was that while I was lying on Ken's bed, looking out of the window reflecting, Linda a slim and pretty woman of about twenty-six, whom I had met once or twice before breezed into the room. She was about three years older than me, and I had always found her a bit assertive, anyhow if I was a bit backwards, she certainly made up for it by being quite forwards, it was the beginning or middle of woman's liberation and experimentation; along with the freedom afforded by 'the pill', although at that period I had little awareness of any of that.

I was just aware that she came into the room and over to the divan where I was sprawled on my back at about midday. Then rather like in an erotic Levi Jeans advert, quite unannounced and in no time at all, she had my zip down and hypnotically subdued and seduced me. What interested me was that while she looked down at me in that free-flowing moment, our eyes just seemed to melt into each other's, and she smiled like she had another conquest. Yet there was nothing negative about it and felt sort of right for that moment. Even so a few days later she encountered me on the stairs, and I think she wanted to teach me a lesson; as she told me she was pregnant, and seeing she had made an impression; she then laughed it away as a tease, from then on I was more aware of possible consequences, and became more reticent and self-contained.

I hadn't really considered the possible consequences of such impulsive behaviour. Thus, in due course I decided to try to return towards chastity, and in any case stay celibate, and be less easily seduced. My childhood had made me feel that while family life may have light and joyful moments, for me all too often it seemed to be fraught with all sorts of pain and sorrow; and I just didn't feel or believe that the nuclear family was the best or only 'way of life', for me or humanity to follow. Also, even if I had wanted to get married, in various respects I didn't feel either mature enough, or financially able to start a family.

From another perspective I felt that the planet was and is populated quite enough, and that if anything I wanted to be part of a 'spiritual community', where I could live with others on a basis of shared values. In short, I didn't feel I had really grown up myself, either emotionally or spiritually, and didn't want to be in a relationship based on mutual dependence or addiction, since as a child I had already seen and experienced the effects of that. Also, to me it seemed that sexual experience is very brief, and doesn't compare with the satisfaction which can be derived from cultivating new and deeper or higher levels of consciousness through meditation practice. Furthermore, to me it seemed that in helping each other to develop in this sort of way, we are learning to care for all forms of life and may also be able to live more meaningful lives while also putting less strain on our environment.

* * *

Regents Park

Of course, actualizing one's aspirations is not always as straightforward as one might like it to be. And so it was that at some point in this period, still being a bit impulsive, I decided to take one more L.S.D. trip. Not for old-time's sake but because I was feeling the pressures of a squalid situation, as well as being a bit lonely. And also because when I had my previous psychedelic trips a few years back, apart from good experiences some of my latter ones had been quite rough, and rather like getting back on a horse after a fall, I felt it might be a worthwhile gamble to take one more trip to try and redress the balance. There again all the above could just be excuses, but anyhow someone had given or sold me a tab. (L.S.D. trip) and I took it one morning and then stepped out onto Prince of Wales Crescent. I had hardly walked a few yards when I was accosted by an unusual 'tramp' who frequented the area. He had often seen me playing my Yamaha flute on the street, and he had asked me for a small sum of money which I gave him. I continued on my way to Regents Park, where as a little boy I had whiled away many a day on the swings and roundabouts, and as a schoolboy had been taken to the playing fields for football. I had also had teenage jobs at the zoo, and later had discovered and spent many a day reflecting in the Rose Gardens.

    Anyhow now I sat on a bench in a quiet spot and tried to relax and let myself go into the trip gently, after a while I went from the bench onto an expanse of lawn. Then for some reason, unlike other trips where my consciousness seemed to expand, in this instance my mind seemed to contract to a tiny point which itself then disappeared, and I just seemed to lose consciousness for about six hours. When I came to my body seemed to be having a fit of convulsions but after a while these subsided and over the next couple of hours I gradually started to come back to earth. During this period people were starting to pass by returning home from work, and at one point what seemed like a vast Alsatian dashed over and pounced all over me, and seemed to lick me all over my face and hands and later I found his large muddy paw marks all over my copy of 'The Psychedelic Experience' which I had with me. (Penguin modern classics, Timothy Leary, Ralph Metzner & Richard Alpert). The light was fading, and it was a cold and gloomy day, and I felt like I was an alien in some sort of wasteland or purgatory. I realised that the bulk of the 'trip' was over, but that there were still a few waves to come, and that my state of mind was very suggestible and that I was been affected by intense cold and increasing twilight and that it was important to find a more congenial setting. Apart from it being sordid, I didn't feel like going back to Prince of Wales Crescent, as I felt I needed some sort of human contact. Then I thought of Colin Ferguson and Annie Leigh, a couple of friends who lived not too far away.

    On my way there I was crossing a busy junction when the traffic seemed quite menacing and the headlights seemed to turn into tigers' eyes, and I was at a loss for what to do, when on the far corner of the junction I spotted the same tramp I had given about fifty pence to that morning. He was beckoning to me, so I made a bee-line to him, sort of veering through the traffic. He seemed to realise something was up and took me into a nearby workman's cafe for a cup of tea. I was grateful to him for drawing me out of the traffic. Even so I found the cafe quite bizarre. For me the place was like a jelly with everything wobbling and swirling in waves of energy. Then I looked into my host's face and I seemed to be able to read his entire life-story reflected in the countless lines in his face and he seemed to have been through so much that I just burst into tears. He didn't know what to make of me, as my tears flowed. After a few minutes we parted and he quipped that I should keep on playing my flute.

Eventually I got to the street where Colin and Annie lived. The only trouble was that I couldn't find the house as the tail-end of the trip was still affecting me, and the houses kept dissolving away. But somehow I got to the right door, and fortunately they were both in, I don't recall what I said, if anything. Annie who opened the door informed me I was half frozen, so I took her word for it, and she quickly settled me down with a blanket and a hot water bottle and made me a drink while Colin at my request read to me some sections from my simplified version of 'The Tibetan Book of the Dead', mentioned earlier. (A many decades later Aloka is married to Padmajyoti and their resident cat also seems acute and sensitive).

I was very grateful for the help I received from Colin and Annie (who respectively became Aloka and Varaprabha, after being ordained individually into the Western Buddhist Order) also I appreciated their cat who came and purred by me, till until I was more and more at ease. The next day I went back to my place, and after a few days started to feel I had my feet back on the ground. I concluded that I had been quite lucky as my experience, unlike previous ones, had been neither very good nor very bad, but had been quite 'middle of the road', and I felt happy to leave my dabbling there. Subsequently it was increasingly clear to me that altered states of consciousness induced by the haphazard use of drugs; can in no way compare with the careful and systematic development of higher states of consciousness, which can be gently explored and entered into with the help of a good conscience; and developing mindfulness and positive emotions through the practice of meditation, and thereby becoming more at one with the universe and kinder towards both oneself and others.

* * *

An Official Appointment

About this time I received notice that the place where I was living was going to be pulled down, but that over the next month I would be offered another short-term place to live. Then, as if to add to the general turmoil, a friendly uniformed London bobby, turned up at my door to inform me that a date had at last been set for my forthcoming trial at the Old Bailey, and to my surprise, the date my case had been fixed for was to be on my twenty-fifth birthday August 1974.

Although I was innocent, I found waiting for this court case caused a lot of stress and strain in my life. And the prospect that after so long, the case might in the next few months be sorted out one way or the other seemed some sort of relief. Meanwhile, life went on. I continued with my involvement at 'Pundarika' the (Friends of the Western Buddhist Order) Buddhist Centre in Balmore Street Archway. I continued going to have flute lessons, and I continued doing various film jobs of one sort and another, as well as also continuing working for Mrs Floyd doing gardening, painting and that sort of thing.

CHAPTER SEVEN

Old Bailey (24-25)

Lyndhurst Gardens & law study

My new place was in a less run-down part of Hampstead. In fact it was quite pleasant and not far from the Heath. The house was impressive from the outside, but the inside was a semi functional mess. There was one sink and a few cooking rings in the basement, which were shared by about a dozen people in various states of mental health. About half the people were caught up in drugs or alcohol and the rest into various alternative lifestyles. Not wanting to be side-tracked into drugs or alcohol I mostly kept myself to myself. My own room was at the top of the house, and large and apart from a quarter of the ceiling missing which made it difficult to heat, it wasn't bad especially as it looked out onto the back garden. For some reason or another I decided I should have a big shrine in it, to symbolize and remind me of my values and aspirations. A few days later the police raided the place; probably looking for drugs, when they came to my room, I asked to see their search warrant which they treated as joke, I then went a step further and asked them to remove their shoes. They didn't comply but at least they didn't turn my room upside down, they just looked around a little bit and left in a polite fashion.

This brush with the law reminded me of the advice that I had received from the friend of mine David Gerald Annsley who was an Anglican vicar. He had observed that people often get stage-fright or tongue-tied by courtroom procedures. So since as well as being represented by a solicitor and barrister, I mainly intended to defend myself in court, I decided it would be prudent to make myself familiar on a practical level with what goes on in court houses, as part of my preparation for my Old Bailey debut. So I started the practice of occasionally visiting public galleries at various trials, where I could observe the behaviour of defendants, lawyers, police, juries and judges. I had assured my friend I wouldn't be tongue-tied, and to help this I decided that as well as studying law at a basic level, I should also have all the facts of my case clearly memorized, and that I should deepen my practice of yoga and meditation and make sure that I tried to be in good health in the few days running up to the trial.

* * *

Comparative religion

There were still about four months to go, till my birthday appointment with Her Majesty's officers. Meanwhile having found that observing how people go about things in law courts, is quite a practical and effective way of learning, for various other reasons I started to extend my first-hand experience of how various adherents of different religions practice their faiths. I was twenty-four and a bit restless, and I wanted to have more meaningful communication with other people. The place where I lived didn't really meet my needs, and I felt isolated and wanted some sort of meaningful contact with other human beings. This is not to say that some of the other inhabitants of the house in Lyndhurst Gardens were not friendly in their own ways. So it was that one day when I had gone out for a short walk, I saw on a small board outside a large house on the corner of Haverstock Hill and Pond St, the photo of yet another guru, complete with beaming face and his right hand in a gesture of peace or fearlessness. Because he looked quite attractive and it was only a few minutes from where I lived I decided to go to the advertised meeting, which also included free vegetarian food.

Funnily enough it turned out Sri Keshavadas had been trained in India as a lawyer, but his main interest since a child had been bhakti yoga, which means 'union via devotion' with whatever you want to call 'it'! The house and temple were owned by Mr Benares who had come from India as a young boy. To my surprise when I arrived for the meeting and had settled myself down I found that Sri Keshavadas, who himself sang and played the accordion, was to be accompanied by his own son who played the tablas. For me this was a totally entrancing experience; the youth seemed to be very absorbed, with hands so lithe that they seemed to dance over his tablas, while the rest of his body moved or swayed to his mesmerising beat, the expression on his face seemed to remain calm and absorbed in the rhythm.

Sri Keshavadas seemed very alive and warm hearted and had quite a positive effect on those around him, and another time at one of his meetings I found myself having a very pleasant sensation in the area of my pineal gland in my forehead. Subsequently on another occasion it was in this same area that I was given some sort of initiation with a shell on my forehead and a new name, though this happened, unexpectedly and off the cuff, without formal preparation. After Sri

Keshavadas departed, his followers seemed to vanish as mysteriously as they arrived. Personally, I continued to develop a bit of a friendship with Mr Banares, who at about seventy-five was about fifty years my senior. Apart from finding him a bit of a character and appreciating his jovial nature and his cooking, he also expounded to me on the Bhagavad Gita and started to teach me a little bit of Sanskrit. Around this period, I continued the slightly odd practice of engaging with various other religions, on a practical basis at grass roots level. So for a period I developed the practice of participating in the religious activities of various traditions, thus on a typical day I would attend the Zen Centre at about 5am for a double period of intense meditation, then at 10am I would sometimes attend a Catholic Church partly because I liked the architecture of the church and partly to come to terms with some of my childhood experiences, and review it from an adult perspective, then in the middle of the afternoon I would sometimes go to the (the more well-known) Hari Krishna temple, and do some dancing and chanting and get a free vegetarian meal, and then in the evenings I would go to Sanskrit classes or the F.W.B.O. Centre in Archway and hear lectures on the Higher Evolution of man and related topics.

One or two of my fellow 'Buddhist' friends did not much approve of my activities; and at different times I was playfully told that "I was mad", that "I was a Hindu", and at another time that "If I was to be really dedicated to the F.W.B.O., then I should stop going to my general adult education classes, if they clashed with a class at the Centre ". Anyhow I became a bit alienated from some of the people involved at F.W.B.O. Centre, but I didn't let this undermine my strong connection with a few people who seemed to be able to relate to and had more patience with me, and I continued to be deeply impressed by the teaching and practice of the Dharma (Buddhist teaching) as taught by Sangharakshita.

* * *

Community Café

One day I was sitting in Community Cafe, a very good and cheap vegetarian co-op which was near Swiss Cottage swimming baths. The staff included some Buddhists whose friendliness often seemed as much a tonic as the food. I had spent part of the morning busking with my flute, and was sitting there feeling decidedly content, when a man came in and sat at my table and engaged me in conversation and told me about a place nearby that he was going to visit and that he thought I would find it of interest to come with him and meet the people who lived there. Since I wasn't busy and it wasn't far, I agreed to go for a short while. The place was a large old Hampstead house, which was well kept and may have been owned, rented, or a high-quality squat. My companion rang the doorbell, and the person who answered looked like a doctor or teacher and not what I expected. He asked if we had an appointment, and then told us to wait. Shortly he came back and told us we could come in and have some tea. Inside the place was very clean and highly polished and more like a convent or monastery than a squat, and I remembered this was the place where I had previously passed one evening and noticed someone playing a violin by candlelight.

We were taken straight to a room at the back where about five men and three women were seated around a long wooden table; they had a well-scrubbed appearance and didn't seem disturbed by our arrival. We were directed to sit down and were given tea and whole-meal cake. I was aware of becoming affected by the atmosphere, as if one had just stumbled into some kind of retreat, and I found as I sat there that my mind felt less cluttered and more relaxed. The fellow who brought me left, they were asking me questions and I felt as if they were trying to draw me into something, though I didn't know what? And yet I didn't feel like leaving.

One started to emerge as their leader, he took a position in front of me while the others sat to the sides, and there was something both strange and yet familiar about him. The questioning became more and more pointed and critical. They said things about how I was dressed and slightly ridiculed me, I was embarrassed, yet the more I defended myself the more they teased me. Then all of a sudden his mind and mine seemed to be suffused with white energy. It was both inside and outside of us. My mind just for a moment seemed to dissolve, and to become quite naked like a white flower unfolding its petals, and all the words gave way to a deep and satisfying silence. While I appreciated this fleeting experience, essentially it wasn't any more unique than 'experiences' I had in formal meditation practice, as well as an occasion when I had a spontaneous experience which was quite similar. Though I went back a couple of times, it became clear I was not compliant enough for them. I never did find out who they were, or if associated with any teaching, in retrospect I wondered whether the tea or cake contained some added substance. Years later Bhante suggested to me they may have been a group related to Gurdjieff.

* * *

Poetry and Irregular Steps

About this time, I was much inspired by another event; one evening I visited the F.W.B.O. Centre 'Pundarika', and to my surprise learned that Sangharakshita wrote very engaging poetry, such as his poem 'The Awakening of the Heart' and many others, and could hardly believe that someone who gave such profound lectures, and actually seemed to embody what he taught, could also be the author of such beautiful and meaningful poetry. I didn't stay for the evening's event; but went home after taking down some notes about a forthcoming lecture "The path of regular and the path of irregular steps" which Bhante was to be giving, not at Archway but at the London Buddhist Society in Eccleston Square, near Victoria bus Station.

I was quite keen to go to Bhante's lecture and when the day came I set off to Victoria to find the Buddhist Society. The fact that I was wearing pyjama bottoms was more to do with influences I had picked up in Afghanistan, than that I had just got out of bed. But it hadn't really occurred to me that wandering about Victoria like that might attract unwanted attention but it did. It had started to rain and somehow my striped pyjamas under a large black umbrella made me look like I had escaped from some sort of institution and I shortly found myself being interviewed by a plainclothes detective who looked as if he was himself from India. Along with his white colleagues who emerged with him from a squad car, they questioned and searched me and then made checks back at headquarters over the radio. After about half an hour I was free to continue, and still managed to get to the Buddhist Society on time, but only to discover that I had got my dates wrong, and that the lecture was not to be for another month. To add to my consternation; I was also surprised to find the lady receptionist smoking a cigarette, meanwhile she appeared to be no less baffled by my looking as if I had just climbed out of bed. But anyhow she was quite polite and suggested I came back in a month's time.

* * *

The Old Bailey

As my twenty-fifth birthday, which was to include my debut at the Old Bailey, started to loom large, I realised I was going to be a nervous wreck on the day, if I didn't start to make a special effort to be in good health both physically and psychologically. It seemed to me that the law-system was like an impersonal machine, or even a snarling dog, which somehow had got the corner of my shirt-tail in its teeth, and that if I didn't swiftly get through this ordeal which had been weighing on me now for almost a year, then not only was there a danger that it would wind me in and chew me up, but also quite possibly it would not even bother to spit me out. To off-set these fears, I decided that it was not enough to have all the facts of the case both at my fingertips in the form of documentary evidence and at the tip of my tongue, but that I also had to endeavour to be in tip-top condition. I determined that if I was to be thrown into prison, then it would be because 'The Law is an Ass' and not from my lack of trying. And so as well as keeping up with my flute, yoga, and meditation practice, I took to donning a pair of shorts and going running each day, all of which I found quite helpful in putting aside the general pressures I was feeling, both from the court case and my general living situation.

Despite all that, I have to admit that when the day came I felt nervous and had butterflies in my stomach. There seemed to be quite an entourage what with my mother, my solicitor Patricia, my lawyer who had my own name Patrick, there was also Gerald the Anglican vicar friend as well as Mrs Floyd. Yet despite all this support I felt lonely and on my own as we entered the building, and I found myself being taken into custody, with the understanding that I wouldn't be set free again unless I won the case. Meanwhile locked in a cell adjoining the courtroom, there were a couple of preliminaries which occurred. My lawyer informed me that the police would possibly be making contradictory statements about when they picked me up, he added I shouldn't worry if what they said wasn't quite what had gone on, and that it didn't necessarily mean they were trying to distort the case. On the other hand he told me I had been unlucky with the judge, who would be presiding over the case, and of whom he did not seem to have a very high opinion, and he seemed to imply that anything could happen. To some degree I read between the lines, and in part took this to mean that my lawyer and this particular judge were not on very good terms.

To add to all this slightly disturbing information, to my further consternation and slight disbelief, my lawyer then added that he had been instructed to inform me that the judge was prepared to offer a deal, if I consented to change my plea to guilty there and then. This came as quite a shock to me and I felt a bit insulted, and told him to convey back a message that, 'since I was totally innocent of the charge, there were no grounds for me to change my plea'! After all that I felt slightly indignant and a bit shaken, and so for a while I did some meditation, and then feeling more centred, I started to do some soft chanting, but apparently they could hear me in the court-room and a policeman came in and told me to keep quiet, until they were ready for me to be brought in, and so I stopped chanting and instead did a little yoga including a headstand on my jumper. After a while I was brought into court, and after a few technical hitches the process of choosing a jury began, which to my surprise seemed to involve my lawyer rejecting almost every other candidate on various grounds, but eventually a complete jury had been sworn in. Despite having familiarized myself a bit with what goes on in courts, I found the atmosphere of the place both imposing and intimidating, and so to offset this I decided I should pay careful attention to what was happening both within myself and about me. To me it seemed the attitude of the court was very impersonal, and that the case on which my future hung would be conducted almost like a game of chess, and that even though I was not guilty of the charge, I should make every effort to be coming from a strong and yet relaxed position.

While I appreciated the slightly surreal experience of having a box-seat all to myself, in what was a piece of real life-theatre, I also felt cooped up and restricted, inasmuch as when I realised my body didn't feel quite right, and that I was starting to shiver, I wasn't able to just go and get a jacket, but had to repeatedly distract my solicitor's attention until finally she arranged for my jacket to be fetched. Having sorted out my body temperature, it then dawned on me that I wanted to go to the toilet, but the hearing had already started, and I didn't want to miss what was being said, but on the other hand I realised that later on, it was going to be hard enough being cross-examined in the witness box, without finding myself wanting to be somewhere else.

On the contrary I wanted to ensure that my attention was not divided and was fully focused on what was happening. So I had to tell the policeman (not to say usher), who was standing outside my box; that I needed to go to the toilet, and he in turn had to write and send a note to the judge, who in turn read the note and then looked at me and then looked at the policeman, which apparently signalled; that I was to be excused. As we plodded down and down the stairs, I felt too much time was being lost and so I quickened my pace so that my jailer had to call to me to slow down. When I did get there I found I felt inhibited and embarrassed by the policeman standing within listening distance just out-side the half-sized door, but not to hold up the process of justice I did what I could, and then somewhat to my poor jailers consternation, I bounded back up the stairs so as not to miss any more than I had to.

While various bits and pieces were being discussed, I found my seat in my private box, and started to regain my composure. On my solicitor's advice I had agreed that since I insisted on wearing my flip-flops I would at least wear socks. As the case progressed having only flip-flops on happened to turn to my advantage. Inasmuch as I was able gradually to take up a sitting posture, which helped to maintain my feeling of well-being. In effect what I am saying is that since only the policeman standing beside my box could see below my waist, I took a slight liberty, and sat first in the half-lotus and then when my jailer had adjusted to this slight oddity, I flipped up my other leg and sat in the full lotus, which due to gradual practice in the previous few years, I had come to find quite comfortable for short periods. Perhaps it also gave me a sense of feeling removed from the present procedures, but at the same time I continued to pay full attention.

In short, I remained moderately 'cool, calm and collected' as the police read out their various statements and eventually called their star witness, in fact their only witness, which was the woman who about a year previously had come to the police station and asserted that she thought I looked like the person she had seen removing some antiques from somewhere in Hampstead. To my surprise she now seemed less sure and less stable as a person, and confirmed this by making statements which didn't seem like the sort of thing a prosecution witness should be saying, she said that one of the reasons she had registered my face, was because she had found me attractive or good looking or something to that effect and then she seemed to start bringing in various irrelevant factors, until she was asked to sit down.

***

Eventually my own turn came.

When I had made my way to the witness box I was asked whether I wanted to swear by the bible or 'affirm', I pointed out I had already made clear that I was happy to take the oath, though I felt it would make more sense to do so over a Buddhist text inasmuch as I considered myself to be a Buddhist. After a bit of scrambling about, to my surprise the usher came back with a copy of the Bhagavad Gita. My attitude already seemed to have caused a bit of a stir and rather than push the point any further, somewhat bemused I took the oath. In the witness box realising I was now physically much nearer to the judge, I took a visual swipe at him, to my surprise as I gazed straight into his eyes and he looked straight back into mine, some form of quite positive communication took place, and quite unexpectedly some unspoken 'energy' seemed to flash between our eyes. This all happened in a split second, and I started to feel like some sort of unexpected possibility was there, simultaneously I realised I should balance this by staying 'earthed' and be careful not to be conceited or cocky. I quickly lowered my head and turned back to the court in general, I now felt that even if the judge had been on poor terms with my lawyer, he wouldn't be unduly against me.

Conversely the prosecuting lawyer seemed to be both cocky; conceited and very much against me. So much so that I couldn't help but feel slightly amused by his cheek when, after he had started to cross-examine me in his public-school drawl, after a while he whined very assertively "And so I put it to you Mr. Burleigh that you're lying?". Managing to contain my pique I retorted somewhat to his astonishment "And I put it to you sir, that you're 'just doing your job', and can assure you that I feel quite able to defend myself", at which point I turned to the court in general and declared "The fact is I'm totally innocent of this charge, and it should never have been brought against me", at which point the prosecuting lawyer changed his tack, and invited me to say whatever I felt I had to say and in general to put my case. This was an invitation which I eagerly accepted, and I then proceeded to make a number of points pertinent to the case which had been laid against me.

To start I reiterated that apart from the fact that the charge was quite out of character since I held a completely clean record without so much as a parking offence, I had also produced documentary evidence which showed that during the first five days that I was back from Afghanistan, on days one and two in the opinion of my doctor I was still quite unwell and hardly fit to look after myself (let alone lug bits of antique furniture about), and for days three, four and five, I also had evidence which showed that during that time I was engaged by a television company and working on of all things the T.V. series Special Branch, this caused a certain amount of mirth in the courtroom. Continuing for a while and having generally made clear my innocence, I started to draw attention to the flimsiness of the prosecution's case which far from proving my guilt, seemed to hang on the testimony of one woman who had picked me out alone in a police cell and apparently hadn't even been required to have her eyes tested.

This experience for me was cathartic, and everything seemed to fall into place, so much so that the prosecution lawyer interrupted me and asked me to sit down, but to my surprise and I think also his, the judge said I should continue, which I did though I shortly rounded up, but not without first looking at the prosecution witness; and in a friendly way stated I was under no illusions about her need to have her eyesight checked, after which I looked at the jury and reiterating that I was completely innocent of the charge, and then returned to my box-seat.

I hadn't realised it, but apparently the case might have already taken a decisive turn earlier, after the prosecution witness had been cross-examined. This later became clear when it emerged that the jury had wanted to retire early as they already felt able to come to a verdict, but the judge didn't see eye to eye with my lawyer on this, and then it was declared we would have to adjourn till after lunch. While the friends and relatives went off to lunch, I was not at liberty to join them, and was taken down to the 'dungeons' under the Old Bailey where I was about to be placed with a varied bunch of characters, supposedly to relax and eat lunch, but I didn't feel now was the time to be subjected to a social intercourse of whatever nature, and so I told the bloke who had brought me down that I needed time and space to reflect, and asked to be locked in a solitary cell, and so I was taken back out and put into a cage about six feet by six feet, where I ate my vegetarian lunch and perused a book on Zen Buddhism.

In due course I was taken back to the courtroom, where things had apparently started to move. By about mid-afternoon the jury retired without having bothered to hear any defence character witnesses. Not surprisingly after having gone through the various formalities, the jury quite speedily returned a unanimous verdict of not guilty. After a year of frustration and persecution and anxiety this was certainly a relief. I was also satisfied that even the judge at some point had expressed his surprise that the case had been brought to court, taking into account my not having any sort of police record and the lack of any sustainable evidence other that one person's perhaps 'well intentioned' but inaccurate and damaging flights of fancy. I was surprised that as well as my solicitor and lawyer who came and congratulated me, as if I was about to graduate from Oxford or Cambridge, the detectives who had brought the case also came and shook hands with me, which seemed like a positive gesture despite all the trial and tribulation. So it was that I wandered out of the Old Bailey on my twenty-fifth birthday with a sigh of relief. There was also a feeling of anti-climax after having been obliged to build an entire year of my life around that case. But despite a slight feeling of emptiness; my predominant feeling was that I was very glad that that ordeal was over and I resolved to do my best to make good use of my new situation.

* * *

Quandary

The place where I was living continued to be an unsettling and at times difficult situation. I felt out on a limb without very much contact with people and I knew of no job or training prospects that I would be eligible for. Up until now I had been prevented from joining a Buddhist community because of the court-case, but with that cleared the situation had changed, and so I thought of trying to throw myself more in that direction. In this respect I approached Subhuti at the Pundarika Buddhist Centre and asked if he would consider becoming a Kalyana Mitra to me. In Buddhism Kalyana Mitra means good or intimate friend (in the platonic sense). In fact this was asking rather a lot of Subhuti, as he was already a very busy person even so he didn't say no, but said something like he would check about to see who else might be available. Anyhow not much came of it, other than that on a subsequent occasion Subhuti mentioned there might be a place for me in a new community starting in about a month or two, when work would begin revamping an old fire station in London's East End. to turn it into a Buddhist Centre (Later named Sukhavati) to replace Pundarika (the current Centre) which shortly had to be vacated.

Partly due to my previous experiences, where I had 'thrown myself' into a spiritual group situation in New York, without first having some idea or understanding of what I was doing, I was now wary of consciously or unconsciously losing myself in some sort of group situation, basically I was confused and uncertain as to what was the best thing to do. About this time the date arrived for Ven. Sangharakshita (the founder of the Friends of the Western Buddhist Order) to give his public talk 'The Path of Regular and the Path of Irregular Steps', at the London Buddhist Society in Eccleston Square. This was the talk which I had previously tried to attend, this time I arrived properly dressed and on the correct date.

Later hearing this talk on tape, I found it to be relevant and helpful, but at the time I wasn't so receptive and seemed to feel awkward and distracted by the large audience, who all seemed to know each other. The place was packed, and I wasn't able to see the speaker, and remember afterwards feeling slightly dejected as I cycled off. For various reasons in the previous few weeks I had been considering going to India. I was a bit naive and seemed to think I would find what I was looking for there. I hadn't really given much thought to the reality of what it meant to arrive in India without connections or friends or much money or even a clear idea of what I was looking for. In retrospect I realise I just needed a retreat or a place to live, where I could assimilate and consolidate my various experiences so far and put them into some sort of perspective.

* * *

Factors for retreat

Alongside feeling I was not connecting enough with people or friends to want to stay on, I was also affected by coming back to the place where I lived, which was short-term housing and home to about fifteen other squatters, to find yet another police raid taking place. At first, I assumed it must be another drugs raid, but to my dismay and sorrow, it turned out that Ian (A lively character and an artist from Glasgow), and one of the people in the house whom I had known, had apparently committed suicide. This event just further disillusioned me with my situation in London and added to my impetus to leave. Other factors included that because of my previous spell in Australia, I still had the right to go back there, though this option was due to run out in a few more months. I felt fed up with living in squats and being unemployed and decided on a course of action. I was aware that the Friends of the Western Buddhist Order were established in New Zealand and considered that if I entered Australia before my previous ex-emigrant visa expired, after working in Australia to earn money, I could then apply to enter and work in New Zealand if allowed to.

After I had decided to leave London and had got the necessary arrangements underway, I visited the Buddhist Centre to see Subhuti, as well as other friends to let them know what I was up to. I explained my plan to spend a few months in India, and then travel via Australia where I would earn some more money before going on to New Zealand, where I planned to re-establish my contact with the Friends of the Western Buddhist Order. As I was leaving Subhuti whom I felt to be a good friend, told me that I would be back, I was glad to hear this, but at the same time it added to my sadness and mixed feelings about leaving. It's hard to explain but I felt that I had to conquer some sort of mythical mountain inside myself, before it would be appropriate for me to return. I had already made most of the arrangements for leaving and to boost my funds I had managed to sell my flute, camera and bicycle. To my surprise a young French/Canadian fellow (Michelle) who also squatted in the house where I had been staying, caught me as I was leaving and gave me a second-hand flute to replace the one I had sold, which was very kind.

My last evening was spent at Ken's place as he was going to give me a lift to the airport the following morning. Though I had a cold, I agreed to his suggestion to spend the last evening at Gerald's his eccentric Anglican friend. So eventually we turned up at the vicarage, where Gerald true to form rolled us a joint, to which I partly succumbed. Soon I found myself feeling increasingly anxious as I was regaled with all sorts of unsolicited information about how to survive in India, and as the night went on I experienced all sorts of fears about my forthcoming trip. By the next morning when I got to the airport, my cold had got worse, I hadn't had much sleep and I felt pretty dreadful. After various formalities I made my way towards the departure lounge, suddenly quite unexpectedly I found myself overcome by a wave of emotions and broke down in tears, much to the embarrassment of myself and the friend who had brought me to the airport. Anyhow I found my composure, told my friend I was alright and said goodbye.

As I sat in the departure lounge, instead of having my usual fanciful romantic notions about flying and travel, I found my mind seemed to be assailed with all sorts of unwelcome thoughts about plane crashes and poisonous snakes. I seriously wondered whether I was doing the right thing, but having told everyone I was leaving and to some degree having burnt my bridges, I couldn't easily about-turn. So it was that I stayed put, and tried to make myself feel better, as I waited for the announcement to board the plane.

CHAPTER EIGHT

India and Australia 2nd time (25-26)

Plush and Poverty

After the flight had departed with myself on board I started to feel less anxious inasmuch as a decision had been made, and a few hours later I had unwound and started to relax. Along the way we had a stopover at Rome airport, where an incident happened which quite surprised me. An Indian man with a friendly face who was dressed in a dhoti, whom I recognised as one of the passengers on the same flight, came up to me as I was strolling in a corridor and gave me a bright smile and then without any explanation to my astonishment gave me a big hug, I sort of received this, not really knowing what to say. He then told me that his name was Yogi Shanti (which means peace) and that if I was passing near his neck of the woods in India I was welcome to come and stay at his ashram if I wanted to do so, after which he gave me his card and continued on his way.

My ticket to Madras included a night's stopover in Bombay at the airline's expense. To my surprise I found myself lodged in a very plush hotel that seemed reminiscent of the far-gone days of the British Raj, in fact I found the servile attitude of the staff a bit discomfiting and felt like asking them to relax and be themselves. I had the sense to go straight to bed and get some much-needed sleep, after which I had a shower and a meal, and then it was time to return to the airport. Thus my first taste of India was rather insulated though this was soon to change. After the few hours flight to Madras I stepped out on to the tarmac, not really having a clue which way to go next. During the process through customs I helped a young woman with her luggage (I didn't have much myself). We talked a bit and she told me she was going to Pondicherry, which was a few hours bus ride from Madras where she was staying at a large ashram which had been founded by Sri Aurobindo and a lady known as the Mother. I realised to my surprise that this was the same place where Sri Chinmoy had spent many years and it was suggested I might come for a visit after I had sorted myself out a bit, and we said goodbye.

Somehow I didn't have much luck finding accommodation in Madras, I was partly hindered by not speaking or reading any of the languages used, and I was soon feeling exhausted by the very hot weather. While I had an airline ticket which would depart from Madras to Australia in about three months' time, I didn't actually have much money. So this contributed to my ending up in a very murky and dingy room, with bars on the small window and an open drain running by the door. That evening I seemed to be accosted by mosquitoes and the temperature was stifling, and the only drinking water was lukewarm and tasted absolutely foul as I had to add water purifying tablets. It also happened to be November the fifth, and during much of the night, fireworks which sounded more like bombs kept exploding all over the place. So that I spent most of the night lying on my bunk feeling totally bemused by the absurdity of the situation in between the few moments during which I managed to sleep.

* * *

Pondicherry

The following day I decided to leave Madras which seemed a big vibrant city teeming with life, and took the long bumpy bus ride to Pondicherry. I soon found myself being charmed by vistas of rural India which constantly changed with the setting sun, all of which was seen through bowing palm trees which stretched far into the distance on either side. As we sped along the dusty roads I was amazed at how the driver never slowed down for animals or people who happened to stray near the road, instead there was an almost continuous blaring of the horn. To my relief we eventually reached our destination without any mishaps, Pondicherry seemed to be the size of a small town, the pace of life felt a bit more manageable, though it may also be that I was starting to get over my jetlag. More people seemed to speak English and I soon found the Ashram office and was allocated some dormitory-style accommodation in a large hall, which had very high ceilings with large old-fashioned fans hanging from them. I also was relieved to notice the beds were all hung with full-size mosquito nets, and looked forward to the prospect of a good night's sleep.

After a few days I was transferred to a shared unit, this comprised of two single rooms and a shared shower in between, my window looked straight out onto the beach, which each morning would become a sort of public bathroom and I soon got used to seeing people there each day performing their various ablutions and other such activities. I soon found myself being affected by heat-stroke and didn't seem to have much energy, till gradually it dawned on me that I should get up at about three or four in the morning and take siestas during the day. I was intrigued to find that even after I resorted to hanging foodstuff from the ceiling on a piece of cotton the ants still detected this.

Some mornings would be spent sitting on the sea wall and watching the sun gradually rise up out of the ocean and high into the sky, while others were spent just lying naked on my bed under the mosquito net dreaming of cooler climbs. After getting around to hiring a bicycle, I had easier access to the main ashram buildings and would sometimes go there to meditate in the mornings. The main shrine area was very colourful and was all decked out each morning with what seemed like vast quantities of fresh flowers all very carefully arranged, along with countless sticks of incense filling the air with wafting fragrance of various sorts. There was also a strong atmosphere of stillness and quiet, especially in the relative cool and peace of the early mornings.

The place seemed to be run, or even to run itself like a large spiritual co-operative, with all sorts of activities going on in which one could participate or not as one pleased. In my own case I was asked if there were any skills I wanted to develop or that I had to share, and this led to my facilitating a very basic hatha yoga group and I in turn funnily enough, attended a class where I started to learn some basic typing and shorthand. At some stage I was invited to go for a short bus ride out of Pondicherry, to visit a place which was called Auroville. This was to be their new purpose-built city, at the centre of which there was an impressive large spherical building which was about half completed, which was to be the meditation hall and would be the heart of this new society. The idea of having real values at the heart of the city, instead of yet another shopping complex, seemed to me like a very good idea. Though this is not to say that there were not social circumstances in Pondicherry and elsewhere in India which I found shocking, such as the odd-looking fellow who had missing limbs and appeared only to have part of his torso, who would call at me from his spot on the pavement, if I tried to pass him by on my way to the ashram, and conversely would show great appreciation for whatever little I gave him.

On another occasion I was invited to go on a picnic, in the event the group seemed to be made up mostly of Indian ladies. Earlier in Bombay I had noticed Indian women doing building work carrying things to and fro, and was very impressed by their general composure.

The women on the picnic were no exception, and all seemed to be dressed in vivid saris, which seemed to display all the colours of the rainbow. The day itself was also very bright, and the spot where we had our picnic seemed to take on an almost magical quality. After a while I could hardly believe my eyes when a boy came by and at the bequest of the women, proceeded with confident agility, to dart up one of the tall trees to dislodge coconuts, while in the distance the ocean shimmered and sparkled in the slightly hazy afternoon sun. To my surprise they looked nothing like 'English' coconuts, they were coloured bright green, yet after he cut the tops off they produced a refreshing drink which we shared, none of the ladies spoke much English so we mostly communicated through silence with punctuations of laughter, I don't recall which hand I ate with, but no one looked too concerned about my etiquette or lack thereof, and the afternoon seemed to be enjoyed by everyone.

The rent money for my room also included meals which were taken in the very large ashram dining room, I noticed one fellow who would occasionally fast and instead of taking a meal would just sit there with a glass of water, I didn't really know quite how to respond, but settled for just eating away, though he appeared to register all that one ate. What I found far more disconcerting was a little crippled boy of about twelve or thirteen strapped to a board on wheels; he used to park nearby to the ashram dining room. If I remember correctly there was a rule that one wasn't to feed 'beggars' directly outside the ashram, but of course to me this was one of those rules made to be broken, and I generally made a habit of keeping a bit of food or money for him. Apart from his heart rendering gratitude for the little that was given to him, what was remarkable about this boy was his radiant smile and joy which seemed to beam forth during our occasional meetings.

* * *

Steam train to Agra

After about a couple of months I decided to make the effort to move on as I felt I should try and get about a bit during my last month, so I made my way back to Madras. While I was in a bank trying to get some money a cow wandered in and did some 'business' on the floor. Even more bizarre from my perspective were some of the idiosyncrasies of Indian bureaucracy. Having eventually got hold of some cash, I went to the station assuming that buying a ticket would be quite uncomplicated. In the event after queuing for hours, to my slight disbelief the clerk told me I couldn't obtain a ticket without first filling in a form, which among other things required details about my parents' names and addresses. Despite all the fluffing about I did in due course find myself boarding a train for a journey to Agra between Delhi, and Lucknow which was to take about three days.

The train inevitably was very crowded, but I did actually get a bunk of sorts, though it was right next to a toilet and wash basin which proved to be in perpetual use, and at times I couldn't get off my bunk because the floor just below was in use by a Moslem while he performed his prayers. At some stage on the journey I was accosted by a small group of American 'Children of God', who did their very best to convert me. Part of the journey was also spent sitting by some Indian nuns who became quite friendly. Being a long journey I had to get some exercise and at one of the stations I did a session of hatha yoga on a quiet spot on the platform, only to find myself surrounded by many onlookers. Gradually I adjusted to life on an Indian steam train, and at times sat with my feet hanging out an open door, though I stopped doing this after we went under a tunnel and got a bit covered in a mixture of sooty steam. I also struck up a bit of conversation with the driver and his mate. Occasionally vendors or performers of one sort or another would board the train, one young boy singer was so vibrant and wholehearted in his performance that it was almost like being at an opera.

I disembarked at Agra, I had mainly stopped off to have a peep at the Taj Mahal, which was indeed very impressive, especially under the almost full moon, and being late evening the place seemed almost desolate, except for a young man who told me that he was suffering from hepatitis. I spent the night in some non-descript place, and next day returned to see the Taj in broad day light. I was surprised that while impressive, the inside of the building then seemed to have little internal lighting. Also I recall my amazement when near a large archway; suddenly I encountered a large and magnificent elephant, beautifully turned and with his mahout or driver. I also recall at some point, paying for a photo of myself in a dhoti, which the chap did kindly post to my mum.

That night I caught a further train to Benares (Varanasi), this was not such an easy ride, there was a shortage of seats and at one station there was almost a riot which was a bit frightening, personally I ended up sleeping on a luggage rack. I spent a few days in Benares which for the Hindus is a very holy city. Soon I was feeling exhausted from repeatedly getting lost, as well as from the effects of the heat, and also the large numbers of people. By now I was feeling flustered and wasn't in the best of states when I came across the burning ghats, and encountered human bodies being burned. I wasn't sure what to make of it all, but it certainly reminded me that death comes to us all, and sooner or later my own body would be disposed of in one way or another.

I had a phase of feeling a bit depressed and confused, and in a way had a sort of delayed culture shock. I seemed to be surrounded by sickness, poverty and constant signs of the inevitability of death, and I realised I didn't feel in the least bit ready for dying. This awareness of my aversion to death seemed to reach its peak while I was at Varanasi station. I was in the process of making myself take a train to Nepal, even though I didn't really want to go, since I had come down with a touch of flu or illness of some sort, and somehow as I was wandering about the station, I kept stumbling over bodies wrapped in what appeared to be white bandages or sheets. Perhaps they were just people sleeping I really wasn't sure, but I reflected that I needed to recuperate a bit myself and that I was in no state to face Nepal, or another long journey. So I decided instead to go to Bodh Gaya the place where the Buddha had attained Enlightenment.

* * *

Banares to Bodhgaya

This turned out to be a very fortunate move. The last leg of the journey to Bodhgaya was by horse and cart, through quite attractive countryside which had a soothing effect and was more relaxed than the hustle and bustle of trains and buses. Compared to the previous period of travel, arriving at Bodhgaya to me seemed like discovering an oasis of peace, after stumbling out of a desert of noise and confusion, and I soon started to feel much better. Various factors contributed to this, perhaps most significant of all is that it was the spot where the Buddha as an ordinary human being had sat under a beautiful tree, and eventually achieved or entered into Supreme Enlightenment, and I certainly detected and felt influenced by a very strong atmosphere of peace and calm which seemed to pervade the area. It may be that in part this could be attributed to the presence of the many monks of various sects, who seemed to be living peacefully and in harmony with each other. I recall noticing a Tibetan monk who was in the habit of discretely giving portions of food to beggars. Various schools of Buddhism had temples in the area each of which seemed to have their own particular charm. On one occasion I encountered some Theravadin monks, who seemed to have a kind and friendly disposition towards me.

There were a number of Tibetan refugees or travellers in the area living in tents, and they ran a sort of cafe which provided very good vegetarian food, and had a very friendly atmosphere. One of the highlights of this spell was my experience of doing prostrations. I wasn't aware that when Tibetan monks prostrate themselves before a shrine, in many cases they are not just physically prostrating themselves, but simultaneously visualise the object of their reverence and devotion within their minds' eyes, as well as reciting a mantra.

My own practice of prostrations was less developed than this and just a simple act of reverence, which I felt spontaneously inclined to give expression to as many times as I felt able to. For this purpose I borrowed one of the monk's wooden prostration boards set aside for this, which was already well worn from use. After setting the board in the direction of the stupa (a symbolic structure) and area where

Siddhartha Gautama the Buddha to be; had sat under a tree in deep meditation and attained Supreme Enlightenment. Later I think it was in a Burmese temple, where to some degree I engaged with a meditation session though I was a bit distracted by the heat and mosquitoes. Elsewhere in Bodhgaya, in an apparently empty Tibetan Temple; I sat silently in half lotus on a monk's pew; until a wee boy appeared and let out a scream of surprise; then a Lama appeared; saw me and just laughed and smiled. In general I found the effect of performing prostrations quite moving and uplifting, and at times I felt almost feelings of inexplicable happiness and joy. After a while the time drew nearer for me to consider returning by train to Madras in South India, from where I had a seat reserved on a plane to Australia. But by now I felt sorry and had some reservations about leaving Bodh Gaya, even so after careful consideration I realised that my desire to stay on could cause all sorts of complications, and so I accepted that in due course it would be time to leave.

*　*　*

Madras to Melbourne via Canberra

After another long train journey, I arrived back in Madras (Chennai) worn out and in need of a good rest, with a couple of days to go before my flight departed. I was fortunate to find a room within the station complex itself, which was relatively secluded and had real hot showers which despite the warm weather I found very refreshing. These facilities along with the vegetarian food available in the station canteen, made my last few days in India relatively easy, I didn't have to do anything in particular and could just relax and meditate or wander about Madras taking in various sights. The flight from India to Australia was straightforward. I decided not to stay in Sydney; instead I took an overnight bus to Canberra which also solved the problem of finding somewhere to stay for the night. Although I had jetlag and was tired, the coach journey seemed like sheer luxury after my travels in India. Once in Canberra I expected to connect with another coach to Melbourne, but somehow this didn't work out and I ended up having to stay overnight in Canberra.

After India, suddenly finding myself in a sterile motel room with a large colour television stuck in the corner seemed quite odd. It occurred to me that I had started to take for granted the often colourful and vibrant people of India, and now by comparison colour television seemed an artificial and inadequate substitute. In effect I realised I was now having culture shock in reverse, whereas in India much of life's activities take place on the streets, by contrast Canberra seemed quite different and almost at the other end of the spectrum. While my experience was limited to half a day's wandering about, I got the impression that Canberra (designed by an architect from Chicago), was designed more for cars than pedestrians. Though perhaps walkways have since been installed.

The following morning, I wandered about the city and went swimming at a public pool in preparation for continuing by coach to Melbourne. I had some conversation with a swimmer, and mentioned how I had just come from India and was finding the contrast of India to Canberra very different, his response was a sort of remote look, so I let that go, and just plunged into the pool. Many years later thanks to 'insurance, health and safety policies', public pools where one can springboard or plunge in, are a rarity. Still, I much enjoyed the swim, then after some lunch in due course continued by coach to Melbourne.

* * *

Melbourne to Sydney

Melbourne is quite a cosmopolitan place with 'new' Australians from all walks of life. The city itself reminded me a bit of San Francisco due to the trams which ran up and down some of the steep streets. Through the local paper I soon found a bed-sitter in a family house on the edge of the city, the room was a bit dull; but did have a small balcony where I could sit outside occasionally. The landlady and her husband were both very friendly, and they insisted I make good use of the lush apricot tree in their garden. I was amazed at how plentiful the fruit was from one well-established tree, and appreciated lots of apricot crumbles, and in return was asked if I would like to play cricket with their boy who was aged about twelve, and so I responded to this request as best I could and enjoyed tree climbing and playing international cricket in the late afternoon sun. Apart from occasional drunks, the people seemed friendly and I wasn't averse to the idea of spending a few months in Melbourne while I earned some money.

During walks I discovered the botanical gardens, and to my surprise a very impressive public library, in terms of its circular dome, as well as the range of books. To find a job I went to the council administration building, though they didn't have any vacancies in the parks dept., I was told to go to another floor where I was offered a job as a tram-conductor subject to my passing the medical. After a few days of red tape, interviews and form-filling I got taken on, was fitted out with a uniform and told to report for duty at the beginning of the next working week. This job only lasted a short while, when after a week or so it became apparent, that my basic ability in numeration meant that I had idiosyncratic ways of doing sums, and while they were quite satisfied with my resulting figures, they had noticed it took me longer to total up. I wasn't too upset, as I didn't really seem to fit into their world. I was aware most jobs can be awkward in the first few days, and that my arithmetic methodology might have improved.

So it was that a few mornings later I woke up and thought 'what am I going to do today', I was fed up with looking for jobs and I wanted to do something different, I recalled I had seen a poster advertising a Hari Krishna festival and decided after meditation and breakfast to go and see the event. Shortly I was on the street and heading in the general direction of the festival, then I started to notice lots of confetti on the pavements and by following this I soon caught up with, and was surprised at, the size of the floats which were very colourful. As a result of going to this event I made the acquaintance of a young Canadian fellow named Graham, who at least ostensibly was a Hari Krishna devotee complete with close-cropped hair and Indian clothes. For no apparent reason we seemed to relate to each other quite well, and as I was about to leave he asked if I would come back to their temple for a while.

Later it emerged that he also wanted somewhere to stay and he asked if he could come and spend the night at my place, I explained that I only had a single bed-sitter but he persisted, so I agreed. He then asked me to wait and shortly came back, somewhat to my surprise now dressed in a smart suit and clutching a set of golf clubs and a few other possessions. As we walked to my place, he told me how his father had come to Australia because of his work with an oil company, and that he had left their new home in Sydney as he wasn't getting on to well with his dad, though they were still in contact. He also explained that back in Canada he had been very keen on golf and that if necessary he might sell his clubs to raise some money. The following morning Graham who was also a poet, asked if I would come to Sydney with him where he had a job he hoped to return to, his idea was that we could share a flat. At first I declined partly as I couldn't afford to be on the move again so soon, but he said he would pay my fare and so since I hadn't got much else happening I agreed.

* * *

Sydney to New Zealand

My second experience of living in Sydney was very different to the first, partly because at twenty-five I was now a little more mature (or so I thought) and partly for objective reasons. After checking the papers we found a double room in a large old rooming house in Neutral Bay. The landlady seemed a bit peculiar, as were some of the inhabitants, but somehow having a companion seemed to help us both to take things a bit more lightly. On one occasion when Graham and I attended a lonely old tenant, who reeked of alcohol and was having some sort of fit, and clearly having a rough time; I couldn't help but feel saddened. Our living together was in a way my first experience of creating and living in a spiritual community, a positive world created within the environment we found ourselves in. While we had been attracted to each other, the basis of our friendship was platonic and we sought not to exploit each other either sexually nor emotionally, but instead to complement and encourage spiritual aspirations. One might think how peculiar to have spiritual aspirations, yet filling one's life with smoke, alcohol, or television as one's main resource, may be detrimental and unsatisfactory, whereas music, art, literature, meditation and friendship is a more meaningful alternative.

From our room, which was often bright and sunny in the day, I was able, while lying on my bed, to look down on the harbour and was sometimes a little intrigued at the presence of a large black American submarine as well as various other crafts, while Graham would sit at his desk trying to write poetry on his portable typewriter. One of the charms of Neutral Bay was that living there involved often travelling on the ferry across Sydney harbour. The sort of pattern which developed was that after coming back from work or whatever, we would go jogging and then after a shower do some meditation and sometimes we would do some sort of devotional practice with the help of the F.W.B.O Puja Book which I had brought with me. Later we would cook tea together, which Graham found helpful as though he was vegetarian; he wasn't used to fending for himself and I was able to introduce him to at least the basics of vegetarian cooking. So we often enjoyed having tea together, after which we talked for a while before washing up, at which point we would sometimes be joined by a slightly tame possum, which was in the habit of making appearances at the window in search of supplements to his or her diet.

To start with we both registered as unemployed and received some benefits but in due course we both managed to find jobs. Graham was taken back on at a hotel where he had worked previously, while in my case I continued to apply for various positions, including a job which would have involved cleaning windows on the outside of a skyscraper, which I wasn't sorry about not getting. Eventually I applied for an ordinary office cleaning job, thinking there wouldn't be much competition only to find there were about fifteen other applicants. As we sat there waiting to be interviewed, suddenly this incredulous character who seemed just like Groucho Marx burst onto the scene and declared 'right which one of you prefers cleaning toilets', so I put my hand up and he said, 'right you got the job'. Then he took me into his office and told me he was only kidding about the toilets and after a brief interview, gave details of my terms of employment and asked me to return the following day for what would be part-time cleaning work in the evenings.

While the boss had seemed a little odd, my foreman on the job seemed even odder. He was a small French man who was friendly and had a sense of humour, but no matter how hard you worked he always insisted that it wasn't fast enough, so that after just a week or two he had really pushed me into the job, and trained me up to work fast and efficiently. I soon got used to turning up in shorts and a vest, knowing that for the next few hours I would be drenched in perspiration. This was partly due to the workload but also because the air-conditioning was turned off after the office workers had left, except for the computer room which was a large area filled with large computing machines of various sorts.

I must admit I didn't think it was proper that the air was kept cool for the computers as if they were somehow more important than the cleaners, who apparently didn't get a very high rating. To make up for this I didn't waste any of my energy preventing the large and heavy polishing machine from bumping into the metal sides of the computers, and instead conserved my energy for the office areas where one had to be very careful that the polishing machine didn't get out of control and whack into any of the furniture, which it would have sent flying. When I eventually left this job the foreman told me that he was obliged to get out of his workers what he could, and that I was one of the best he had and that he was sorry to see me go.

During the few months that I lived with Graham it emerged that he really wasn't sure philosophically which direction he wanted to go in. He explained to me, a little to my surprise; that prior to his spell with the Hari Krishnas he had been involved with the organisation popularly known as 'The Moonies' and that he was still interested in them. On another occasion one Sunday, he said he wanted to go to a service at the church which he had attended while living with his parents, and also to visit his dad and would I come with him, and so I agreed. Graham had a racing bike which he had previously picked up from his parents' home which was about seven miles away, and he showed me an obvious and yet ingenious way for us both to cycle there on the same bike. This was alternating turns, with first one of us cycling as far into the distance as the other person could see. Then dismounting and parking the bike and walking off. Then the other person would collect the bike and repeat the process; this made us both laugh as we kept riding past each other. Eventually we reached our destination, where suddenly we found ourselves transported into a different world. I don't recall which denomination church; it wasn't one of the mainstream ones. The small flock seemed elderly and conservative in appearance. Most of them were pleased to see Graham again and we were directed to one of the pews. I felt a bit like I was at the theatre, except that from time to time I was obliged to participate in the various activities, so as not to embarrass Graham nor upset the proceedings.

What I found more awkward was the bit afterwards where Graham had to talk with lots of people, who in turn asked me about my background, which wasn't easy for me to put into a few words. Though I am aware that for some it is possible to sum up the essence of one's life in a few words, as exemplified by the Tibetan Buddhist saint and poet Milarepa (1052-1135), who once roundly declared:

"I renounced all worldly affairs, and no longer lazy devoted myself to the Dharma ('Truth'), thus have I reached the state of eternal bliss, such is the story of my life".

Milarepa was renowned as a sage and poet and for composing and singing many songs. After the church attendance, at which I don't think we sang any songs, which is the bit I might have most enjoyed, we then visited Graham's parents which basically went alright, at least so far as I was concerned, but Graham still wasn't getting on to well with his dad. It was obvious they cared about each other; and that he was going through a period loaded with lots of emotive issues which would probably sort themselves out in the next year or two.

A few weeks after our visit to his parents, Graham asked if I would do a seven-day fast with him just drinking water each day. At first this seemed a bit radical, but after a bit of discussion I agreed and a few days later we commenced and completed a seven day fast on water. This went quite well, even though at times I felt a bit lacking in energy and lightheaded. It wasn't too difficult as the weather was warm, and we had both stopped working. By now we had both saved enough money to shortly go to New Zealand, which was a plan we had decided on a few weeks before. Due to my having previously emigrated from America to Australia, I had residency status which in turn allowed me to enter and work in New Zealand, so all I needed was my one-way fare, which was about how much I had. In Graham's case he was required to have a return ticket, which didn't bother him; as he was only intending to go for a few months, while in my case I was open to the possibility of perhaps staying for about a year. Though I really didn't have any plans, except that after I had arrived and perhaps found my feet a bit, I would contact 'The Friends of the Western Buddhist Order' in Auckland or Christchurch.

So in due course we both arrived in New Zealand at Auckland airport. The customs didn't take long and very soon we were on the bus winding our way, towards Auckland along roads, occasionally lined with colourful fruit trees, into the world's largest Polynesian city. My first impressions of Aotearoa the 'Land of the Long White Cloud' were favourable. The land looked fresh and green, and I imagined in my mind, that perhaps New Zealand could become a sort of retreat centre for the world, where people could come from the congested cities and for a period, enjoy a process of unwinding and becoming more at ease and refreshed; before returning. I dare say many other countries also have regions, which could provide real holidays, which could leave people feeling revitalised and rejuvenated rather than exploited and exhausted.

Auckland was very hospitable from the start, on our first night we slept on top of a public toilet in a small park, we thought out of sight; then about 3am a couple of police with torches; interviewed us; and then much to our surprise took us to a free hostel, where we stored our small packs; showered and later were given breakfast, of course we were grateful for that kind hospitality. Then in due course we were to discover as well as kindness; Auckland does have lots of other attractive features. Something which did make an early impression came not so much from the architecture but from one of the indigenous Maori people, who one evening when I was apparently looking a bit destitute, came up and asked me if I needed somewhere to stay. To me he undoubtedly seemed quite sincere in his friendly gesture, though I didn't need to have recourse to his offer, as Graham and I had already managed in our first two days in N.Z. to obtain an adequate if somewhat seedy flat, but I did obtain his advice on where I could get a tram back to Herne Bay, which is where I was due to be meeting up with Graham in our new abode.

CHAPTER NINE

'Land of the Long White Cloud' or Aotearoa (26-30)

Unification Church (The Moonies) Auckland

When I was about sixteen somewhere on edge of London, late on a freezing night, I had nowhere to stay and was so cold that I naively phoned a police station and explained that I was desperate for somewhere to get warm. Perhaps I struck unlucky, inasmuch as the guy on the other end of the line wasn't in the least bit interested and curtly used the eff-word to make it clear to me, that police stations were not hotels. (Incidentally in difficult circumstances, I may use an expletive, but I don't like to just 'show-off' or use expletives as a badge of 'honour'.) Anyhow almost the reverse situation happened in Auckland. By contrast I reiterate more fully how, on our arrival we couldn't afford the rates at the Y.M.C.A. as we needed to conserve our funds for a deposit on a flat and we ended up sleeping in a city park, on a flat roof on top of some public facilities, where we thought we wouldn't be noticed and would be able to sleep quite well as the weather was dry and warm. But to our surprise at about 3am we were awakened by torches shining in our faces, and with policemen at the end of the torches. At first, I thought we were going to be prosecuted or some such thing, but to my surprise after ascertaining what was going on, they checked our passports and then said, if we were that hard up they had better take us to a hostel where we would be able to stay for a few nights, until we found a place to stay. I didn't know if they were kidding, and was slightly in disbelief when they actually took us to a relatively plush place called the James Listen Hostel, where we were well looked after without being charged a penny and even given a free breakfast.

By contrast the flat which we found a couple of days later was not so comfortable. Due to the warm weather and despite cleaning, it was and remained infested with some insect to which I seemed to be a bit allergic. Even so we tried to make the most of it. On a less itchy note, we were surprised to find how cheap food was, especially simple things like bread and milk. We had only been in the flat about a week when Graham who had previously been involved with the 'Moonies' came across a newspaper advert that had been inserted by the Unification Church, also known as the 'Moonies', as a result of which later he spoke to them on the phone and was invited to tea. The next day he came back with a softly spoken and smartly dressed fellow who was president of the N.Z. branch of the 'Moonie' organization which operated both in Auckland and Wellington. He then mentioned that Graham had decided to move in with them and that since I couldn't afford to keep the flat on my own, I was welcome to come and stay with them as a guest for a few weeks, even if I didn't want to get involved with them. At first I declined and so they said to give them a ring if I changed my mind in the next few days.

After a few days, due to practical considerations, as well as being interested to see what Graham was getting involved with, I accepted their offer to stay as a guest for a short while. A couple of days later I vacated the flat and made my way over to Remuera, the smart part of Auckland, where the Moonies' large house was situated, I was slightly surprised to see that quite a few of the streets were lined with grapefruit trees most of which were swelling with fruit. To me it seemed a little strange that an odd sect like the Unification Church should happen to have a fine mansion in Remuera which is one of Auckland's wealthier and select areas, and it seemed even more peculiar when I shortly discovered that the inhabitants of their household, were each morning dispatched on various missions, one of which was selling bags of peanuts. They also had other business interests such as a Ginseng Tea Shop situated on the High Street. I was excused these excursions as I was only a visitor, though I was expected to help with the household chores.

There were about ten or twelve people aged between about twenty and thirty staying in the house, though a man and woman who seemed to be in charge may have been a little older. They all seemed to dress smartly, and to like living in a large family type of situation. For the first couple of days nothing was asked of me as I was just a guest and Graham's friend, though I was invited to join in singing and other activities, but was mostly free to just come and go. Then on about the third day I was asked to go with one of their experienced members for an excursion into the countryside as he wanted to have a talk with me. Along the way we stopped in a remote spot where he asked a bit about my own views and proceeded to embark on introducing me to their teaching or philosophy. After about three hours of trying to bring me round to his way of seeing things, he eventually became a little exasperated, as I would go along with what he said but immediately there was any point which I couldn't accept I would refute it, till eventually he concluded I wasn't that interested and decided we should go back, but we remained on friendly terms.

Though I didn't show any signs of coming round to their way of thinking, I continued to get on quite well with the various people that lived there, though I noticed I wasn't seeing so much of Graham perhaps because they didn't want me to dissuade him from his involvement. Then after a couple of days, their president/leader whom I'll call Peter, disclosed to me that they had taken Graham on some excursion up north and that I couldn't stay in the house anymore, but that he would be driving to their Wellington headquarters, where I could come and stay for a while. Peter informed me that Graham was quite happy doing what he was doing and he had asked him to say goodbye to me, he added that I could stay at their place in Wellington for a couple of weeks if I wanted to. Since I hadn't got much money and didn't feel like sleeping out, I accepted the offer of a place to stay for a couple of weeks and asked them to pass a message on to Graham. The next day about three of us set off on the long drive to Wellington. About half-way we stopped off at some indoor hot-pools, not knowing them that well, I felt shy about being required to strip off naked and share a pool, but they had paid, and I soon felt more relaxed as we just rested in the pool, soaking in the warm water and enjoyed the stillness and silence, along with a refreshing N.Z, bottled drink like UK Seven-Up before continuing for another few hours' drive.

The place in Wellington was no less smart than the house in Auckland but it was different in that it was a bit more regimented, and I found myself sharing a room with several young men who like me were aged about twenty-five. Over the next few days, it became clear I wasn't succumbing to their various efforts to draw me into the situation, thus Peter declared that if I didn't start to shape up in various ways then he would have to ask me to ship out, and so it was that a few days later they, they returned my few possessions and bade me farewell, and I played them a tune on my flute before I departed.

I can still remember one of their songs: 'Come together Friends of The Earth', also their way of using secluded spaces for certain practices.

* * *

Christchurch (South Island)

I had managed to keep aside a small amount of money hidden at the bottom of my things, and so I was able to pay for my passage across the Cook Straits from the North to the South Island. After disembarking at Picton I hesitantly stuck my thumb out as the cars rolled off the ship, and was relieved to quickly get a lift, since it was already dark and it might have been a long night. I was fortunate in that my host was going to within a few miles of Christchurch, which is where I was dropped off at about 4am. While I was looking for somewhere to shelter I stumbled across a half-constructed house, where I was able to have a few hours' sleep, and then in the morning at about 7am caught a bus into Christchurch City. As I sat on the bus, I became aware that I seemed to be in an almost dreamlike state, I seemed to have gone back in time by about twenty years and to have entered an almost different world. As I looked around I noticed a large proportion of the passengers were school children; all looking rather quaint with their bright faces and neat school uniforms. But it wasn't just the children; the adults also seemed to look fresh, composed, confident and ready for the day ahead.

It dawned on me that I probably looked a bit of a sight, and that some of them may have wondered what I was and where I had come from, and I wondered myself, how it was that I had never really felt I belonged anywhere. Even so whereas in my adolescence I had felt like a 'reluctant outsider', nowadays I felt more like an 'insider', mainly thanks to the phase of Buddhist meditation practice which I referred to as 'beginners luck' which had quite changed my perspective on my place in the world, and imbued me with a sense of worth and vision and made me realize, that I am a part of the cosmos, and furthermore that life does have meaning and purpose. Christchurch seemed very English and a bit like a mini version of Oxbridge. Coursing through its centre is the River Avon, by the sides of which I occasionally sat and played my flute, while at its heart is the large Cathedral Square.

Within a day or two I found a small room in a large wooden house in Cranmer Square, which was not too far from the city centre, and so my next task was to find work. As a Buddhist my livelihood needs to be, if not always creative, fruitful and worthwhile, then at least harmless to myself, the environment and all sentient beings. Thus I wasn't prepared to work in non-vegetarian restaurants, or to promote cigarettes or alcohol, though I respect some people may need these things some of the time. Personally I would feel able to enjoy sherry trifle or an aperitif with a friend, and though mainly vegan, partake of food even if it had a miniscule amount of dairy product in it. From about twenty-one it had become clearer to me that I should endeavour to have a good conscience, and thereby be more inclined to cultivate mindfulness, kindness and insight, which is helped by the Buddha's Noble Eight-fold Path: Right Vision and Emotions (wisdom), Right Speech; Behaviour and Livelihood (ethics), and Right Effort, Mindfulness and Communion (Meditation), and thereby to share with others what one believes to be of real worth and value.

Thus it was that I still felt motivated to re-contact The Friends of the Western Buddhist Order, when I was in a position to do so. Since I was aware that affiliating oneself with those that share one's ideals is of importance not only to help prevent one from being crushed by worldly pressures, but also in that, just as a musician benefits from practicing on his or her own, of no less importance is the stimulation and development which comes from interacting with others who share your aspirations. Thus it was that after just a couple of days of being in Christchurch I phoned the F.W.B.O. at their Christchurch Centre and mentioned that I was a friend who had been involved for about a year at the Pundarika Centre in London and that I still wanted to continue with my involvement with the F.W.B.O. and asked when I might visit their place in England Street which functioned both as a public centre and a small residential community.

The fellow who answered whose ordained name was Indrajala seemed a little curt at first, and he made it clear that they were not a 'drop-in centre' but did give me the time of their next public meeting. Eventually I turned up at their centre in England Street, which had a large cherry tree in full bloom by the front door. Here I met Indrajala and started to experience some of his good qualities including his homemade bread. I was to find out that previously he had been among other things a Franciscan monk and a baker, and at present was employed with the tax department. While Indrajala impressed me with his head of long curly hair which made him look like he had a judge's wig on, Megha who was very petite impressed me with her friendliness and astute character, and along with Vijaya, who later gave me a lift home in his van, they all made me feel quite welcome.

Meanwhile I started looking for work and the least offensive position that I was able to find was with a large Dutch firm of wool-brokers called Hart-wool who needed someone to take on a contract to clean their plush office block. I was pleased to get the job, which involved turning up at 4am and then checking the security and doing general cleaning till about 10am. The route between where I lived and my office block was a couple of miles, and always had an airy empty silent dreamlike quality to it, partly since often I had hardly woken up. Along the route in pre-dawn darkness, there was a large full-size billboard of Maharishi Mahesh Yogi whose jovial face and benign eyes somehow seemed to speak to me, and console me as time and again I dashed along the route (sometimes running in snow) and not always feeling up to it. I usually interspersed my work with a spell in the executive suite at the top of the building, where I would practice meditation or do some yoga after which I would swivel in one of the fancy chairs as I watched the approach of dawn and some very beautiful skies often streaked with pink and red and enhanced by the silhouette of silvery mountains on the horizon. My involvement with the Friends continued to develop and so did my job, and after a few months I was called into the assistant managing director's office. Mr B who seemed Dutch, kindly offered an extra job of about two hours as a courier which I accepted.

The place where I worked also housed the Dutch Charge d'Affairs and the courier work involved flitting between various customs offices, banks, post offices and that sort of thing, and at times I quite enjoyed just engaging with business people and I made a practice of amusing the staff who dealt with me, like telling those at the bank that "none of this paperwork would be necessary if we could trust each other". On one occasion I got back to the office and my lady boss informed me that I had just managed to lose the company over a million dollars, she then laughed and explained that I had just delivered a cheque for a sum well over a million dollars and had forgotten to get the book stamped, so I had to go back and get a receipt. Somehow the larger the sums, the more nominal receipts seemed to become, but receipts were important in case they had any hitches in the future.

Occasionally I went on retreats with the F.W.B.O. One of which was at Taylor's Mistake, a beauty spot a few miles out of Christchurch on the coast. Here I made acquaintance of Keith Downer who was a medical student and later as well as passing his exams, was also eventually ordained into The Western Buddhist Order and thus became Dharmadhara. There were about five on the retreat, which wasn't difficult, and it could as well have been described as a holiday by the beach. The difference being that it included meditation, vegetarian food and human communication, by which I mean instead of losing ourselves in alcohol or tobacco, we enjoyed each other's company, as well as occasionally swimming, running on the beach, studying, and just enjoying silence. The place I lived wasn't too bad and after a while I discovered that one of the tenants, Greg Knight, was involved with the Friends and we got to know each other a bit. The landlord was quite amiable and even wrote off part of my rent in return for doing a little caretaking, but after a while he decided to lease the entire building to his cousin who was quite a different character, and having decided he wanted to turn the place into a tourists hotel, set about trying to get us all to leave by means both fair and foul. So that one day when I came to have a bath I discovered a notice declaring only ladies could use the baths, and men were now allocated the use of the showers. But of course this hadn't been the case when I moved in so I ignored it, only to find twenty minutes later when I was in the bath, a loud thumping on the door and someone asking who was in there, and then to my surprise, his officious daughter stuck her head over the bathroom door, and we both seemed to be embarrassed by her intrusion, and I thought it was a good thing I hadn't been doing anything 'unladylike'. In the event I was just relaxing in the water wondering how I was going to get back from bathroom, but now it was clear to his daughter that my gender did not match the notice on the door, and off she went to fetch her dad. In due course all the tenants were evicted and I moved in with Vijaya and his girlfriend, who had become good friends. In particular what I recall about my spell in their place, was a few nights, when in the warm weather I slept out in the garden, while being entranced by classical music and The Moody Blues 'In Search of the Lost Chord' with a borrowed 'Walkman', and gazing up into Southern Cross and the vast starry heavens for long periods, until falling asleep.

Another feature of Christchurch which attracted my attention was a fellow who had been a lecturer in psychology at Melbourne University, but had given up academic life of the normal sort and appointed himself 'The Wizard of Christchurch' and over the years had become officially recognised as such. I first came across the wizard when one day while at work I noticed a small crowd around a figure outside the entrance to the cathedral, as I went closer I noticed an odd figure dressed in a single sackcloth, I noticed he had sharp eyes and a penetrating gaze, and furthermore his discourses were not just ranting and raving and he seemed to be having a strong effect on his listeners, and in a way he was stimulating his listeners to think about the nature of their lives and that sort of thing, though I'm not saying he had all the answers, though he did cast a few spells. Also on one occasion (prior to mobile phones), he produced a telephone from under his sackcloth and proceeded to have a lengthy debate with God which gave him plenty of scope for his performance. I didn't get to hear the whole dialogue as I had to get back to work. Apart from the antics of the Wizard on the outside of the cathedral, I also on weekday evenings, occasionally ventured into the cathedral and enjoyed sitting in a meditation posture on a pew, and listening to the choir singing beautifully.

Towards the end of my year stay in Christchurch it was suggested to me that I might like to come on the Xmas retreat which was to be held at a place called something like 'Waikari' and I decided to go. By now apart from getting to know the Christchurch Order Members (OMs) a lot better, I had also met a few of the OMs from Auckland. Before the open retreat there was about a week's Order gathering and I was invited to stay on my own at the Christchurch Centre for that week, and so I moved in there and in that week, had some repeatedly strange and disturbing dreams. As a last resort I resolved on future nights to stay aware and try to relax when feeling accosted by a suffocating and frightening green figure on top of me, then to my relief, gradually I was able to stop struggling and relax, then the dreams started to change into blissful states and eventually dissolved into bright light. Thus by the end of the week these seemed to have been positively resolved. Then the morning came for me to load up my CG110 Honda motorbike, which I had acquired for use with my job a few months previously. The ride to 'Waikanae or Waikari', which is near Wellington, was a long way for a small motorbike, but I got there in one piece, and after a few days had settled into the retreat.

During this time I deepened my acquaintance with various Order Members and Mitras, both local and from Auckland. A Mitra is someone who hasn't yet been ordained, but has decided to affiliate him or herself with the F.W.B.O. with a view to perhaps eventually being ordained. As a Mitra one is expected to fulfil some criteria such as: 1/ To have stopped 'shopping around' other groups. 2/ To keep in regular contact with Order Members, 3/ To keep up a regular meditation practice, and 4/ To help out with the Movement in whatever ways one can. Thus it was during this retreat, that I made the decision to ask if I could become a Mitra. The day after I asked, I was told by Purna that this had been accepted, and so during the course of the retreat, a ceremony was led by Akshobya, or Purna, during which I offered a candle, a flower, and a stick of incense in front of the retreat shrine, and also chose to make a full-length prostration, since I wanted to emphasis an individual commitment, to the Buddhist path, of trying to cultivate the practice of ethics, meditation and wisdom/compassion, for the benefits of all sentient beings.

* * *

Wangapeka Track and Riverside Community

During the course of the retreat where I became a mitra, apart from meeting Dennis Iverson who later became Udaya and Peter Joseph who later became Priyananda I also met Akshobya who had played a large part in establishing the F.W.B.O. in New Zealand and had originally himself come from England. Anyhow it was he who quite strongly suggested that I move from Christchurch up to Auckland and though I didn't immediately agree, I did start to consider this as a possible next move. After the retreat I had a very cold motorbike ride back to Christchurch, where after further reflection I decided I would move up to Auckland. I told Vijaya with whom I was still staying and tried to explain my reasons for leaving, which were not particularly clear even to myself, but anyhow while sorry I was going at least he was able to take over my job which he found of use, and of course I planned to keep in contact with the friends I had made in Christchurch. I didn't move straight up to Auckland as a friend whom I had met at the Christchurch Centre had told me about a place called Riverside Community in Nelson a picturesque part of N.Z. where she was going to pick apples for a few months and so I wrote away and arranged for a temporary job there en route to Auckland. Catherine also told me about the Wangapeka track which we decided to walk together, our acquaintance was platonic and remained that of travelling companions.

The Wangapeka Track was for me an enchanting and refreshing time, and entailed what seemed like an almost classic experience of spending each day for about a week trekking over remote terrain, covered in verdant bush which seemed especially magical since most of the flora and fauna was new to my eyes. There were also the antics of fantails and other birds, as well as their strange sounds and many sweet fragrances lingering in the fresh clean air. As the walk progressed we found ourselves at times fording rivers, ascending steep peaks or descending via massive gorges, so that usually by the end of the day we were exhausted, and would have just about enough energy left for the chores of chopping wood and fetching water, before having tea and sitting around the fire, and then collapsing into our bunks. The huts which we used were located at strategic points along the way, at one location we slept out because that particular hut was over-run with rats, and we were then kept awake by sand-flies and the like, but early in the morning I did have the chance to make my first observation of a Kiwi in its natural habitat. Apart from observing Kiwis we also observed each other in our natural habitat, since while our friendship remained uncomplicated, we were not too coy to take advantage of our unspoiled surroundings, and usually by about midday were more than ready to cool off, when we would both enjoy bathing nude in idyllic ponds of fresh crystal-clear waters, like Eve and Adam in wonderland.

The larger part of my interlude between Christchurch and Auckland was the three months spent at Riverside Community near Nelson. While earlier we had not succumbed to the symbolic fruit of life and death. Now we picked apples endlessly and little else. At first, I slept on a few apple boxes but after a few days I was given the use of a small caravan. So much time was spent plucking fruit, that at night when I lay down and closed my eyes I would continue to see clear blue sky and bright red apples still brilliantly vivid in my mind's eye. Life in general was very simple, occasionally there would be time off for river bathing, or trips into Motueka but mostly it was work and sleep.

Although now and then I would get shaken up, like the day when it rained, and I was silly enough to let my wet legs and shorts encounter an electric fence which just about caused me to jump out of my skin. On another occasion there was a small forest fire which all of us who were nearby helped to extinguish. The community had been started about thirty-five years previously by several people who were against wars and fighting and believed there could be more harmonious, creative and peaceful ways to deal with difficulties other than just repeatedly resorting to wars. While I don't completely describe myself as being a pacifist, I do wholeheartedly concur with the truthfulness of a verse in The Dhammapada (A classic Buddhist scripture) which asserts in one of its verses that "Hatred is never ended by hatred but by love; this is the law eternal". I would choose to be a medical assistant.

I enjoyed living life close to nature for three months and even found being relatively happy in myself, I seemed to be quite content being chaste. Though this state of relative harmony and integration within myself was in part helped by my practice of yoga and meditation which I managed to keep up occasionally when I wasn't too whacked from all the apple-picking. Though I wasn't formally qualified occasionally I led a hatha yoga class, and at other times I played my flute. Anyhow in due course the season came to an end, and I had to make some plans with regards my next move, and so I contacted someone in the men's Buddhist Community in Auckland and asked if I could come and stay for a period and was invited for a few weeks and confirmed it was alright to send my things up ahead of me by post. I needed somewhere to store these as I had arranged with Megha, a Christchurch Order Member, to spend about ten days solitary at her parent's community-land on Waiheke Island.

Megha's parents had a share in a community on the Island, and she had been able to arrange for me to camp for a week at a sheltered bay, where I would be able to spend some time on my own, it turned out to be an attractive area and very much like an archetypal desert island. The period of the retreat was to be seven days, not being very experienced in solitary retreats I hadn't made any particular plans, other than that I decided to fast for the seven days, while drinking water and fruit drinks. In fact, the weather was so hot I hardly needed to eat, and the sky stayed blue and cloudless for the entire week; which was just as well since I didn't have a tent; but just a bit of cloth hung over a few old bits of wood to keep the sun off. Though far from giving myself a hard time I revelled in the elements, and enjoyed throwing off my clothes and for seven days living naked and alone under a clear blue sky with just the white sand beneath my feet and my own thoughts for company.

Of course my thoughts were not always perfect and I soon realised that while sand, sea and solitude can be fun for a while, even so one still has to deal with passing moods and what have you. After a few days of not eating, I found it less easy to have sustained meditation practice, and so I mostly just meditated if and when I felt like it, I also spent time reading: "To see a World in a grain of sand/ And a heaven in a Wildflower/ Hold Infinity in the palm of your hand and Eternity in an hour". (Auguries of Innocence/ William Blake/ Dover Thrift Edition). Swimming came naturally, since one could just dip in or out and soon dry in the sun, and by the end of the seven days felt I'd had more than enough sun and solitude. Towards the end of the week, a man appeared on the beach, who to all extents and purposes was dressed like a City of London banker, consequently I felt distinctly undressed and quickly searched around for my shorts. To my surprise he came over and conversed a little, and though he seemed real enough, I'm not totally sure this wasn't perhaps the result of my having had a bit too much sun, but perhaps he was just an eccentric person on a day's excursion, who had somehow happened to pass that way.

(In due course I heard of the five hindrances: Craving, Aversion, Sloth & Torpor, Restlessness & Anxiety, and Doubt & Indecision, which are countered by the five antidotes: Consider the consequences, Cultivate the opposite, Let pass, Suppression, and Going for Refuge... All well communicated in Kamalasila's book on Meditation.

Subsequently I had quite a few retreats on Waiheke Island at the spot which came to be known as Padma Bay. Apart from Megha's mum (at whose suggestion I had read and much enjoyed 'Cider with Rosie') and who was later ordained and became Vajrasuri, Akshobya also had some property on the island. This included a bungalow which he had built high up on the peak of a big hill with sweeping views of the island, and so I had an occasional solitary retreat there during one of which I enjoyed reading the book 'Coral Island'. Although a lot of Waiheke (which means something like 'sparkling waters'), is used for retirement homes and the like, there were also lots of untouched parts including a bird and forest reserve, where some years later I came close to obtaining a quarter of an acre; but then chose to the U.K.

Apart from occasional retreats and low-cost day excursions from the city to Waiheke Island which offered swimming at the naturalist's beach and relaxing in the open while reading, or just spending the day dreaming, another aspect of Waiheke Island which enchanted me was the modes of transport available at that time. On my first few crossings over the few miles stretch from Auckland, I went by 'Sea-Bee' which entailed flying in a small and slightly ancient sea plane, and was amused to be told by the pilot that for my return flight I had to be down on the beach at such and such a time. A few days later, on as I looked and listened for his arrival through the clouds, it seemed not a lot different from waiting for a London bus, but I was the sole passenger, and though late when the plane did arrive there weren't three other planes bunched up behind him. When I was not affected with seasickness, as was the case during one rough winter crossing, I liked travelling on the ferry which apart from being cheaper could at times have a slightly mesmerising effect on me, which on one occasion I tried to capture in this verse:

Waihake Island retreat.
Din of the engine, roll of the waves,
Gentle breeze, cloudless sky,
Green Island beckons, as city slips away.
Warm sun on my knee,
Entranced by glistening foam,
And swirling blue sea.
Reflecting the ocean depths.

Coming back to the matter in hand my first retreat on Waiheke, having finished, I made my way by ferry and then an old-fashioned tram, complete with its pole and sparking wires, to the Buddhist community at Stack Street in Herne Bay Auckland, where I was expected.

* * *

Aryasangha

Aryasangha, as the community was subsequently named, was housed in a very large wooden mansion, set in a spacious garden especially lovely in the summers for the large Monarch butterflies which would often hang singly or in pairs from the overripe figs which seemed to attract them. The garden also contained fresh supplies of oranges or grapefruits and feijoas which made delicious crumbles and provided juice for breakfasts. Though the resident kitten Sooty (it was a single sex community), was attracted to legs, so one had to dart in and out of the garden with caution. The house was owned by the family of Peter Joseph (later to become Priyananda) whom I had met briefly in Christchurch and had immediately impressed me with his bright and friendly nature as well as by his good looks.

The community included among others Dennis Iverson (later to become Udaya) who was no less friendly and a very energetic and warm-hearted fellow, Tony Joseph who partially participated in the community and lived in his own quarters in a flat under the house, which looked out over the back garden and also had a trapdoor from which he would emerge in the mornings into the common room, Tony was tall, softly spoken and a crusader for whales and dolphins. He knew lots about lots of things and was very good at counselling and was influenced by various teachings from California and even had a 'Sensory Deprivation Tank' in his quarters which he let people in the community use occasionally. There was also Purna, a friendly deep and mysterious person with an engaging personality, whom I had first met and grown to like at the retreat where I became a mitra. Others included the quaint and interesting figure of Dave Moore (Later to become Ratnaketu) who came along not much later, and John Peacock a bubbly chap who had been involved with the Freemasons, he later died of cancer and was given a Buddhist funeral, which at the time I found very moving and my own contribution was to recite an excerpt from Shelley's poem on the death of Keats. There was also Geoff Bing, who reminded me a bit of a slightly mad professor, he was only about twenty with curly hair a bit overweight and often exuberant in his excitement about whatever he happened to be up to. Later Dave Rice moved in (who was subsequently ordained…), who created a plush and trendy bookshop on the high street called 'Heads & Tails', he also had an interest in vitamins and kept quite an array of them in stock, so that along with the large selection of herb teas the kitchen might have been mistaken for a health-food shop. There was also myself, since within a few weeks I had been accepted as a member of the community.

While everyone in the community was vegetarian, in due course I became mostly vegan and had a phase of occasionally doing fasts. My experimentations with fasting soon taught me the truth of the saying that "Any fool can fast, but it takes a wise person to break it properly". I noticed that towards the end of a fast I would often be feeling light and very clear-headed, almost as if there had been a sort of chemical change in my body, but that after starting eating again, I would lose the high to which I had become a bit accustomed, and then there would be a tendency to want to derive pleasure from eating, to compensate for my feeling of loss. Eventually I started to appreciate that for the most part, it would make more sense to neither starve nor stuff myself, but instead to work on bringing about more effective changes to my experience of life, with the help of meditation, spiritual friendships and going for refuge to the Three Jewels: The Buddha, Dharma and Sangha. The Buddha may be symbolized by The Moon in the night sky, the Dharma or teachings is like a finger pointing to the Moon, while the Sangha is all those practicing the Dharma.

A few weeks after I moved into Aryasangha community, I started to feel like I had inadvertently been drawn or side-tracked into some sort of deva-realm or heavenly state. The weather was warm and seductive, and the people happy, friendly and intelligent, and the house and external environment, was pleasant, spacious and charming, with its lovely grounds, and serene and sunny sitting room with sweeping views over the garden to sparkling waters in the distance. Despite the attractiveness of the situation, I didn't feel particularly at home or at ease, and was weary that I was somehow in a dreamy trance which might titillate for a while but ultimately would just leave me marooned on the rocks, which may have been why I had taken to experimenting with occasional fasting, to try and put my experience into some sort of perspective. Perhaps I could benefit from having time and space in which to just stop for a while and to assimilate and come to terms with my previous few years. With my disrupted schooling, homelessness and later the Old Bailey court case, it was hardly surprising that I felt insecure and a bit at the end of my tether, and now at twenty-seven I just seemed to feel the need to stay put somewhere for a while.

Yet on the other hand Subhuti, for whom I still felt a lot of warmth from my meetings with him at Pundarika in London, had sent me several postcards in which he suggested perhaps I should like to come back and get involved with things in London's East End where he was still spearheading a large new Buddhist Centre. By now I had to some degree come under the spell of Udaya who was very friendly and supportive towards me, and I found myself oscillating between staying and leaving. The fact is that if I had received these cards earlier, before I had left Christchurch then I probably would have returned without any hesitation. But somehow the pull of the situation I was now in, combined with practical considerations, all made it difficult to extricate myself. Despite getting encouragement to stay and sort myself out from those around me, I was undecided about what to do and deep down I could feel there were bits of me that were unresolved and not happy with me being in N.Z.

On the other hand, I seemed to be fed up with being on the move, and so for about two years I had a very ambiguous situation and felt like I was being pulled in two directions at once, and my fasting was one of my ways of trying to figure out what was the best thing to do. I found myself starting to occasionally enjoy being in the community which in fact at times was brilliant, and at least on the surface they were relatively happy times. Though at other times, whether on retreats, or floating in the 'Sensory deprivation tank', or swimming in the nearby attractive bays, I still felt I wasn't really acknowledging my unconscious depths, but there was also general life to deal with. With regards underlying stuff, there was a secluded bay nearby, where I would occasionally jump naked into deep water and swim about two hundred yards to the further shore and back, though I was always aware a peckish shark attracted to Auckland harbour area, unsatisfied, may then have strayed around the coast, looking for a little something, with which to break its own fast and satisfy its inner yearnings.

Our community meetings were generally looked forward to and happily participated in. At evening meals we all came to the table, sometimes we lit a candle and then had some silence and chanted together before eating. There seemed to be no negative strands in the community to undermine our efforts, and there was lots of laughter; though not surprisingly there were also less harmonious times when disagreements had to be sorted out. To help facilitate change as well as giving each other open and direct feedback, sometimes we all laid on a large carpet in a star formation, with our heads toward a candle in the middle, then did some shared chanting. Then the following week was approached almost like we were a new community, seeing each other afresh with new eyes, and with renewed openness and commitment to practising and sharing the Dharma with each other, as well as taking it to other people via the Auckland Buddhist Centre.

There was an advert for early morning cleaners needed at the university which I was going to apply for, as I felt it would be good to do some basic work, but Udaya pointed out this would disrupt the shared community meditation in the mornings. Instead, I started various odd jobs such as working at a place making whole-food sweets though that didn't last long, and then for a while I had a job as a life-model for the Auckland Society of Arts. After a while it was necessary for the Auckland Buddhist Centre to move to a new location in Hobson Street which created scope for lots of work as the place was a dilapidated top floor of an old building, and in due course with lots of helpers the place was transformed into a bright new centre.

Apart from helping with various odd jobs, over the coming months and years I also helped to support classes at the centre, which introduced people to meditation practice and Buddhism for those that were interested. Also I helped reorganise the centre's library which I looked after for about a year. I mention this to make clear that not always being in paid employment doesn't mean that I wasn't at times occupied with unpaid work of one sort or another, even when it was only collecting buckets of surplus fruit from the garden and taking them down the road to an old folk's home.

With the help of Priyananda I got a job along with him stacking books at the university for a few months, which in turn led to my getting a job as an assistant gardener, this job was quite a lot of fun at times and I particularly used to enjoy watering and tending various plants on hot sunny afternoons. My section included a pretty enclosed garden area outside the fine art library, and at times I felt like I was a performing work of art as I stood in my shorts and floppy hat gazing at the patterns the water made as I cast my hose over all sorts of strange and delightful botanical wonders. By now I had been in New Zealand about five years, and had written a number of times to various people in England including the Venerable Sangharakshita (Bhante), and it was in one of these letters that I first requested to be ordained. Sangharakshita was due out for a visit to N.Z. in the coming months, which for me was quite exciting, as by now I had been on lots of F.W.B.O. retreats as well as a number of solitaries and generally felt I had a better appreciation of what the F.W.B.O, was about, and so I planned with some regrets to give up my job after Bhante arrived, so as to be able to participate in those activities open to mitras.

* * *

Suvarnaketu

By now Aryasangha community had gone through a few changes, which after a few stopgaps eventually culminated in the acquiring of a rented property a few streets away which was in a bit of a state and had to be made habitable and moderately fit to live in. This potential new community was named Suvarnaketu, and consisted of some of the people from Aryasangha including myself, after I had made a request to be included. As the date for Bhante's arrival drew closer, various people from other parts of the country came and joined the community, these included Trevor, Bruce Henson, Bernie Tisch (later Gunapala) and Hum Wol a New Zealand-born Korean monk who to me always seemed to be very friendly. (Hum Wol made clear to me that he was sorry I wasn't one of those ordained on that occasion).

While Bhante's modest rooms had been carefully made ready, the rest of the place continued to be a bit of a mess, which wasn't helped by the fact that a large section of one of the walls was missing and for some reason the place was buzzing particularly at night with hordes of thirsty mosquitoes. Fortunately I had obtained some cheap net curtains which I used to improvise mosquito nets. Despite the mosquitoes and the general mess, the place did have some charms including a garden with fresh grapes, and a front porch which boasted bunches of ripening bananas, but the real charm of the place was the prospect of the forthcoming visit by Bhante, which was drawing closer and closer, so Udaya and Purna were endeavouring to finish work on the plush old Rover, which would be used to take Bhante on a tour to Wellington.

Not long after this I was coming back to the community when Bhante was due to be arriving, and I found as I made my way to the community, that I felt drawn to run, and as I came to the front door I seemed to be charged with energy as I ran up the stairs; and there to my surprise were Bhante and Purna. Bhante looked younger than when I had last met him about five years previously, but what I wasn't expecting was that on this occasion a contemporary form of a 'Padmasambhava' figure, like an angel/bodhisattva manifested before me, which just stopped me in my tracks, a sort of idealised form, it's hard to explain but I found it a deep and inexplicable experience. Perhaps Bhante did or didn't appreciate what happened, though it was like meeting Bhante face to face, he could hardly be unaware of it, (later I had other 'experiences' with Bhante). He didn't comment, nor did I, but I was interested to note that the next day Purna said to me something to the effect of 'don't think I didn't see what happened'.

The next few months were at least a partial turning point for me, so far as the F.W.B.O. was concerned. I had asked to be ordained, though

I realised this wasn't likely to be accepted until I had stronger links; that is to say friendships within the Order, It was Udaya who had suggested I write and ask for ordination, but then when he returned from one of his UK visits, he seemed different and at some point, slightly fell out with me. As Bhante put it to me on one occasion "I could be the Buddha himself, but he would be unlikely to ordain me, if I hadn't got satisfactory links within the Order". Since in N.Z. and elsewhere I had at times tended to be a little outspoken with some Order Members, these links had become frayed, though not irretrievably broken, and it was during these months with Bhante (some of which he was away touring) that I found the impetus to hang on, and clarify my involvement with the W.B.O. Somehow it came about; that along with the future Ratnaketu, I shared the role of housekeeping, doing errands, cleaning, cooking and occasionally showing visitors in to meet Bhante, which I was happy to be doing. In short I mostly much appreciated those few months of closer contact with Bhante, and while I didn't get to be on any study seminars, I studied what was going on around me and had occasional interviews, as well as spontaneous communications with Bhante and generally tried to contribute to and make good use of the situation.

After Bhante had toured the country visiting various centres, he returned to Auckland where he was due to lead an ordination retreat, the names of the six or so people to be accepted for ordination; were not going to be announced by Bhante until the actual retreat itself. I already accepted that I was unlikely to be in the running, though I was quite serious in my request, I didn't share the obsession or compulsion which apparently some had about 'getting ordained'. While I was quite happy to dream about and work towards perhaps one day being accepted for ordination into an association of aspiring individuals, committed to cultivating a way of life imbued with 'goodness, beauty and truth', for the benefit of all sentient beings, my main concern was to continue to grow and develop from where I actually was. So I didn't let the slightly edgy atmosphere at the start of the retreat bother me; and instead quite enjoyed the intrigue of waiting to see who would be ordained, though I hoped no one would be too disappointed. So far as I was concerned it turned out to be quite a good retreat, and I found the public ordination ceremonies towards the end of the retreat quite beautiful, and inspiring.

While I'm not one to put Bhante on a pedestal, I'm sure he has more right than most to be on one. Sangharakshita the person may have his own idiosyncratic shortcomings, even so I was very impressed by his warmth, humour, diligence, directness and other qualities which until now I had mainly encountered in books and taped lectures which had already convinced me of his erudite learning and bright intelligence. In this respect I'm reminded I did also attend a 'question and answer session', and I was impressed by Bhante's fielding of questions from all sorts of people, and his presence of being, and certainly he seemed to me to embody and at times to radiate that which he taught. Perhaps I should also add Bhante did not play upon or lay great store by psychic powers or the like, which in Buddhism are treated as not particularly important developments. Instead it is pointed out that they can be dangerous distractions along the way, and are not necessarily indicators of the quality of a person's character or the validity of what he teaches. The Buddha himself exhorted his students not to take what he taught on blind faith or mere intuition, but to critically investigate his teachings and to put them to the test of one's own experience.

Coming back to the ordination retreat, the highlight of my experience was towards the end, when I had an interview with Bhante in the old gypsy-style wagon, where the private part of the ordinations had taken place a few days earlier. Bhante seemed to be in very good form, and we seemed to relate with even more ease, depth and openness than usual, I was aware this would probably be my last interview with Bhante before he left New Zealand and I was pleased that it was such a bright and even refreshing experience, and I felt afterwards that I was sort of 'up to date', and that quite a lot had been resolved. Previously I had asked Bhante to have a look at the details of a Buddhist meditation practice, which I had become acquainted with some years earlier in London's Swiss Cottage Library, and to verify whether he considered it appropriate for me continue with it, which he did though he elaborated on a few details. Not long after the retreat back at the community, I got up very early one morning and made tea for Bhante and Ratnaketu who were about to be departing overseas as Kiwis say, I had by now myself become a N.Z. citizen. Although I had been getting used to the idea, I did feel sad at Bhante's departure and later cried a few tears, but I also felt a sense of happiness and freedom.

After a few days or weeks, it became clear that the community would soon be breaking up, mainly as a number of the Order members were going for visits to England. In due course I obtained jobs first temporarily at 'Western Springs Park' and then at 'One Tree Hill', while the work could be enjoyable it could also be a bit tedious, and I started to develop the practice of taking Poems and Dharma verses to work which I would keep in my back pocket to refer to through the day, and thereby commit them to memory. Having memorised a piece, I would then be at liberty to reflect upon it and thereby take it more to heart. And I soon realised I could do this even while driving the tractor to the top of One Tree Hill to collect the rubbish, or while sitting through a 'works depot' tea-break. In this way I became aware that though Bhante had moved on, it is true as he has pointed out that 'there is a lot of him in his books, lectures and poetry', and studying and reflecting upon these can be a very effective way of being in contact with him. I'll finish this chapter with one of Bhante's shorter poems.

Meditation

Here perpetual incense burns
When the heart to meditation turns
And all delights and passions spurns.

A thousand brilliant hues arise
More lovely than the evening skies
And pictures paint before our eyes

All the spirits storm and stress
Is stilled into a nothingness
As healing powers descend and bless

Refreshed we rise and turn again
To mingle with this world of pain
As on roses falls the rain.

.

(Ven. Sangharakshita, Complete Poems, Windhorse)

CHAPTER TEN
New Zealand 2nd part (31-36)

Shelley Beach Road

It was now that I embarked upon a change of approach during my time in New Zealand, in which I undertook to put more emphasis on directing where I was going, rather than letting myself be led by whatever the demands of the moment happened to be. So this was helped by now needing to live on my own for a while, and to my surprise within only a few days, I happened to find quite a good flat at an affordable rent just a mile or two away in Shelley Beach Road. My new abode was situated in a large and atmospheric wooden mansion, with quite a lot of character, part of the roof sported a large dome and the main gate had big posts on either side, topped with large spheres. The owners, who seemed to me an unusual couple, also had character. He was rather a big man and she was thin and with pointed features, and while I liked them as they were quite friendly, they reminded me a bit of a 'witch' and a 'giant'. Apparently they kept a large part of the house empty, as they didn't like to have too much disturbance, though they had to let out a few flats to keep up with the costs of repairs. The woman told me they didn't mind if I brought friends back to stay, but that I wasn't to repaint any of the rooms. Gradually I settled in and became accustomed to living on my own again. While visually the flat was a bit dull and drab, but was spacious and there was a park nearby with beautiful blue jacaranda trees where I could go jogging and I wasn't far from the bays that I was used to go swimming in.

After a while of being on my own and unemployed, I started to feel a bit cooped up. Though I studied and meditated and did prostrations before my small shrine, I still felt at a bit of a loose end, so eventually to offset this I made more effort to obtain some sort of work. At first, I found a job as a gas-meter reader, but though I got on very well with my supervisor, I only stayed for a few months, as my arithmetic wasn't quite good enough. After that I enrolled for a 'new start' course at Auckland University, which would prepare me for provisional admission to the university. The course was interesting and included lectures on various subjects including economics, the latter which I expected to be dry was made meaningful since the lecturer, an American woman, was keen on E.F. Schumacher the economist who wrote 'Small is Beautiful' (A study of economics as if people mattered).

Auckland summers tended to be warm, and since quite a few of the local people were pacific islanders, I sometimes felt reminded when I went shopping that Auckland is the largest Polynesian city in the world. More than a few of the islanders still seemed to retain quite a sunny disposition to life, and when they wanted could be quite warm-hearted and friendly. The next position to which I was appointed was working at Selwyn College (high school) as a resource room assistant, this entailed handing out photographic equipment, sorting out sets of books and that sort of thing, later after about a month I was asked to help in the library during the afternoons.

The atmosphere in the school seemed good, the work was quite pleasant and the staff were friendly. They included Mrs Butcher the English teacher, who I found a bit daunting partly because of the state of my own written English. Then there was the woman I worked under in the resource room who was quite a strong-willed and witty person and reminded me of a character whom I had once met in a children's book. There was also the librarian, a very proper lady, who reminded me a bit of an owl in her tree with her big round eyes and sense of always being in control, so that I could hardly believe my ears when one day she told me she took quite an interest in going to the horse races, where most weeks she liked to have a little flutter.

My work also fleetingly introduced me to various classics of literature both in book form and occasionally on video. I don't suppose Bishop Selwyn (whom the school was named after) would have approved, but feeling I would like to give something to the College, (with the librarian's consent) I made a point of introducing some Buddhist literature into the school library. Apart from being quite happy with the work, I enjoyed the journeys to school each day, (unlike in my childhood, when I longed for the bus to break down) since the route was very picturesque and ran along the shoreline, which looked out to Rangitoto Island. My position at Selwyn College was under the auspices of T.E.P. (the temporary employment programme) and so only lasted about six months. I might have stayed longer since my employers had mooted the idea of trying to get my term extended another six months, but I was starting to feel a bit like I was just treading water. I was also influenced by the behaviour of a new fellow who had moved into the flat next to me who was very noisy and with an unfriendly disposition, though I didn't react to his inconsideration other than trying to respond to him in a friendly way.

At about this time I learned that the retreat cottage in Otorohanga, which the Buddhist Centre retained on a low rent of about $10 a week, needed someone to take it on while a number of the Order Members were away in England and so I arranged to go to the cottage for three months, I had been on a couple of solitary retreats before, the first was a bit of a flop as the weather was too hot and the place seemed to make me feel uneasy. The second was a lot more successful, it was after a shared retreat when I borrowed a small tent from someone and went with my flute and a few provisions deep into the local bush and spent two weeks living very simply and read The Bodhicharyavatara by Shantideva, a very inspiring Buddhist classic. Recently I had been reading a commentary on this text called 'The Endlessly Fascinating Cry' by Venerable Sangharakshita, and this also contributed to my decision to complete my present term at Selwyn College, and to give notice on my flat and prepare to go on what for me was to be a foray into the unknown in the form of a three-month solitary retreat.

* * *

Otorohanga

While I was completing my notice at Selwyn College, the time arrived for me to complete the formalities of becoming a naturalised N.Z. citizen which involved formally swearing allegiance to the Queen, at an immigration office in Queen St, which I was pleased to do. By now I seemed to have roots in both N.Z. and UK. I felt connections with both regions, as well as with all of life. Now I felt the need to pull up my roots and to go on a retreat, and to try and figure out what to do next. Even so I hadn't long arrived at the cottage, when it dawned on me that I had bitten off more than I could chew, and that I really wasn't ready or prepared for a three-month retreat, and that three weeks would have been much more sensible and relevant to my needs, but by now it was too late to turn back as my job was terminated and my flat vacated. So, I thought there was nothing to do but make the most of it, and decided I should try to stay for the full period, even though I felt like a fish out of water, and so that was that.

Soon I started to be disturbed by minor problems, I didn't find the area particularly attractive, and this was made worse by the duck shooting season apparently having just started, so there was quite a bit of gunfire which I found unsettling both in terms of noise and because I consider ducks to be quaint and harmless creatures. To add to this, within a few weeks the farmer who owned the cottage and surroundings put a raging bull in a field nearby, which constantly made anguished noises in protest at having had its horns sawn off. In fact rather than settling in I was starting to feel quite unsettled and to add to all this, the weather was freezing, and I was only just able to stay warm enough at nights, though after a month the weather perked up. The first half of the retreat was a struggle, and I mostly followed a regime which included listening to Sangharakshita's series of lectures on the Sutra of Golden Light. In the second half of the retreat I started to feel more at ease and relaxed in my surroundings, and less adversely effected by my various states of mind, and in fact at times I was even starting to feel glimpses of happiness and occasional joy.

In the first month I became familiar with the local terrain, I could either go for walks over a large hill or follow the winding river. For the most part, the area was flat with grazing sheep and there were few trees. Someone had left behind a tin of Nescafe, and I was surprised when I succumbed to a cup, as I distinctly felt a surge in my body like my heart was speeding up, over the first month I finished the tin but I didn't bother buying any more. Though I did go into the small town about once a month to get provisions and found this a particularly enjoyable walk, as I would encounter various large and magnificently coloured trees en-route. My meditation practice wasn't anything spectacular, in a way I didn't really have the experience or confidence to really push my practice in a systematic way, and I felt it was better just let the retreat unfold in a moderately steadfast way, and so I made do with a period of meditation in the mornings and a meditation and puja (act of worship) in the evenings, combined with yoga practice, study and going for walks. Funnily enough despite my occasional slip-ups like oversleeping, overeating, or once getting briefly drawn into sexual activity, the overall effect of the retreat did start to accumulate.

I was made more aware of this when towards the end of the second month I went into town. I had to go into a department store and it being a weekday the place was fairly empty, I spoke to one of three young woman assistants, and our energies seemed to spark each other; my appearance and behaviour were straightforward, and we seemed have light and easy communication, but something set them off, and all three of them broke down with laughter and when they regained themselves started to blush a little, after which I asked for whatever it was that I had come into buy. In contrast to their friendliness, earlier a similar thing happened with the farmer, but in his case, he quickly tightened up his stance, scratched his head and walked of, after which I saw less of him. Except one night when I had a peculiar dream about him, or his forbears, in which disturbed ghostly figures woke me up. Thus I felt anxious but that settled down. Conversely, I related quite well to one of the young male farm employees whom I encountered on the hills. The Otorohanga Librarian had kindly loaned me some art books, and I enjoyed doing painting exercises with water-colours, as well as reflecting as I walked up and down a longish driveway which did have a few trees, while at other times I walked along the river bank, and continued the process of learning by heart the 'The Six Root Verses' which are the nucleus of the Tibetan Book of the Dead, or recalling reflecting on the nature of: The five Hindrances: Craving, Aversion, Sloth & Torpor, Restlessness & Anxiety, and Doubt & Indecision. And then reflecting on the five Antidotes: Considering the Consequences, Cultivating the Opposite, Letting Pass (sky-like mind), Suppression and Going for Refuge to the Three Jewels: Buddha, Dharma and Sangha.

As well as disturbed ghostly intruders, I inadvertently encountered a large rat which disturbed both of us, and I had to use a broom to shoo him/ her out. A few weeks later there was a red flowering bush in the garden of which I was particularly fond, one morning I ran out from the meditation still in my pyjamas, having seen cows in the garden, and one of these dreamy creatures had his very large mouth open and was in the process of chomping his way through the flowering bush. As I ran outside, my pyjamas started falling down, simultaneously I endeavoured to persuade the rather uncooperative creature to desist from her anti-social behaviour. Though I was irritated by the damage, I couldn't help being entranced at the cow's big, beautiful eyes staring at me with incomprehension. As I danced about barefoot trying to shoo the creatures out, until I realised, I was going to have to take a more systematic approach, if I was to successfully to evict the gate crashers back into the field from where they had strayed.

I had no phone or radio, and I recall lying in the bath at times, trying to come to terms with inexplicable feelings of anxiety or fear, then again at other times, I felt inexplicably joyful, rapturous and peaceful, while at others I felt content just to lie under the vast black night sky and let myself be absorbed in the vast array of glittering jewel-like stars. In the last weeks of the retreat which was now nearly over I started to prepare myself for going back into the world, I spent a day in Hamilton, and just looked at all the people coming and going and remember it all seemed a bit magical like some sort of dream and I was relieved that people seemed quite healthy and positive.

I also made an excursion to the not too far away very beautiful Waitomo Caves, which literally and metaphorically, were a deep and wondrous experience, and somehow seemed to symbolise all the innate riches which are deep within the hearts of humanity, some of which all to easily skims through life, without really fathoming the depths and heights of our fragile human lives; and even though myself I had perhaps only scraped the surface, I felt my few months had been fruitful and worthwhile. The day came for me to leave the cottage, after cleaning up and packing, I made my way to the main road and soon had thumbed a lift going to Auckland. My host along with his son turned out to be a Jehovah's Witness, and before long had put into my hand a booklet, on the cover of which was printed 'Know the Truth and The Truth shall make You Free' with which I didn't disagree, and so I smiled and listened and also wondered where I was going to stay that night

* * *

Unfixed abodes

Not really being in much of a position to make arrangements for coming back into society at large, I had to make ends meet as best I could. Since it was evening when I arrived in Auckland, I just turned up at the Buddhist centre. Vipula was leading the class and gave me a warm and friendly welcome, and either then or not long after Megha offered to put me up for a few days in Alan Millar's place (later to be Sarvasiddhi), which she was looking after while he was in England. Apart from myself and Megha, there was also Alan's large and impressive statue of Vajrasattva the bodhisattva of purity in residence, whom I mention as its presence seemed almost tangible. From there I moved to a place with some other order members, whom I think were Buddhadasa, Dharmamati and Dipankara each of whom impressed me in different ways, they had kindly offered to put me up for about a week while I found a place to stay. After the first week, I took the only flat I could, which I soon realized was flea-ridden, rowdy and generally not very conducive to positive mental states, despite my efforts to clean up the place.

My transition back into the 'world at large' was more bumpy than smooth, as I hadn't the resources for much else. Alongside this, after his return from the U.K., Udaya seemed different, and our communication seemed to go a bit askew, and I started to feel a little let down or confused. This eventually culminated with me directing my feelings of frustration onto my few possessions, it was the most harmless way I could vent my feelings of exasperation. Though afterwards I felt sorry and ashamed, and realised I had only gained more heartache by my silly outburst. So I resolved to just start afresh.

I decided that in future I should be careful to take full responsibility for my emotional states, and not to depend too much on anyone, or expect too much from other people. Though if I did manage to develop more sustainable friendships in the future; well so much the better, so long as I wasn't going to be upset if these didn't last. The following day I was feeling a little more light-hearted; and I took what was salvageable from my bits and pieces and gave them away to a charity shop. Not long after I obtained a second-hand flute; and to get away from my seedy abode, I spent occasional lunchtimes or evenings busking, on Queen Street or K-Road. Much to my surprise not only did I enjoy myself, but I also found most people seemed to be quite appreciative and generous, considering my flute playing was unskilled and improvised. As well as feeling stimulated by being a lunch-time performer, and chuffed by the bags of loose change which were starting to accumulate, I also realised I needed to dance a bit more lightly with life, and when necessary to roll with the punches and not take problems so seriously, and instead to be creative and practical.

I had let it be known that I was interested in finding somewhere else to stay, and after a week or two I was contacted by a Friend or Mitra like my-self. Pete Radford, a slightly eccentric ex- schoolteacher and hippie who lived in a few acres of wild bush where he had built an unusual dwelling, part of which was like an oversized treehouse. The place had slanting walls, sliding doors with bells, numerous cobwebs and nooks and crannies and on the roof was a triangular room, of which any or all the sides could be dropped back with the use of pulley ropes to reveal the beauty of the surrounding bush, or the wonder of the heavens above, unspoiled by city lights. I was very glad of the offer to have a spell in the country, and in no time, Pete had picked me up in his old van with its built-in skylight and whisked me through various patches of urban blight to his colourful and hideaway.

A change was as good as a rest, and I enjoyed wandering about in the bush or gazing at the stars or being able to throw off all my clothes and just laze in the sun on the wooden patio. At first I lived in a funny little room with colourful walls and a floor lined with a patchwork of carpet off-cuts. At other times I stayed in the dome which opened up to the skies and for a while in another dwelling a hundred yards or so into the bush up a path, which was unique for its splendid array of glow-worms and also a bit hazardous due to the exposed electric cable, which tried to supply the hut but tended to short whenever it rained or one happened to trip on the wires in the dark. The place also contained a nuclear shelter which had been dug into a hillside, where lots of large Wekas (large insects) tended to reside. Though looking a little intimidating, their bite I'm told is fairly harmless. Other wildlife which frequented the area was lots of possums which I considered quite quaint, though Pete wasn't too fond of them as they kept coming into his room at night and kept him awake.

While I appreciated the spell, I did started to feel like I needed to be in a situation, where there were fewer mosquitos and more running water, and also where there would be more chance of finding some paid employment. It was a bit different for my host, inasmuch as it was his place and so he was able to have lots of projects going on, as well as having his own transport at hand. Probably my main contribution while I was there; was my suggestion that we should convert one of his less-used huts into a meditation room, which once done was soon realised to be very worthwhile. A mile or two from Pete's section was a bamboo farm, run by a neighbour who was a Baptist and looked very much like a figure out of the Old Testament. I visited the place partly out of interest but also to see if he had any vacancies for work. Though there were no jobs to be had, I was intrigued by the character who ran the place; and by the numerous different types and sizes of bamboo which had been grown, often to quite a height, which all around one, could be seen swaying in the gentle breeze.

A new community called Suvarnaketu (ii), had been started in an Auckland suburb and after a while in response to my request I was offered a place and so I moved. I had my bedroom in a motor-van parked on the side of the house owned by Rick who later became Satyananda. I liked living in the van till one day I came back to find it had been put back into service and my stuff moved into the house. About this time Sangharakshita's book 'Human Enlightenment' was in the process of being published, for which people had been asked to fund-raise, and so I absorbed myself in organising a showing of a film called O Lucky Man (which I had worked on, shortly before leaving England) and pre-sold the tickets, so as to ensure money was actually made from the event. Around this time there was a sort of country-fair-cum-body & spirit festival called Sweetwaters or Nambassa, in which the F.W.B.O. took part, mainly through providing a large meditation tent and giving basic introduction in meditation.

Apart from helping with this, I also during this time, happened to come across (Baba) Ram Dass, the ex-Harvard professor who along with Timothy Leary and Ralph Metzner had popularised L.S.D. through their book 'Psychedelic Experience' and then later Ram Dass turned to spiritual ways of 'becoming' rather than 'getting' high, as described in his later book Be Here Now. Meeting with Ram Das was a complete surprise, I became aware of a man walking parallel to me and his energy or spirit was shimmering like a blaze of light, he noted I had seen him, and a day or so later, when I queued to meet him, while giving me a hug, he gave me a kiss on my neck, and then said to me 'nobody cares' a sort of zen-like koan. It was a positive and friendly experience; I had not known he was at the festival, and his presence of being, made an unexpected impression on me. During the next few months it became clear that Udaya wasn't relating to me very well, and that he wanted me to leave the community, I found this a bit difficult to accept. To try to get some perspective on things I hitched to Ninety Mile Beach to go 'walkabout' and think things over. En-route a hundred or so miles north of Auckland, I was given a lift in a large station-wagon by a friendly and hospitable family called the Harrisons, who put me up for a few nights. Though they didn't evangelise directly, it soon became clear that they were born-again Christians. Because of the warmer climate towards the Bay of Islands' and the character of the area where they lived, it seemed a bit like I had stepped back in time, such as nineteen sixties American Bible-belt.

Leone loved painting wildflowers, and Evan was a senior teacher at the local school, on the first night she came to my curtained Alcove which had a crucifix at the head of the bed, and asked for my underwear so she could wash it. They fed me vegetarian/vegan food, and took me to meet the pastor at their local church, and had friends take me out on local excursions. After about ten days, my hospitable hosts, who had kept extending my stay, waved me farewell, and I returned to Auckland, where Udaya gave me notice to leave the community, I was quite upset by this, and after a few days departed. I wasn't initially able to find anywhere that I wanted to move to, and for a few weeks I was discretely sleeping at the centre in the reception room, with Tara hanging on one of the walls to keep me company.

From there I moved to Judith and James Dubignon's place, as I had been asked if I would like to mind their house, and water the large Bonsai collection while she and the rest of her family were on holiday. Judith, whom I liked very much for her steady and positive outlook, was by profession a Doctor of Clinical Psychology and taught at the university, she was later ordained and became Jayasri. The bonsai collection was a hobby/ interest of her artist husband James, who first took a shine to me, when we were doing Tai Chi on a F.W.B.O event. He was an accomplished artist) It was he who had designed their stylish house complete with underfloor heating and Japanese influences, I already knew and related well to both James and Judith and enjoyed my various spells looking after their house and plants. While at Judith's place I received a phone call from another (F.W.B.O.) friend, Marion Feasy, a bubbly, generous and vivacious lady, who was later to become Punyasri, who wanted to know if I would be interested in looking after their place out at Kaucaupercauper for an indefinite period. (At some point she played me 'Bridge Over Troubled Waters' and later gave me a copy of Sangharakshita's poem 'New'). Marion and her husband Ron had their first home in the city and a small animal-friendly farm in the countryside, where they needed someone to move the goat about and untangle him when he got caught in his rope, feed the chickens, keep an eye on the few pet sheep and occasionally ride Captain, a largish mare. So, I spent three very enjoyable months, which at times were idyllic just doing a few chores, and courtesy of James reading various Penguin Classics, and being absorbed in relative quietness and charmed by the environment, where sometimes colourful parrot-like birds would make appearances, while one occasion I opened the front door to find a wild-looking white pony rearing up before galloping off.

In due course I learned to call Captain over, put on the bridle, and then use the fence to climb on bareback, as he could be ridden without a saddle; even so I stayed within the fields so as to have a softer landing if I came off. On another less happy occasion I noticed on the farm nearby cattle being prepared for transport and I couldn't help observing how fraught and distressed the creatures were. The farmer had difficulty loading them on the lorry, and it seemed a bit like the animals were experiencing conditions not unlike those atrocities of the past, when human beings were subjected to being forcefully loaded onto wagons.

Towards the end of my spell looking after Marion Feasy's place in the country, I had one particularly beautiful period during which I read The Symposium and Socrates Last Days. One afternoon, I considered that perhaps I should make a concerted effort, to try insofar as possible to resolve any 'unfinished business', so that when my time is up and I am about to die, I might feel at least a little more able to accept it. Thus, I decided that in a few weeks I should go back to Auckland and find a place to live and a job, in order to save some money and prepare for the journey back to England. Where I was aware I still had a few friends and connections, and imagined, that now with a different perspective on life it might be easier to let go of the past, and be open to some sort of new life.

* * *

Remuera to Rarotonga

There was quite a contrast between the quality and style of the Feasy's farmhouse with its plush white-tiled bathroom and other spacious rooms, and the dingy bedsitter in a rooming house to which I moved. To my surprise I later discovered that though removed a few steps, my new landlords were actually the Anglican Church. My room was about three yards by four and included the use of a seedy kitchen and sitting room. The other tenants were a mixed bunch, the young woman who supposedly slept next door kept me awake at nights, since she and her boyfriend who made clandestine visits, were very vigorous in their lovemaking, and not only was every deep sigh audible, but the partition/wall would vibrate with their movements. The first few days she would look at me in the kitchen in the mornings and I would smile and she would laugh, which was about the extent of our communication, even so it was certainly better than the person on the other side of my room who seemed to be a bit sour and sullen. Though the bed-sitter didn't afford me space to do things like yoga or flute practice, it was situated in an attractive area with hill walks and a school playing-field nearby where I could go jogging, and my plan was to use the room as a steppingstone to finding a job and a better place to live.

Soon under the auspices of T.E.P. the government temporary employment programme, I found a position working for the Auckland City Council in their 'Valuation Department'. This involved my driving a car and with a colleague; measuring the size of houses, so that they could be valued and have their rates set. Then in the late afternoons we would come back to the office and spend an hour or so drawing up the data we had gathered onto graph paper. I was teamed up with a Chinese girl called Janet who had been brought up in N.Z. At first she seemed quite nervous and distant but over a month or two without having intended it we became quite good companions. Janet had a flat in Parnell with a spare room and when I had to vacate my bed-sitter, she suggested I move to her place. While we did become quite intimate our friendship was platonic though it did have its moments during occasional hot sunny afternoons, when after we had finished our quota of houses to measure, we sometimes would go back to the flat for a while. Even so basically we managed to keep things from getting too out of hand. Janet was intelligent and good-looking, but also self-conscious though she did come to the Buddhist Centre, and went on an occasional retreat, and I encouraged her to be vegetarian, and having learned to meditate she seemed to get on quite well. At times there was the suggestion of starting a family and even a business with her parents' help. But it was clear that I was already preoccupied with meditation and The Dharma, I felt that I couldn't get involved; since sooner or later I would be going to England. Even so it wasn't easy to extricate ourselves from the developing situation, and we continued to have quite close feelings for each other, but by continuing with a platonic friendship, we were able to stay friends without getting totally entangled in a mutually dependent relationship; though this wasn't easy to maintain, since we were both living and working together. These verses written during my employment with the city's 'Valuation dept', expressed some of my feelings at that time, with regard to the material life and the pull to normal values

Temporary office job. (N.Z.)
...."Stagnation blues
Frivolous gossip
Grey walls and
Incessant phones
Beyond the double glazing
Cars roll silently by,
In the distance looms
A haze, of tomorrows.
Sustenance comes rolling down the corridor
Tea break blossoms, cups appear

Newspapers flower from nowhere!
Old news lethargically perused
By 'sleeping' heads
Grey matter hanging
Over, grey matter.
Walk out of that
Office-zoo-daze!
No need to blame
Clarify your aim
Cease to feel lame, tame your desires
Rekindle your fires
Let go of strife.
Transform your life…

    I bought another Honda motorbike so that I could create a bit more space, and also more easily visit the Buddhist Centre. After a while I happened to hear about a flat which was going to become vacant in Mt Eden in Kingsview Road, so I arranged to meet the owner who agreed I could move in when the place became vacant in about a month's time. Meanwhile one day at work Janet mentioned she had read in the paper that a film company was making a movie with David Bowie in it called "Happy Xmas Mr Lawrence" and that they were auditioning for extras, and the filming would take place on Rarotonga Island which is a pinpoint in the middle of the Pacific. At first I didn't want anything more to do with film work, but I let Janet persuade me into going for the audition, and being white and underweight was deemed suitable to play the part of a prisoner of war in a Japanese camp.

    In fact this wasn't my first connection with Dave Bowie, since my mother had once taken me to a party, where I had met and had a conversation with Lindsey Kemp (the mime artist), he was dressed in a sort of gown, and we lay on a couch as we talked. It was he who had taught David Bowie mime. The Anglo/Japanese film company's terms of employment didn't involve much money, but I fancied a free trip to a remote Pacific island and I was eligible for two weeks leave from my job. Initially this excursion to the South Seas was a bit of a fiasco.

    When the plane to Rarotonga touched down it was 4am in the morning and pouring with rain. At which point we were loaded on to Lorries, and taken to some accommodation quite different from what they had offered. Then after a few hours' sleep we were expected (after having our hair cropped) to start work early that morning. As a matter of principle, I decided to go to the production office and clarify the situation, after which they apparently decided it would be better to keep me out of the way, and so they informed me that, I was free to have a holiday, and they transferred me to a beautiful beach chalet. There wasn't any acrimony, and if anything they seemed to respect me for expecting them in as far as possible to stand by what had been agreed, I went on to enjoy my visit to Rarotonga with its blue skies, white sands and turquoise sea, and island fruits like papaya for breakfast, served with pancakes cooked by large island ladies who looked like figures out of a Gauguin painting.

While I enjoyed my South Sea sojourn it did occur to me that fancy hotels and exotic surroundings were not all they were cracked up to be by travel agents, and truth be told I had enjoyed hot summer days no less magical while swimming in the Hampstead Heath Ponds; and then lazing in the sun watching beautiful dragonflies hover about. After a few days I had to go back to the production office to see the assistant who was going to arrange my ticket back to N.Z. I supposed I would be going back on a cheap night flight similar to the one which I had been brought out on but to my surprise the assistant who was a young and friendly Japanese lady wanted to know if I was interested in having a stop-over in Fiji, since this wouldn't cost them anymore and it was to be a day flight. And so after leaving Rarotonga, I winged my way to Fiji where I had four warm and balmy days retreat staying at a youth hostel. In the nearby cafe I wrote a short verse to try and capture some of the ambience of the place:

Red hibiscus flowers
peeping out of leaf-lined shells
in the midst of local music.

I had some years previously touched down in Fiji when I first emigrated from San Francisco to Australia, but now I was enroute for New Zealand; where in a few days I arrived back from my Pacific excursion courtesy of the British and Japanese venture which was producing "Happy Xmas Mr Lawrence", feeling refreshed and happy to be back in N.Z.

* * *

Kings View Road

Not long after being back at my job I moved into my new flat, which consisted of the front half of a lovely old wooden mansion set in its own small grounds with a large tree in the front, a Norfolk pine tree outside the kitchen window, and a large mass of tall bamboo swaying outside the sitting room window, while another window in the same room exhibited a stained glass design of bending reeds and red blossoms. The place was very spacious and good value for the small rent which I was paying, but was likely to be put up for sale after about six months' time. Meanwhile Janet's place got sold and so she came and stayed for a while until she found another flat. My temporary job finished and combined with being on my own, I at first felt at a bit of a loose end and wasn't sure what to do with myself. About this time there was a trend at the Auckland Buddhist Centre for 'progressive dinners', which was a method of fund-raising (for various causes). This involved those who had bought tickets proceeding to various addresses, at each of which one of the courses of the meal would be provided. And so I participated in this event and was amused to suddenly have about twenty people turn up for their starters or pudding as the case may be, and then after they had eaten their food and finished chatting they would disappear as suddenly as they had arrived. Though I practised yoga and meditation I didn't always manage to keep things together, and sometimes ended up masturbating or oversleeping, but more often than not I had a fairly creative and positive approach to things and even though I slipped a few times I tended to bounce back, even if it was only to lay on my bed eating, while reading about other people's spiritual endeavours.

My own efforts during this period did include going on quite a strict retreat for ten days. I had seen an advert some months prior to the event, giving the dates and details for a Vipassana or Insight retreat which, was to be led by the Burmese meditation teacher Sri Goenka-ji. I was intrigued that they asked for no money other than voluntary donations at the completion of the retreat, and that the brochure spelt out quite carefully that the retreat would be in silence, with the day starting at about 4am and would include a lot of meditation. Being at least aware of the Five Spiritual Faculties introduced in Sangharakshita's 'A Survey of Buddhism', which explain that Energy & Concentration, and Faith and Wisdom, all need to kept in balance through 'Mindfulness', I felt I could benefit from the discipline of such a retreat, even though it concentrated mainly on the faculty of Meditation, but I was a bit concerned that the retreat might be too much for newcomers to meditation. Though I did note that the application form and other preliminaries seemed designed, to some extent, to put off people who might not be able to cope.

Of course I wasn't sure how well I would cope myself, but in the event I had a very good retreat which focused on three main practices: developing mindfulness, contemplating impermanence and cultivating an attitude of universal loving kindness. The retreat was held in school accommodation, in the meditation hall, the females sat too one side and the males to the other. At 4am we meditated in our own accommodation, then later in the main hall, there was access to drinks and one meal before midday; it was probably early summer, as generally I was in shorts and a top. The vegetarian/vegan food was exceptionally good both in quality and quantity, so that I felt quite satisfied until the next day. In the evenings, there would be some sort of encouraging talk from Sri Goenka-ji. Perhaps I should reiterate the whole retreat was in Silence. With the exception that about two-thirds of the way through the retreat, without having requested it, I was pleased to learn I would be having a one-to-meeting with Sri Goenka-ji. As I walked into the room he instructed me to, thus I sat at his feet, and I could feel he had a strong radiant aura, like I had entered into his bubble. I don't recall the exchange, though at some point he stated either I must be in a committed marriage, or I must be practicing chastity, and that there must be no 'in between', which reminded me of a Tibetan adage that 'Chastity is the parent of human happiness', anyhow I didn't disagree, and after a few more words, the interview concluded. While the retreat wasn't always easy and I did at times feel tired or a bit alienated, I felt Sri Goenka-ji seemed a strong, sincere, good and warm-hearted man, and I came away feeling quite refreshed and enlivened by the experience.

Back at Kingsview Road I tried to keep up the momentum of the retreat but in a balanced way. I started going jogging again and was often moved by the beauty of the blue jacaranda trees, which I would pass on my early morning sprints. Another activity of sorts, which I started developing around this period was writing letters to the press on various issues which I felt to be socially important and worth pursuing. Not having really gone to school, I felt some sense of achievement in having occasional letters published and a little satisfaction from being able to express some of my thoughts and feelings and was amused to see what sort of headings they got. Though I have to admit that even the simplest of letters often took me hours to complete, such as this first one on vegetarianism, which was written in response to strikes in the 'freezing works', and was published by the Auckland Star under the heading:

END MEAT STRIFE------FOREVER

(N.Z.1980ish / P.Burleigh)

There seems to me to be perpetual strife in the meat and freezing industries. I suggest one of the roots of this problem is that no worker, however highly paid, could ever really be satisfied or happy spending all day killing helpless animals. It seems to me that the obvious and immediate solution is to phase out all the meat-works and initiate a new industry, through which instead of being confined to the horrors of slaughterhouses, the same workers could be tending and cultivating health-giving crops, while breathing sweet air, in green fields under blue skies. From the soybean alone many money-making and high-protein products are possible that require neither killing nor freezing. Of course if you're a confirmed meat-eater this idea may not appeal. Even so, I would ask people to put aside prejudice and bias and consider the validity of these points: 1/ It's a scientific fact that an acre of beans, peas or lentils can produce ten times more protein than an acre devoted to cattle (see Diet for a Small Planet, Ballantine Books). With a little common sense this protein can easily be turned into delicious foodstuffs and at the same time would drastically reduce the world food shortage, so fewer people would need to die of starvation. To quote Gandhi "There's enough for every man's need, but not for every man's greed". 2/ It is obvious from the first point that there is no justification for the violence, cruelty and exploitation that animals are subjected to. To quote Voltaire "If animals could speak would we kill them?". 3/ Speaking from my experience and honest observation, people who eat vegetarian food, (and I don't mean carrot juice and limp lettuce), tend to be healthier, to live longer, to take up far fewer hospital beds, and seem to have less weight problems. So, I would suggest apart from these personal benefits, this change could help mankind to a healthier and happier relationship with the world in which he/she lives.

The knowledge that this letter had been printed and perhaps even read by thousands of people, did galvanise me from then on, into writing letters on various social issues such as the following letter published in the N.Z. Listener:

***

SPORT AND TOBACCO

(N.Z. 1980ish / P. Burleigh)

With reference to your article ("Cash and smoke", May 5) about sponsorship of sports clubs by tobacco companies, I'd like to suggest a few points. First the tobacco companies could review their values and admit they are pushing a product that is detrimental to society and does not have a healthy future. And thus they would be best to bow out graciously and turn over a new leaf. Second, I'd like to dispel the illusion that has been created---- that the sporting world must depend on tobacco companies or breweries. On the contrary, any healthy sport can stand on its own feet. In fact, to take support from companies that exploit human weakness (I imagine) goes against the Olympic ideal of healthy and fair competition in the pursuit of "excellence". Third, there is a viable alternative: the money these companies spend on advertising could instead be given back in the form of a "health levy", which would pay for, or towards, the upkeep of sports clubs, as well as providing free swimming pools in our cities. To conclude, when the tobacco companies decline, we shall not need a levy, as we'll save millions on medical expenses, and many people will have extra cash and less ash, with which to finance healthy pursuits!

Having letters published in the Auckland Star and N.Z. Listener, and some years later in the U.K. Listener (before it went under), as well as in the Observer and other papers, was a way for me to express my thoughts and feelings on various issues. It also helped to slightly bolster my lack of self-esteem; I experienced both as a youngster at school, and later from prospective employers. They could only define me in terms of my not having been through the normal school system, other than sporadic periods which didn't count for much. Since I hadn't sat any exams and therefore seemed to be deemed a 'non-person'. While I derived some satisfaction from writing and having published what I felt to be socially worthwhile letters, I did still find myself wanting to have more tangible interaction with society and after a while I obtained a job as a school caretaker.

* * *

Parnell District School (Est. 1873)

Parnell is a fancy part of Auckland and from my Londoner's perspective its tone is akin to Kensington or Hampstead. Mr Whimp the headmaster of the quite large primary/middle school of which I was now caretaker, seemed quite conventional when he took me on, and I wondered how I would fare with the position, but in due course it became clear that he wasn't the officious sort and that so long as I kept the gardening, cleaning, swimming pool, school security, general maintenance and ordering of supplies all ticking over and running moderately smoothly, he wasn't too concerned how I went about it. As schools go I quite liked the place as on the whole the atmosphere was a friendly and positive one, and the children except when they were sent to the Head's office, seemed mostly 'happy go lucky'. The wooden buildings were set in spacious grounds (compared to the playground on the roof, at a primary school I had attended in London) and were frequented by an old English sheepdog, which helped make the place feel less institutional and along with the mostly sunny climate, I soon started to feel relatively happy with the position.

After a while my routine developed and went something like: arrive early on my 125 Honda motorbike, open up the school, turn off the burglar alarm, check for break-ins, turn the water back on and sort out heating needs etc. After which I would retire to my care-takers cabin, a large and bright room with the advantage of some seclusion, being positioned at the opposite end of the school to the Head's office and administration area. Apart from containing a large stainless steel sink with its own hot water heater, my caretakers' room also had its own toilet, which I rarely used as such, but instead used it for short periods of meditation when I needed to consolidate my state of being, thus at this point in the morning I would recover from the journey, with a short meditation, unless some school crisis came up; heralded by a member of staff looking for me, in which case I would pull the chain before coming out and cheerfully attend the arisen need.

One afternoon when the headmaster was checking on me, he was relieved to find me at the other end of the grounds, where it was obvious, I had pruned and cleared a lot of stuff. On another occasion, after he had suggested the need for a 'hop-scotch' area, with a pattern of squares containing numbers, he was checking, and pleased to find I was on that task, and had done some quite elegant lettering. Another time he really put me to a test. The school had a fundraising bottle drive, and the majority of parents had come and dumped tons of glassware, mostly wine and alcohol bottles, which they had accumulated. Then someone needed to sort out the large mess of sometimes broken glass, which took a couple of hours to clear out. Surprisingly they added an extra payment to my wage, after which he checked on me less often.

At other times, there would be various chores like gardening, putting up goalposts or mending windows. The afternoon would commence with a daily fire ritual; incinerating rubbish from the bins, which the children would bring to me from their classrooms. I got on well with the kids, and found that by not reacting to mild misbehaving of some, and not becoming unduly familiar with others, I soon had quite a good rapport with most of them, as I did also with the staff. The kids were amused with my lop-sided effort to erect the rugby posts, and other innovations like trying to recycle waste paper, and also collecting all the leftover lunch sandwiches from their bins, which would often amount to a third of a dustbin full, which I would then chop up with a spade before distributing to the large flock of mainly sea birds with some unusual visitors, which started to turn up at that part of the day. Usually by mid-afternoon I would be starting to feel tired and after I had sorted out the dangerous chemical process for keeping the swimming pool up to scratch, there would then be various cleaning jobs, which included vacuuming all the classrooms and would take at least a couple of hours, by which time the staff would have left and I would then read the water meters and close up the school.

* * *

On a less mundane note I would usually conclude my duties by playing on the xylophone in the same classroom, where on one occasion I had given a lesson on playing the flute to a class of nine-year-olds. This was at the invitation of Linda, a teacher who one lunchtime had heard me practicing in my cabin. Thus next day while she was meeting with the headmaster, I did a short introduction to my Yamaha flute. During which the kids after absorbing the lesson, then decided to take out their recorders from their desks, and were joyfully dancing around the room playing their recorders at full blast, when she returned. Myself I was slightly astonished at the swiftness of their 'coup', which they had performed, whereas Linda while bemused by their display, clapped her hands and soon had them back at their seats.

In all I spent about a year at Parnell and in some respects, it seemed to serve a useful purpose in helping me to come to further terms with my own childhood experiences. It also created some sort of space in which I could try and assimilate and consolidate the previous few years. I would often find myself in quite reflective moods, whether mowing grass or diving into the school pool on a late summer, afternoon or sweeping up the autumn leaves. At other times in early evenings when the staff room was empty, I would sometimes finish off with a cup of tea and sit gazing at the Paul Gauguin print of a couple of Pacific Island women painted with simple lines and bright colours.

After about eight months at Parnell the headmaster went into hospital for a few weeks for a prearranged operation, and his assistant became acting headmistress. While the acting head was more conscientious about her work than the head, she was also a little more officious and though we continued to get on well, it was her who had sometimes asked me ball game activities and I quite liked her. Now as acting head, I was a little taken back when within a few days of assuming her new position, she came and gave me a 'ticking off' in such a manner, that combined with my being dressed in shorts and tee-shirt, she made me feel like I was about eleven years old, and when I blushed she seemed to be amused by my embarrassment, and satisfied that she had made her position clear. It seemed it wasn't that I had or hadn't done anything, but she seemed to have a need to assert her authority. After a few days she carried her new position more lightly, and things seemed pretty much as before. Even so I did have a little cause for concern, as only a few weeks before Mr Whimp's departure, I had had to vacate my Kingsview Rd home, as the owner had returned from Hawaii to inform me he had sold the place. The understanding had been that I would leave on short notice if, as and when this occurred, thus it was that I hadn't time to find another place.

The Xmas holidays (which in N.Z. means mid-summer) were not far off, and it was the time of year when the caretaker is particularly required to look after the school while the staff go on holiday, and also to upkeep the grounds, and too clean all the floors prior to the new term. Thus, it had happened (after my suggesting the idea of my discreetly moving into my cabin for a short while), that rather than risk losing me, the headmaster had given the 'nod' for me to move in, on the clear understanding that if I got found out, then he knew nothing about it. So, by the time the new temporary headmistress assumed office, I had already become the schools only and probably first boarder. Since I had some weeks previously moved into my caretaker's cabin, lock, stock and barrel. I even had my Honda CG110 (a small motorbike) stored in one of the sheds, which I was quite happy not to have to use for the present, having in the previous months been commuting to and from work, and had already sustained two dramatic, but fortunately relatively harmless accidents. In the first of these, I was thrown into the air with the bike, after hitting some wet railway lines which crossed the road at a slant. While in the other incident my Honda was hit by a car, thereby swinging it into on-coming traffic, but in both cases I was lucky enough to emerge relatively unscathed.

After having moved into the school I became aware that the acting headmistress lived just a few streets away and might therefore at some time happen to come into the school after hours, but I decided there was no point in worrying about what would happen if she did happen to stumble on me while I was in sleeping bag or whatever. In any case I hoped I wouldn't be there too long, as I had learned that there was likely to be a vacancy in a month at a Buddhist community called 'Akashaloka' (Realm of Space). Meanwhile living at the school, I was able to save on rent and of course didn't have so far to travel to work. After following the normal procedure for closing the school, I would depart from the main entrance and then after doing a bit of shopping or whatever, I would re-enter the school via one of the more obscure entrances with my racing cycle, taking care not to be observed.

Once in I could have a cup of tea and relax, before perhaps having a standing bath in the care-takers low sink, followed by a period of yoga and meditation. Then I would transform my caretaker's cabin into a living room, first I had to black out the windows with card, and then I would hang up curtains, pictures, lampshades etc so the place would look quite aesthetic and homely. After which I could set about cooking tea, and then settle down onto my unrolled bed to read, or listen to music on headphones before falling asleep. Of course, it was necessary to be up early in the morning, and everything would be put away again, in compartments or cardboard boxes. In the mornings I would take my bicycle for a short ride, before returning to the front entrance of the school, to open the place up and start my various caretaker's duties, and I shall add that I usually did my job very well and got good references when I left a few months later.

* * *

Akashaloka

Earlier I had attended a 'new start course' with the 'Continuing Education Department' of Auckland University, so towards the end of my year at Parnell I applied for what in N.Z. was called 'provisional admission' to Auckland University, in the application I submitted I stated that I wanted to attend the University so as to develop as a human being; and also, to facilitate the ability to help others. Also I wrote I believed that the discipline of structured study would be time well spent, then I had to explain my lack of 'school records'; after which I added in my late teens, I was influenced by the works of Aldous Huxley, George Orwell, Herman Hesse, and also attended classes in psychology and philosophy, as well as English language, and also life drawing and colour technique at Camden Art Centre. Thus I gained admission to Auckland University, though for financial and other reasons I could only afford to take one paper.

After lodging at Parnell school for a few months, I was able to move into Akashaloka, a community situated near Mt Eden, which consisted of Priyananda, Buddhadasa, Geoff, myself and occasionally others. I was occupied in various ways, from helping to look after the garden, as well as doing 'Bank Jobs' with Buddhadasa. These jobs were usually done at night when there were few people about, I only helped clean out about three banks with him, by which time we had enough cash, and he gave up the business which, in case I didn't make clear, was cleaning carpets. I also had work at weekends looking after a couple of stalls at Cook Street indoor market, one of which sold all sorts of hanging crystals, while the other sold attractive blue pottery which often incorporated dolphins. Spending a day each week surrounded by crystals and turquoise dolphins seemed to be quite enjoyable at times, and I often felt my Saturday or Sunday had been quite well spent, in helping to distribute inspiring pieces of pottery and lots of crystals.

Priyananda was now doing teacher training. When I was investigating which papers to enrol for at Auckland University I decided to do one paper 'Introduction to Chinese Thought', being taught by Dr Ipp, and over the three terms would explore Confucianism, Taoism, and Buddhism. Priyananda had been in one of her classes and considered Dr Ipp a dedicated teacher, and with what he called a dry wit. As it turned out she was quite good, though I didn't always find it easy to follow, because of her speed of delivery with a Chinese accent, even so I did have one of my essays put on 'desk copy' which means it was made available in the main library and recommended for my classmates to read, and subsequently I gained a 'reasonable' pass for my single paper. Though I felt that my main achievement at university was in introducing Dr Ipp to 'A Survey of Buddhism', written by Sangharakshita. To me it seemed since Dr Ipp was responsible for introducing many students to Buddhist teaching, the least I could do was to give her a copy, and I wondered how she might get on find it. I needn't have concerns, since just a few weeks later she told me she had found Sangharakshita's 'A Survey of Buddhism' to be quite brilliant. At this time the F.W.B.O. were teaching courses in Meditation and Buddhism within the context of the University's Continuing Education Department', so I was interested that Dr Ipp also found the time to attend some of those practical Meditation and Buddhism courses, one of which was presented by Jayasri (known to the university, as Dr Judith Dubignon), as she was a member of the faculty, lecturing in developmental psychology. After my part-time year at university, during which I had been living at Akashaloka, I reasserted my main priority was to prepare to return to England, to have clarify my contact with the Western Buddhist Order, as my involvement with the FWBO in N.Z. seemed to have got stuck. Also I wanted to see my mother while she was still fairly well; another factor was that now ten years on, I felt I would be more able to be in the U.K. with new eyes, rather than just stepping back into the past.

* * *

Rainbow Mountain

I still hadn't got adequate money for my airfare and somewhere to live in London or elswhere; and so I applied for a job as a fire-lookout on Rainbow Mountain, near Rotorua. I was called for an interview and was impressed by the work environment, which would have involved living in a small abode, perched way up a big mountain with sweeping views of forests as far as the eye could see, but there were drawbacks: the attitudes of the employers seemed a bit reticent, after I declared my intention to use some of my time to practice meditation and to do some writing. I was told the radio equipment would remain constantly switched on, also there would be visits from schools, and that there was a local lady masseur who could offer services from time to time. It started to feel I was going to be on show and constantly monitored, so I wasn't so sure the position would be as tranquil as it appeared.

Meanwhile while in Auckland, I was offered a position with the City Council, which didn't entail my having to leave the community where I was enjoying the company of Priyananda, Buddhadasa and Geoff, so for this and other reasons, I started my second position under the auspices of a 'government employment scheme'. This time I was working for the Health Department helping to conduct a survey of private swimming pools, to detail to what extent the owners of pools were using safety barriers or other precautions to prevent the accidental drowning of young children. As well as feeling that the job was worthwhile, I soon found I was quite enjoying the work. After arriving at the office, I would sort out the paperwork and then obtain the addresses of about a dozen homes with private swimming pools. After the ubiquitous tea break, which I appreciated as much as anyone. I would collect a car, and then be out on the job until the afternoon tea-break. Homes affluent enough to have swimming pools often included attractive gardens, or even extensive grounds. If the owners were out, as was often the case, I was instructed to go ahead with the survey, in so far as there was access to the pool area via the back gate. Sometimes there would be encounters with dogs, like the occasion when I blithely wandered round the back, to almost trip over a Great Dane, but fortunately he just gave a menacing glance and I gratefully took my leave.

More frightening was the incident at Government House, where at the time Prince Charles and Lady Diana were in residence, as visitors to N.Z. Even royal toddlers are capable of inadvertently falling into pools without safety barriers, and I had been instructed to do a standard survey of the pool at Government House. After explaining my job and showing my card, I gained entry to the grounds and had walked across lawns to the pool in a secluded area, when in the distance I noticed what looked like a Rottweiler guard dog silently speeded towards me, I could see there was no point in running and so had to stand there feeling increasingly tremulous as the menacing hound bounded towards me, it was only in the last few seconds, a few feet from me, that to my relief, the well-trained creature stopped in its tracks and without even a bark, responded to a faint whistle from his controller who had appeared on the scene, some hundreds of yards away. As I measured the pool and took notes, I recalled how as a boy in early adolescence I had been embarrassed to notice I was attracted to a picture on a savings stamp of Prince Charles, (who was about a year older than me). Happily by now this adolescent crush had since passed, and H.R.H was safe.

Much of this pool surveying was done in fine weather, but even on the dullest day I could be positively affected by the blueness of the pools which on sunny days often looked like David Hockney's paintings of pools, transparent and sparkling in the bright sunlight. Despite the attraction on hot afternoons, I resisted the occasional temptation to discard my shorts and dive in, since I realised it would not be appropriate, nor right for someone to come back and stumble across a stranger in their pool. One way I did - on rare occasions - cool down during 'lunch periods', having completed my quota, was to pick up Geoff, from the community where I lived and take him ice-skating. The rink was often quite empty and to strains of classical or Beatles music, we would both enjoy gliding about on the expanse of whiteness. Then after this brief lunch break, I would continue with work for a few hours more, before returning to the health department, situated in the City Council building, where after another tea break and filing notes, the day's work was completed. While I liked having use of a car, I started to see how easy it is to become dependent on their use, and I continued to have more appreciation for cycling and walking, which are less polluting, and wrote the following prose, to question why we have allowed our lives to become excessively dependent on motor vehicles......

Street Star Cadillacs

Shining metallic black
 Rubber tyre cushions
 Idling and forcing past.

Drenching rain pours down.
Headlights befuddled in puddles.
Floating vehicles in autumn rains

Be the solution, abandon pollution.
Break your trance, now is the chance.
Open your doors and silently dance...

Not that I would do away with cars altogether, rather we could move towards a user-friendly transport system, which integrated the use of trains, trams, bicycles, walking, as well as shared cars and ships. Thereby minimising the environmental damage; and pollution from excessive use of cars and planes. Other activities during this period as a swim-pool surveyor which lasted about a year included: a course in 'First Aid' (with the Red Cross), and courses in 'Art History'; 'Human Communication Skills', and a Course in Basic Writing Skills. Along with these activities, I continued supporting 'Meditation Courses'.

At this time I also got to know Jayasri a little more, who along with Dharmanandi and perhaps Punyasri, were leading courses. (I may have mentioned earlier, as well as with Jayasri and Punyasri, also on a couple of occasions I enjoyed a week or so, retreating at and minding Dharmanandi's spacious and relaxing home, as well as meditating, I also enjoyed dipping into a couple of books about Lord Nelson).

Towards the end of the year, I started meeting up with Jayasri on a regular basis at the university, where she had her own office as a senior lecturer. In due course she and the rest of the W.B.O. in N.Z. gradually moved towards a consensus of opinion that I was closer to readiness for Ordination. Meanwhile life had its ups and downs at Akashaloka, the community where I was living. During the summer I made good use of the garden and enjoyed watching the sunflowers which I had planted grow tall and bright with faces constantly turning towards the sun.

During the summer I dragged an old bath out from under the house into the garden, so that on occasions I could soak in the tub, while listening to music and watching clouds float by, or just gaze into blue infinity. On the first occasion of doing this I phoned Damian (later to become Paramartha) who was living next door and asked him to bring me a cup of tea in the garden, just to make him laugh, when he stumbled across me sprawled out in my garden-bath listening to Pink Floyd Music from a speaker under the bath.

It was good fun living with someone like Priyananda, a chirpy good-hearted, friendly person, even though at this stage in his life he was kept quite busy with the training which he was doing to teach at primary school. One morning when his car wouldn't start, I helped push start the thing and while doing so I also managed to somehow damage my spine to the extent that I lost the use of an arm, and had to put up with a certain amount of pain. Fortunately, I was still eligible to use the universities medical services, though after various sessions with a friendly physiotherapist, I felt I needed to seek further help, and I was put in touch with a good osteopath. he carefully investigated my general structure and worked on my back, before manipulating my spine, whereby he released a 'pinched nerve' of some sort, so I was very grateful, then after a couple more sessions, I regained full use of my arm. Living in the Mount Eden area, I was helped by having access to a very good swim bath with its own steam room which I made good use of both on my own and at times with Priyananda.

Not far from the community was Mount Eden, an extinct volcano which was always refreshing to climb up especially early in the mornings. One morning as I sat up there I decided, perhaps partly influenced by what had happened to my arm, that I should soon make the arrangements to go to the United Kingdom while I still had reasonable health; mainly as I wanted to see Subhuti again; and also to see my mother. The N.Z. F.W.B.O. had now accepted me as being ready for ordination, and in any case I also felt that a spell in the U.K. would help me to resolve past experiences. Of course I realised it wouldn't necessarily be easy, but I determined to 'give it a go'! And so a few days later I phoned Subhuti and after asking how he was, I mentioned that I wanted to return to the U.K.

CHAPTER ELEVEN

NZ - Japan - Moscow - UK (age 35)

Rainbow Warrior

Had it occurred to me earlier in N.Z. how simple it is to phone internationally, I may well have gone back to England much sooner.

After phoning Subhuti and talking, he suggested my writing to Vajrananda, who then was partly responsible for the running of Padmaloka, which is a large rural retreat community about five miles from Norwich. Thus I wrote to Vajrananda and introduced myself and asked to be considered for a 'trial' period at Padmaloka, with a view to joining their community, and to help facilitate my participation in the U.K. Ordination 'process'! In due course I received a reply saying that I could come for a three-month 'trial period', though he thought I should come sooner rather than later. So taking this into consideration I wrote confirming my arrival in about seven weeks, which would be early September.

My last seven weeks in N.Z. were not uneventful, David Lange was then Prime Minister and in order to draw attention to the dangers inherent in the proliferation of nuclear weapons, there was a ban on any warships visiting N.Z. harbours, unless they could confirm they were not carrying nuclear weapons, which put a strain on the ANZUS pact between Australia, N.Z. and the U.S.A., since American policy was neither to confirm nor deny what was carried on their ships. One ship which didn't have any difficulty finding docking space in Auckland harbour at about this time was the Greenpeace ship Rainbow Warrior, which was on a mission to try and stop nuclear testing at Mururoa, a small island in French Polynesia. It so happened that a day or so after the sabotage of the Rainbow Warrior, by two French Agents, which killed the Greenpeace photographer Fernando Pereira, I had a meeting with a friend Annie Maignot (who later became Navachitta). Anyhow she mentioned she had to make a brief visit to the Greenpeace office, where to our surprise we both found ourselves immediately 'commandeered' in the service of Greenpeace, inasmuch as that we were requested to go straight to a wharf, where we would find a large boat/yacht which had to have its ballast removed, so that it could be hoisted up for repairs and generally made ready to sail in lieu of the sabotaged ship. Thereby showing that the spirit of the Rainbow

Warrior could not be easily rebuffed and would keep coming back! Thus, it was that Annie and my-self spent a few hours, inadvertently getting our clothes covered in engine oil as we lugged and humped lumps of metal up from the bowels of the hull to the top decks, till after a while other people arrived to continue the task. My own departure for 'overseas', also required a certain amount of preparation, such as selling my motorbike and other stuff. Even so my backpack still weighed too much, and now older I was less robust, and had managed to strain the small of my back which resulted in a certain amount of pain for a few months.

My other preparations were of a more refreshing nature and included a trip to Plymouth' (N.Z.) where, thanks to Priyananda we and Geoff enjoyed climbing Mt Taranaki at least as far as the snowline. Then sometime later I went with Priyananda to Auckland's recently opened 'Underwater world' which was particularly colourful, and after we came out there were one or two double rainbows in the sky. Also, about this time I had a walk with Priyananda in Western Springs Park, where previously I had watched Bob Dylan perform, from a free-view (hill) vantage point, which looked over the barriers. Now as we passed by the zoo area, we encountered a very friendly elephant which already knew my voice from past occasions, and was soon putting his trunk under the fence, to receive peanuts much to our amusement and of which Priyananda took a photograph. On a more practical note I also had to try and learn some Japanese language, since after some investigations and a certain amount of reticence and anxiety, I had decided to travel via Japan. I had worked out that so long as I ate very simply, then a seven-day stop-over in Japan staying at Youth Hostels could be done on a shoe-string budget, especially taking into account that I was able to obtain a 'Seven day Japan Rail Pass' for about 90 dollars, which gave me unlimited travel by tube/metro and train.

The preparations for leaving N.Z. would soon culminate in leaving; fortunately I was able to go on a shared retreat shortly before this, which helped me unwind. In due course it was time to depart, I had seen various people such as Jayasri to say goodbye, and so it was that early one evening, I was given a lift to Auckland airport by Priyananda. Then after further farewells and feeling poignant and nervous, I started the process of embarking on the Japan Airways flight for Tokyo. The previous night I had been up late, and so I was already tired and tense at the prospect of spending the night 'hurtling' through the sky instead of being in bed like sensible people! Anyhow to relax I 'intoned' the tune of 'Hey Jude', and silently recited the 'Bardo Thodol Root Verses'. Then surprisingly and reassuringly I enjoyed hearing Paul McCartney' singing 'Hey Jude', over the public address system as the plane surged down the runway and took off into the Auckland sky en route to Japan via Fiji. The flight was pretty straightforward, I did some Tai-chi exercise at Nandi (Fiji), which along with fresh air is helpful during longish journeys, and helps to rejuvenate one's state of being.

* * *

Three verses from the Tao Te Ching:
"Without going out of my door
    I can know all things on earth.
Without looking out of my window
    I can know the ways of heaven.
For the further one travels
    The less one knows.

The sage therefore
Arrives without travelling,
Sees all without looking,
Does all without doing."

(Thanks to Penguin Classics Intro.p24,
The Dhammapada)

Tokyo, the Kamakura Buddha, Mt Fuji

We arrived in Tokyo at about 8am, and I deposited about half my things at the left luggage office (including my jacket since the climate was very warm), being Sunday the information office was closed, so I started trying out the ten or so words of Japanese which I had learned. Then after getting lost, I found my way on to a train which took me through Tokyo (I fell asleep about three times) to the seaside town of Kamakura, about one and a half hours southeast of Tokyo, which is the residing place of that large bronze statue of Amida Buddha, which as soon as I set eyes on, I found to be both beautiful and inspiring! Some people had suggested that I did some prostrations, and so this is what I did early the next morning, when there were few tourists about, I also offered incense and was able to go inside the statue which has a staircase inside and a window! Amitabha is the Buddha of infinite light and infinite life, and while I didn't get up to the window, I don't doubt that Amitabha's perspective on the universe is undoubtedly very expansive and wonderful. Kamakura the resort (the name also applies to a period in Japanese history) reminded me a little of Brighton during a hot summer, except that here it was about 90 F or 30c. and clammy, thus I was mostly just in shorts and t-shirt.

My first night in Japan was spent at Kamakura youth hostel, which to my surprise seemed a bit like a plush hotel. Much more than the colour television in the common room, I enjoyed my first Japanese bath in relaxing surroundings. Not to my surprise few people seemed to speak English, but the Japanese (men and woman) seemed to be friendly and helpful. Kamakura seemed to be a fairly affluent area; with lots of fancy cars, a bit like the South of France. While the Japanese as a people have many good qualities, as elsewhere they seemed to have developed an imbalanced way of life, reflected by the common 'helter-skelter' into excessive materialism, though perhaps done with their own particular sort of finesse.

The next day I moved on, complete with a small 'doll' of a Zen Monk, kindly given by one of the staff at the youth hostel, en route for Hakone. This entailed about an hour's travel by train southwest, then a period on an up-hill mountain railway which was quite colourful and reminded me of Switzerland, even though I hadn't been there. Then there was a boat trip along a large lake, and finally a bus and a short walk to Hakone youth hostel, which unlike Kamakura was a Japanese-style hostel, i.e. simply furnished and with sleeping mats (futons) for use on the floor etc. It was an intimate atmosphere that evening, the young fellow running the place had an unusual charisma which seemed to enliven all his guests. I was later surprised when he lit a cigarette (smoking seems to be almost endemic in Japan). I talked with some students, and also I had my photo taken a few times, since Japanese girls (who are often pretty) seem to like to have their photos taken with westerners. In the charming (Penguin) Japanese classic The Narrow Road to The Deep North and Other Travel Sketches (by Matsuo Basho) this area of Japan is referred to in his essay 'The Record of a Weather-Exposed Skeleton' where he writes: "I crossed the barrier-gate of Hakone on a rainy day. All the mountains were deeply buried behind the clouds".

*"In a way
It was fun
Not to see Mount Fuji
In foggy rain."*

Basho continued – "On this journey, I am accompanied by a young man named Chiri…"

The weather on this occasion (some two hundred years later) was dry, being that it was late summer. I wondered also whether I might see a glimpse of Mt Fuji before leaving the area. Next morning I meditated at the end of my futon for about half an hour, which seemed to intrigue my Japanese friends. After I had finished one or two asked questions about meditation practice, then one fellow spontaneously offered to take me by motorbike to a point from where I should be able to see Mt Fuji, I was of course pleased by his kind offer, and was also delighted to find the trouble he had taken was worthwhile, since the sky was clear and we both had a good view of Mount Fuji. Then after breakfast and farewells, I walked along mountain roads to Odawara to catch the Shinkansen (Bullet Train) to Kyoto. Needless to say the train went so fast that it seemed like quite a short ride, in fact it took three hours to reach Kyoto. As the train sped through endless miles of lovely scenery with lots of mountain ranges and stretching fields, I refreshed myself with Japanese green tea.

Later it occurred to me, that just a few months earlier, when I had been working on Mary-Ann's crystal stall at Cook St Market in Auckland, I had been quite absorbed while reading a short story about this train journey, and it had never occurred to me, that just a few months later I would be here in Japan travelling on the Shinkansen (Bullet train). While the trains were fast and ran on time, they could be crowded and smoky, and so I was starting to flag a bit as the train drew to the completion of its long trek.

* * *

Nara and Kyoto

I was much surprised by the size of Kyoto and had somehow imagined the place to be smaller and since I didn't feel up to handling a large city just yet, I opted to first make my planned excursion to Nara (which is about an hour out of Kyoto). I stayed at the youth hostel in Nara and in the morning awoke to the sound of clear and enchanting birdcalls; coming through the public address system to awaken us. Most mornings I had quite good meditations in the youth hostels, just sitting at the end of my bunk or futon which helped to prepare me for the day ahead. Despite travelling very light and only wearing shorts and a shirt, I found the weather which was mostly in the eighties and nineties quite warm, and in the evenings when I was starting to flag, would be refreshed by a Japanese bath before tea.

There are many Buddhist temples and shrines in Nara and I visited a very large wooden Buddha image which while very impressive, I didn't feel was as inspired as the one at Kamakura. The temple which I visited at Nara, was set in delightful grounds in what had become a deer park, and I much enjoyed buying 'deer cakes' and feeding the deer which were very tame and reminded me of feeding pigeons in Trafalgar Square, in that the deer were not backward in coming forward. I also visited the Nara Museum of Buddhist Art which was beautiful and impressive (later, I also discovered the Japanese make excellent ice-cream, which was reasonably priced, and as well as satiating my hunger, also helped me to keep cool), more surprisingly I also acquired an appreciation for green tea.

After Nara I returned to Kyoto, my pack had started to upset my back, more because of all the putting down and lifting, than the actual weight. At Kyoto station I sat around for a long while waiting for a torrent of 'warm weather' rain to pass, I just sat and watched all the teeming people, then while discarding some litter I found a discarded umbrella, which I used while I wandered about trying to find the right bus, which would pass close to the youth hostel. At the hostel I had my first and only cooked meal in Japan. Generally I was quite content living on fruit, nuts, rice & sea-weed biscuits, since it wasn't easy to ensure whether food was totally vegetarian, nor what the actual price might be. The dormitory room had about twenty-four bunks in close proximity to one another and the air-conditioning was right by my head but after a bath I did sleep through much of the night. The next morning after a period of meditation, I went to visit a large Shinto shrine, though what I really appreciated on this occasion was the classical Japanese gardens apparently designed to represent the various styles down through the ages, and here I again had my photo taken this time with a bunch of college girls. Later I visited one of the larger temples of the Shin (Pure-land school) which was a bit like visiting a cathedral, after which I called in at a few temples. I didn't go out with any 'geisha girls', but if I spoke Japanese, I would have preferred the uncomplicated girls photographed with me. Anyhow that night I stayed at a Ryokan (Japanese style B&B hotel), which was offering prices akin to youth hostels, which was good, though I accidentally set off the fire alarm while trying to put on the air-conditioning (which amused the owner's teenage boy, though less so the owner), even so the next day I was able to leave my pack there till the afternoon.

On a previous occasion I had visited a vast castle which featured a so-called 'nightingale floor' which squeaked when walked on, which would warn the shogun -who had it installed-, if anyone was arriving 'unannounced'. There were lots of other places of interest, and I was now off for the morning with a young westerner, who had offered to give me a lift on his small motorbike, while I 'navigated' as we made our way to two temples, which I was keen to visit before leaving Kyoto. One of these was situated halfway up a hill in secluded grounds, and while there I signed a 'no nukes' petition. The other place we visited was called Sengaka Hall, which was a very striking place with 1008 life-sized, individually wood-carved and gold-leafed images of Avalokitesvara (The Bodhisattva of Compassion), there was also a very beautiful main figure.

Anyhow by now it was Friday the 13th, and time was starting to press! Even so I decided to take a 'chance' and visit one more place, though I realised I was cutting things a bit fine, and any blunders like getting on the wrong train or getting held up anywhere, then I was aware I might miss my scheduled flight.

* * *

Eiheiji, Moscow, U.K.

Basically I had two choices, I could either continue further south/west on the Shinkansen and visit Hiroshima, or make a more complicated journey over to the west coast off the mainline using local trains, to reach a place called Eiheiji which is what I did. Thus late that evening I arrived at Eiheiji where the Zen Master Dogen had founded his 'Temple of Eternal Peace'. The small town was all quiet when I arrived and it was a clear and starry night, with fresh mountain air and the sweet smell of pines, I quickly passed along the main thoroughfare and made my way over a river and up a hill, to find what turned out to be a very large and active Soto Zen monastery.

The public 'reception area' was not due to open till 5am, so I decided to sleep in the grounds, the place was much larger than I expected and walking up through the grounds, I was wonderstruck by the size of the cedar trees, then I saw some very steep steps leading way up, up and up, and that was where, after a short period of meditation I spent the night hoping for no encounters with snakes, sleeping under the overhanging roof of a temple in what may have been a burial area. In the morning about 4.30am I awoke to bells, drums, running waters and unfamiliar sounds. Thus I was up early and presented myself at the main entrance as a 'visitor', not expecting too much as I hadn't previously written or phoned! Some monks much surprised at my early appearance, with few language skills, indicated that I could wait in the hall and that a 'tour' would take place at about 7am. It was now about 5.30am and so I sat on a bench in the half-lotus posture and meditated. Eventually, though I wasn't pre-booked, they kindly invited me to join with a number of Japanese visitors who had arrived by previous arrangement. We were then led up lots of steps and along lots of corridors to the inner precincts of the place. In some respects the place seemed somewhat like a Soto Zen version or equivalent, to the Tibetan 'Potala' (in Lhasa), with different style.

Eventually we came to what was perhaps the main shrine hall, where about a hundred or so monks and abbots were performing their early morning rites, most likely this had been preceded by a few hours of meditation. Everything was highly ritualised, including the part we visitors played which consisted of a short period of meditation and then a brief ritual, before being taken on a further tour of the various beautifully crafted and aesthetically inspiring buildings. Since the commentary was all in Japanese, I just listened to the sounds and observed what I could, then by about 9am the tour was finished. Thus I made my way (now in daylight), past the massive cedar trees back into Eiheiji. I thought of Dogen who had founded the monastery and lived in the period (1200-1253). Later I obtained Dogen's classic work 'A Primer of Soto Zen' (The Shobogenzo Zuimonki, which a friend, Gunaprabha was fond of.) through which I learned that the Soto School of Zen relies mainly on a 'Gradual' Process of deepening meditation and 'sitting in awareness', rather than the 'Sudden' Methods with Koans, used in the Rinzai School of Zen. Now it was time to make my way to the city of Nagoya, to catch an afternoon Shinkansen back to Tokyo. As I stood on the small deserted platform in the warm sun, looking at the tall grass on the other side of the single track, I appreciated the stillness. A few hours later I was back in Tokyo, where I spent my last night at a youth hostel in a tower block, in a slightly 'run down' area. The next morning I saw various parts of Tokyo, and then caught the 'Sky-Liner' to the airport.

Before long I had boarded the Japan airlines plane and in due course had an excellent flight towards the sun, with a window seat which in due course gave sweeping views of Siberian forests and other parts of what was then the Soviet Union. At Moscow airport where we had a short stop-over, there was a somewhat 'edgy atmosphere', apparently a number of Russian diplomats had just been expelled from the U.K. by Mrs. Thatcher P.M. for some reason or another. There also seemed to be some sort of melodrama going on in the airport, since while I was doing some Tai Chi exercise, on at least a couple of occasions uniformed military personnel ran past me, leaving me slightly bemused. Later I sat on a chair (in a quiet spot) and did the Metta-Bhavana, which is a Buddhist meditation practice for cultivating Universal Good-Will, after which I internally did a 'puja' and chanted some mantras. As we filed back onto the plane, we were closely scrutinized by plain-clothed men and a couple of guards, and just for the sake of it, I looked at them and said goodbye, I felt vulnerable. The flight over to London was good, and I appreciated spending my first night in the U.K. staying near Richmond Park, with the kind mother of Sue Story whom I knew in N.Z. (who became Dharmanandi). Then after a day or so I made my way to Norfolk and the Padmaloka community, to arrive as expected on September-18th -1985, in time for what was to be an Indian summer.

***

Padmaloka Community

I enjoyed the surrounding countryside as I walked the last couple of miles to Padmaloka, and despite a little trepidation arrived in a positive and integrated state. After meeting Vajrananda with whom I had briefly corresponded and some of the other community members, we had tea and before long I was in bed in a small dormitory. Padmaloka, which is situated on the outskirts of Surlingham, a quiet Norfolk village, consisted of three wings 1/ The Office of the Western

Buddhist Order, housed in the main house and run by a small and separate community. 2/ The retreat community (which I had asked to join), whose members resided full time at Padmaloka and who were employed with the general upkeep of the place, as well as helping with the running of retreats. 3/ The participants who paid to come and attend retreats on various themes. The place and grounds were spacious and inspiring, with room for fifty or more people since the facilities in the main house had been extended to a number of converted outhouses. I spent my first day sorting out housing benefit and other red tape in Norwich. The next day I was involved in heavy and hectic work, clearing out the candle workshop and moving lots of stuff into a big barn. I mention this as the next morning I awoke with quite disconcerting pains in the small of my back and these continued through much of the 'Ordination selection retreat' which commenced the next day, with about thirty-five participants myself included. There were five order members on the retreat, one of which was Abhaya who seemed to be leading the event, I was in his group studying The Survey of Buddhism which went well, I also did some yoga with him and a few others on most days before lunch. We were lucky to have excellent weather (an Indian summer) with lots of blue skies which became very soft at dawn and dusk, with cherry blossom colours swathed in faint mists.

Other order members on the retreat included Jayamati who was straightforward and friendly, he (like Abhaya) observed that I was a bit tense and nervous and needed to relax and unwind a bit. Then there was Uttara who remembered me from ten years previously at Pundarika in London, he was bright and friendly, though some of his 'feed-back' was somewhat hasty, as was some of Sanghapala's who during a walk pointed out that I wasn't taking his criticisms on board. I was aware of the good intentions of my well-meaning friends, who were themselves under a certain amount of strain, due to the way these retreats (which have since changed and improved) were set up. Thus while I stood my ground, I refrained from any wrangling and tried to keep things on a positive note and to remain aware of larger perspectives. Of course I probably wasn't perfect and my situation wasn't helped by feeling jet-lagged and not getting much sleep due to the pains in the small of my back. Anyhow I continued going out for walks with people, and tried to respond positively to the situation.

After the retreat, for a short while I felt a little disappointed and didn't find much solace in the community, which itself seemed to be going through a bit of a dip or difficult period. Apparently a number of the community members were away at an ordination retreat in Tuscany, and those remaining consisted partly of those that had wanted to be there, and thus they were a bit wrapped up in themselves. In a way the community was still in a process of organising itself, and while I was useful for paying rent and helping out with chores, people seemed preoccupied and while civil and friendly didn't have much time for welcoming new faces. My situation was later helped by my sharing a room with Tim Crowe (a Kiwi who later became Nityamukta), who was bright, friendly and supportive. Also my bunk in his room had a foam mattress which was less aggravating to my back trouble than the horsehair mattress I had previously been trying to sleep on. Another new arrival about this time was Mike Kenneley, whom I had known a bit in N.Z. and had imagined he would adjust to the situation quite easily, but in the event he only stayed for a few weeks and then decided to go to Europe, and I couldn't blame him.

Meanwhile people in the community became more friendly and communicative. Then after a while Subhuti arrived, who had been in Spain leading a retreat and then in the U.K. launching the book he had recently completed ('The Buddhist Vision'), which had an uplifting influence on the community. In due course we spent some time together, and Subhuti was positive and friendly and interested to know how I had been getting on. By now it was becoming clear that Vajrananda, with whom I thought I got on alright, was reticent towards me and we didn't exactly 'spark each other off'. Also I was starting to lose myself in work, which in my case involved clearing out the aftereffects of a serious fire that had occurred long before I arrived. For however long it took, I transformed what was the candle factory into a reasonable state. Meanwhile, Vajrananda informed me that along with Vajranatha, he was going to decide whether or not to offer me a place in the community, after I returned from my forthcoming visit to see my mother. While there hadn't been any particular problems, I accepted that I may not yet have found my feet in the community, but I pointed out while my first month had partly been a period of adjusting, even so by and large I had done quite well and had already made some contribution in the community. And therefore felt it would be more appropriate for me to stay on for another month before any decisions were made.

* * *

My Mother, Sukhavati and Nine Kids on a Paintbrush.

My excursion to London went well and was worthwhile, though not as satisfactory as I might have hoped. In short, I felt disillusioned and churned up, so that, at times I went out for walks or just sat on the subway and listened to music on my walkman. I stayed at my mother's place; a small one bed-roomed garden flat near Holland Park in West London. My mum surprised me with how bright and lively she seemed and she was hospitable and positive. Though soon, especially when relatives visited, I was in need of extra breathing space, away from the cigarette smoke and television. Fourteen days was pushing it a bit, after having become used to the quiet at Padmaloka, along with meditation practice, pujas and the general sense of space, and I realised four days would have been more appropriate. I found it interesting seeing my father's paintings again (nude figures, abstract art and landscapes), I also took the opportunity to read parts of my father's manuscript 'Nine Kids on a Paintbrush', after which I felt I could understand him and my past a little better. The first evening was spent with my mother, to whom I gave a present from Kyoto. The following evening was a bit more gregarious; with various relatives coming over for my mother's birthday; and before long people were a bit tipsy and I also sipped a sherry, which seemed to keep people 'happy'!

My brothers and sisters from oldest to youngest are Mervyn who had a degree in Zoology and enjoyed surfing in Scarborough, where he lives, he was also involved with the family sports-shop. (I've only met him once or twice), he was brought up by my mother's parents, who were very proper, one of their relatives was a medical pioneer), Mercedes, who is artistic and has performed various roles, and enjoys tending her pot-plants garden at her Brighton home, about ten minutes from the pier and swimming beach. She was married to Simon a friendly Architect, who once took me for a ride in his Porsche. After they separated, she later began a happier and loving relationship with John a multi-talented and kindly person. Ricky (who sadly died from suicide, after buying himself out from the army), was married to Sandra, their son Andrew joined a circus, and I gave him a copy of B.K.S. Iyengar's Book 'Light on Yoga'. Toby was a musician and actor (he died possibly from an alcohol-related condition), Toby at different times had girlfriends, also he had a friendship with Clement Freud. Toby also had a relationship with an Austrian girl 'Christina', and their boy Christoph became a psychiatrist, who is one of my nephews. (With regards to myself, ie 'Patrick', there were three boys and a girl both above and below me, I had sort of 'Cinderella' Role.).

The younger siblings were William who was a successful stage and film actor, though after being given LSD in the USA, for which he was quite unprepared, he was then 'medicalised', from which he hasn't easily recovered. Samuel-Columbus is an artist/musician and actor, and Mary-Honey married Richard a wealthy American 'hippy', they had a big estate in Devon, and had a collection of classic Porsches. She was a child actress, a lovely person, and sadly died from a cocaine accident). Andrew was a child actor and did the lights in the Rocky Horror stage production. By her first marriage Mercedes had a boy Dominic, a talented craftsman who lives with Vicky and two boys in a large house in Hove. Jacinta, Mercedes' daughter, lives with Jonathan who worked on some sort of digital system in Downing Street, they live in a large property within the vicinity of Ledbury. Mercedes' other daughter Zoe (and her daughter Jessika) lives now in Cornwall.

Over the next couple of days, I saw Samuel and Toby. To whom I responded as best I could. The day after that was spent with William who had more on-going problems and was on prescribed medication, I took him out and we also talked, and tried to leave him feeling more positively motivated. In London I was generally sorry to see the number of homeless people, young and old in various forms of dejection or disarray. Later, spending time with other relatives and friends, I learnt I had a cousin who is a defence barrister and had his own 'chambers', and a nephew who is in a British circus. I also visited Ken a friend in Hampstead, whose floor I had slept on at various times over about three years. The walls of the room were still covered with my own primitive murals, which he told me lots of people had asked about, and that he had resisted the temptation to say that he was the 'culprit'. Also appreciated was a walk through Kensington Gardens to the Queensway ice-rink, where after a period of skating I felt enlivened. Then I took the central-line tube to Bethnal Green; and walked along Roman Rd, to the old fire station which had now been transformed into Sukhavati (A Pure Land) and is dedicated to transforming the fires of greed, hatred and delusion into contentment, love and wisdom. I had come for the five o'clock Puja, and being early was able to go and sit in the main shrine-room, which apart from the aesthetic impact had an over-whelming atmosphere of purity and peace. After a Puja and Meditation, I also attended an evening event.

* * *

Change of circumstances

The next day it felt good to be back at Padmaloka, until Vajrananda told me in a warm and friendly way, that he didn't want to take me on a longer trial period and that I should start looking for a place to stay. He implied I shouldn't feel rejected, though I did, I was also aware Bhante (Sangharakshita) and the new Order Members would be due back in a few days, before which I was expected to have left. Anyhow I felt better after I had a dream in which some deva-like beings consoled me, after which I woke up and cried. Of course, I endeavoured to respond positively to the situation, and to 'count my blessings'. Later it seemed to me I had been lured over (earlier than later), to provide free labour while also paying rent, which filled a three-month gap, after which I wasn't needed, as all the new order members could fill any empty spaces.

I visited Street Farm an informal communituy, where I spent three days seeing Aloka (Colin) and Annie (later to become Varaprabha) Annie was now living with Dharmamudra (who was also a good friend of Aloka's), they both lived in a big farmhouse. Most of my time was spent with Aloka, appreciating the artworks inside his railway cabin where he lived, as did also a wee shrew (like a mouse with a pointed snout), as well talking and drinking tea late into two or three nights, which made a refreshing and interesting change, in contrast with the institutional atmosphere at the retreat community, and I felt happier after my few days with Aloka. Then I was back at Padmaloka for the community meeting. We had our first snowfalls, which for me was quite magical. Vajrananda wanted me to find a place within the next couple of weeks and so I arranged to spend three days at a community in Norwich called 'Vajrakula'. The visit went quite well, though they already had a list of applicants, but it did give me a chance to survey Norwich. The bed-sits I checked out were varied, the first was not good, the second had complicated 'undertones' and the third seemed alright, except the landlady didn't seem likely to accept such 'oddities' as my having a shrine and doing chanting.

Back at Padmaloka I talked with Vajrananda, to see if he would let me stay longer and defer his decision until after Xmas. He explained that he was happy with how I got on with people in the community, and with my work and ability to fit into the retreat programme, and he didn't think I had any problems, though he said I needed to relax more, and be less concerned as to what other people thought of me. In short, he felt I wasn't really able to 'be true to myself', in that particular situation. So, I accepted I was going to have to leave and that I should not worry about the rights or wrongs of the situation, since 'fault finding is a source of defilement'.

Trudging about Norwich half lost in the snow, trying to find a half-decent bedsit, while feeling cold and miserable seemed to me reminiscent of times past. My criteria for my bedsit were that it should be clean, quiet, secure, and not ridden with bugs, noise or disturbed people, myself accepted. The place which I took a few weeks before Christmas seemed like it might be temporarily ok. The landlady who seemed alright at first, even to the extent that she insisted on doing my washing, at a price. But she resented my using the heater in the daytime, even though it was the middle of winter, and she soon complained that I used too much hot water in my baths. Being vegetarian I wasn't exactly enthralled to find dead pigeons in the fridge waiting to be plucked, so I kept most of my kitchen stuff under my bed, and tried to do any cooking when the kitchen was empty. I was trying not to spend too much money, to conserve funds, in case I was accepted for the ordination retreat process. I decided to stay put till after Xmas, and in terms of 'human contact', to make do with a small battery radio, and to defer getting a bicycle, since the ground was covered in snow and the weather was freezing, and no place to keep it.

Not knowing anyone in Norwich, I had a cold and isolated Xmas and felt alienated. I had occasional shallow baths, did yoga, and meditated. While at other times I listened to my battery radio and tried to avoid the neurotic landlady, but to responded to her friendlier side. I felt a bit like an alien marooned on a strange planet! I adapted to the situation and did what I could, after the holiday period passed, I started to feel better. My spell at my bed-sitter on Constitution Hill was much helped by the close proximity of the Sewell Barn Theatre, which is reputed to be the barn where the horse was kept which had inspired Anna Sewell to write 'Black Beauty'. Anyhow it was here that I was able to attend performances of various classics such as 'Hamlet', 'A

Streetcar Named Desire' and others, which as well as being well presented and low priced also afforded contact with friendly and positive human beings. Sometimes I listened to BBC plays on my radio earplugs, while I walked on the snow-covered heath, at other times I sat in deserted churches and meditated. Or occasionally feeling particularly pent up or exasperated, I would masturbate, or have half a pint at the local pub while taking advantage of the open fire. In due course winter started receding and I began going jogging and swimming. With the warm weather which eventually came I was able to read and sunbathe in the local park which had lovely cherry blossom trees and started to feel a little brighter. Then Dharmadhara who was based at Padmaloka and working in the order office, as well as a locum doctor, whom I had known in NZ heard where I was, and visited a couple of times. At some point he had taught me the Dhammapala Gatha (Verses That Protect the Truth) and I appreciated his friendliness and humour.

Then one cold day listening to 'Desert Island Discs', my landlady knocked on the door. She switched off the heating during the day and so I was using an electric heater, which she was cross about. Later she complained that the candles on my shrine were making the ceiling dirty, and so she wanted me to leave. About this time I started having more contact with the Norwich Buddhist Centre. I had already on one occasion been to a public talk given by Subhuti (Alex Kennedy) as part of the promotion for his book 'The Buddhist Vision' published by Rider. On that visit I was impressed by the radiant nature of the fellow who introduced the talk, which was Saddhaloka who was the chairman of the Norwich Buddhist Centre, whom I had met previously when I first asked about vacancies at Vajrakula. This led to my having more contact with people in the community, in particular William (later Amoghavamsa) and Patrick Dye, each of whom in their own way encouraged me to keep in contact and stand by my previous request to join the community, and so I started participating in a study course for Mitras i.e. those who have at least provisionally, committed themselves to the teachings of The F.W.B.O.

* * *

Street Farm

Meanwhile I learned that there could be a small caravan becoming vacant at Street Farm, so with a little reticence, I took the plunge and phoned Aloka and asked for himself, Dharmamudra and Annie (who became Varaprabha) to consider letting me stay for a few months in their spare caravan, since I had now in principle been offered a place at Vajrakula community in Norwich when a place became vacant. After the rather sterile nature of the establishment where I had been staying, Street Farm by contrast felt quite liberating with its slightly dishevelled style, its unconstrained inhabitants and its wide-open unkempt spaces. It was brilliant to be able to see the wide changing skies by day from my caravan's windows, and at nights to be able to step out and absorb the vast wondrous starlit skies, while having a pee or letting some ventilation into the van, which had a catch-22 woodstove, in that the door had to be opened every half hour to let the accumulated smoke and fumes out.

After cleaning up and repainting the van it was quite habitable and I used to wash and brush my teeth at a tap in the middle of a paddock, from where I could see horses galloping in the adjacent paddock, as well as the numerous 'swifts' sweeping the morning and evening skies. On the far side of the paddock was Aloka's railway wagon, who I consciously refrained from calling in on too often, since I was concerned not to be too much of an imposition. I also didn't see very much of Varaprabha who lived in the main house with Dharmamudra, as she was kept busy like the others with her artwork and also with bringing up two growing children. Dharmamudra as well as being an active and devoted dad, was also kept busy looking after his Alsatian, keeping his transport going, fixing the roof and keeping up with his art-work, and Tai Chi.

The pattern of living and way of life at Street Farm was geared to a lifestyle which I couldn't expect to step into, partly as I wasn't engaged with any projects there. Anyhow Aloka, Varaprabha and Dharmamudra in their different ways were all of friendly dispositions, and to some degree I tried to fit into the general pattern at the farm, which was to work through the day and have a main meal at about nine or ten o clock at night. Dharmamudra had asked that I do a few days work in lieu of rent, since I couldn't claim rent allowance, as that would have complicated their situation. Meanwhile I continued contact with Vajrakula community in Norwich, which mainly consisted of Monday nights Mitra-Study, and occasionally going earlier to a meal and staying overnight. When convenient, I would take advantage of a cheap matinee at cinema city if there was something worth seeing, or have a hot bath at the public baths. While at other times I went to London to visit my mum. Back at Street Farm my allotted tasks consisted mainly in mowing the lawns, stacking wood, cleaning old bricks, mending and painting woodwork and that sort of thing, and also supporting the meditation class on Fridays. Though I was ready to leave by the end of the summer, the three months at Street Farm did provide me with somewhere to stay and I was helped by having a spell in the midst of nature in the form of frogs, horses and swifts, as well as some contact with Varaprabha, Dharmamudra, and Aloka.

Shortly before leaving Street Farm, one afternoon I couldn't get the lawn mower to start. So instead I borrowed Aloka's bike, and found my way to a nearby aerodrome. The event was little bizarre, in that Aloka's bike had lots of feathers incorporated into its design, and as I cycled up the side of the runway, a glider came into land, and it is likely the pilot got the impression I was trying to get Aloka's bike to take off. In fact per chance, a lift-off did occur, after accepting an offer and paying the twelve-pound fee, and then waiting for a couple of hours for my turn to come. Even so it was well worth the wait; as I was able to fly into the setting sun, and spotted a flight of wild geese go by, before flying over Street Farm. Then coming into land was no less exhilarating, since the flight instructor was positioned in the back seat, and myself being in the front seat, I was able to watch the ground coming up fast, before landing and stepping back onto earth.

By about this time I heard that there was to be a place for me at Vajrakula Community (Vajra: diamond/reality, Kula: family) in Norwich, in about a month, after Abhaya had found a suitable new place and moved out. Meanwhile I continued to be based at Street Farm, though next two weeks were at Vajraloka a Retreat Centre in Wales, on a retreat which would have been led by Kamalashila, but due to low bookings, he decided to continue with some writing work. So Kevala led the retreat which he did well. The highlights being a 'Halloween night Puja', as well as some shared walks and good meditation sessions. Also I enjoyed making a beautiful Green Tara shrine, using lots of ferns. Towards the completion of the retreat, I had a good walk with Kamalashila, and enjoyed seeing him again, and arranged that after going back to Norwich to move into Vajrakula Community, that I would then return to Wales and spend a couple of weeks at Vajrakuta, a study community near Vajraloka. This I did in due course and had a very good couple of weeks at Vajrakuta. During which I read a book about the life of W.Y. Evans-Wentz, who translated the 'Tibetan Book of the Dead' into English, I also wrote a short talk for a Mitra project and completed some work which Kamalashila wanted done. About this time I had an offer of a 'trial period' at Rivendell, a retreat centre in Sussex, but wanted to stay in closer proximity to Padmaloka, and the ordination process. Thus in due course, with encouragement from William (Later Amoghavamsa) and Patrick Dye, I moved into Vajrakula Community.

CHAPTER TWELVE

Padmaloka—Aslacton—Vajrakula (37-44)

A new place

Travelling with a suitcase and a backpack is travelling light, if that luggage represents one's entire household effects. Even so, by the time I had made my way up a hill and out of Aslacton village to the bus stop, pulling my case on wheels, I was starting to feel burdened and wondering how real nomads manage to move about without looking hassled, I guess not having a 'camel' to bear my load, I should have allowed adequate time for the trek to the bus stop.

Anyhow the ride from Aslacton to Norwich was more relaxing and I enjoyed gazing through the strip of tinted blue window at the front of the coach, which created the effect of an infinite clear blue sky. The coach soon arrived at Bonds Department Store, just a hundred yards from a large Georgian house in All Saints Green which was the location of Vajrakula. The aim of the community was to create an environment in which one could live in a spirit of friendship and concern for the world, expressed by practicing skilful means, in body; speech and mind, thus practicing ethics; meditation, insight and compassion.

* * *

In F.W.B.O. terms, the community consisted of three categories of people 1/ Ordained Members of the Western Buddhist Order, 2/ Mitras (or novices) which is people who in a brief ritual ceremony have provisionally committed themselves to the (F)riends of the (W)estern (B)uddhist (O)rder, and 3/ those who are Friends, but who haven't made any specific commitment, though they are experimenting with the F.W.B.O Way. My own position was that of a Mitra. Adjacent to Vajrakula community was the Norwich Buddhist Centre which provided various public classes in subjects such as Meditation, Buddhism, Hatha Yoga, Tai Chi and Massage, as well as various arts and cultural events, all of which have the aim of helping people to be happy, healthy and understanding human beings. It was a few days earlier, during a cup of tea in Cathedral Close with Abhaya, who was the chairman of the centre prior to Saddhaloka, that details had been finalised about my forthcoming move and he mentioned I would be able to use the room space he had vacated.

The building contained many rooms as well as a now redundant dumb waiter (manual lift) and lots of stairs and corridors. Before long I was making myself at home in a corner of a large room on the second floor which I was to share with Adam, and his brightly coloured toucan. Adam was of a warm and friendly disposition and very easy to get along with, as a medical doctor he was now engaged in a period of intensive swatting for an exam which would make him a member of the Royal College of Surgeons and so it was necessary for me to keep quiet much of the time. Adam was himself considering going to London in a few months' time to work and also to live with his girlfriend. By now I was already aware that F.W.B.O. communities aim not to be cultish, but a 'free association of aspiring individuals', and that people that participate in them remained fully responsible for their own lives. The object of single sex communities (there were women's communities in Norwich) was to create a situation where one could live for long or short periods, with others who shared one's ideals and practices and in which one would be less inclined to sexual distraction and more inclined to platonic friendship.

The single-sex aspect had nothing to do with liking or disliking either sex but was to create a situation where one could study and practice the Dharma in a situation which is non-exploitive, straightforward and friendly. Within such a community people may have quite different lifestyles so long as their work is ethical and of a worthwhile nature, though this doesn't have to be grand, it could just be sweeping floors. Other people in the community were William (later to become Amoghavamsa) a big warm-hearted fellow from Sheffield who had been at university with Saddhaloka and was now doing bookbinding and massage. Then Patrick Dye, a friendly, considerate and good-natured person, who was generous with the use of his van until it fell apart, and went on to start a small business venture distributing Buddhist books. Also there was Satyapriya who hailed from Grantham, and could be described as a happy-go-lucky fair-haired 'builder', who also had a black belt in Aikido of which he was a dedicated teacher; he also had a lively mind with a serious interest in literature and Buddhist studies, as well as interests in his girlfriend. Then again there was Saddhaloka, the chairman of the centre and a fine and devoted spirit, with a methodical and selfless dedication to helping humanity by making the Dharma teachings available to the public. Previously he had attended a public school 'Victoria College' in Jersey, where he was brought up before earning his degree in history at Leeds university, subsequent to that he did social work with handicapped people on a farm in Ireland, with Padmavati an arts-graduate, to whom he was married and from their union sprang Aidan, a fine and bright young man. It was while in Ireland that Saddhaloka and Padmavati (at that stage having not yet ordained) made their first contact with the F.W.B.O. Previously they had also spent time travelling in India, and as a result of a letter sent by Saddhaloka to Sangharakshita the founder of the F.W.B.O. they moved to Norwich, and became more involved with the movement. Before I come back to my own immediate experience, I must make mention of David Havers a kind person, now deceased, who while not resident at Vajrakula, was actively involved with the various chores which needed doing in and around the place and was a sort of associate and honorary member.

Most of the people mentioned so far were aged about thirty to forty, Dave was a bit older being about fifty, his previous career had spanned from lance corporal, to holding a small business franchise, to milk-rounds-man. At the time of coming to the centre he was overcoming a minor nervous breakdown, but very soon developed a devoted friendship with Saddhaloka, and over the following years served in many ways, and became much loved by many people, both for his Norfolk charm and his general warmth and readiness to give as well as various other good qualities. I continued to live in the big room with Adam (the doctor) for a month or so, and then after his departure to London, Jonathan (later Sthiravajra) who had a chemistry degree from University of East Anglia, and recently returned from travelling in Asia moved in, as he wanted to renew and deepen his contact with the F.W.B.O. At first our contact was a bit difficult we were not ideal room partners, though despite the awkward beginnings, we continued to get to know each other and as time passed friendship developed.

After a few months I moved to a small room in a wing of the house, which had just been newly renovated, and where in its previous dilapidated state I had helped Saddhaloka to re-paint the centres twenty or so chairs. My new room was adjacent to a new meditation room, and overlooking the courtyard. I appreciated its secluded atmosphere and its only drawback apart from not getting much daylight light, was that after a few months a washing machine was installed in the room below, though it was quiet at night and in early mornings, and there was an over-hanging tree, from which came early morning bird songs. There was also a large and splendid copper beech tree, best viewed from the kitchen window. Outside the kitchen on a branch fixed to the windowsill I erected a small bird-table and bath and I was pleased to soon notice Blackbirds, Robins, Yellow-tits and Sparrows all becoming confident and regular visitors to Vajrakula for breakfast. In due course I started making various small improvements to the place in the form of aesthetic and practical innovations, from cleaning out the cellar and carpeting and painting floors, to re-designing part of the entrance stairs and clearing and repainting hallways.

I was also engaged with various classes and was attending the three-year Mitra Study Course, being led by Saddhaloka which though at times very good, was geared more to newcomers than those that had perhaps been over the material a few times. I was also about this time experimenting with tai-chi and doing a massage course. At Saddhaloka's suggestion I gave some thought to visual improvements at the Centre, and in due course various innovations were made and I introduced more plants which I've since been looking after. After a while I occasionally went back to Padmaloka for retreats, I didn't always find them particularly relevant, I did partly enjoy working for ten days on an Order Convention and staying in a tent, especially since I was given the job of serving meals to Sangharakshita. Back in Norwich I continued with pottery classes at Wensum Lodge where I made a large vase decorated with leaves of grass, which was quite satisfying since after it was fired its colours worked well, and it has since added a touch of brightness to the stair landings, and on a visit Bhante expressed some appreciation.

At the back of Vajrakula a big copper beech tree, gives relief from the multi-story carpark of Bonds dept store. While in the courtyard in early mornings I sometimes did tai chi exercises, there is a white blossom tree. Nearby are various Norwich Union Insurance buildings, whose grounds I sometimes go jogging through, while watching as the sun rise over their new head office which looks a bit like mammon's temple, and at nights is slightly surreal when its peaks lit with blue light. Their first head office also nearby, is more traditional and contained an unusual entrance hall, built entirely from a shipment of marble which they obtained cheaply, after it arrived too late to be used in building Westminster cathedral. Opposite Vajrakula is another large Norwich Union building from which flags flutter on royal birthdays, while on its lawn is a string of pink cherry blossom trees, near which patrons of the Top Rank bingo hall (just down the road) park their cars. To the left are the B.B.C. studios and a little further on Sainsburys and near-by 'corner shop'. Living in Norwich is only a few miles from Padmaloka, where I was able, in my first few years, to have a few meetings with Sangharakshita which was very good, but I realised I also needed to have more contact with people in my day-to-day life. Saddhaloka had already shown himself to be a kind and ready friend, and on one birthday gave me a cassette tape of very beautiful music by Tallis. At other times he invited me to tea when he was looking after his and Padmavati's children at their Salisbury Road house. From my own childhood I had not forgotten the difficulties of family life, I was moved by the quaintness of these little tea gatherings and wished that they would all attain true happiness. On another occasion when I looked after the place while they were all away, I stayed in Padmavati's room, and was struck by the beauty of a small shrine she had created and also on a warm afternoon was enchanted by the pretty layout of their small garden. The nuclear family when functionally positively, may well be an appropriate way for some people to live some of the time, and it is important that parents support and help each other in the very real responsibilities of bringing up their children. Even so the nuclear family unit is not the only option or model for living.

* * *

Community

To me it seems parents and non-parents are human beings, they too have needs, social, cultural and even spiritual and if these needs are not catered for they can very easily start blaming each other or their children. These situations are compounded by alcohol abuse, from which family life easily degenerate into difficult situations. Then teachers find they have pupils unable to settle down or show much interest in learning. Education begins at home and what's important isn't the type of family, so much as whether children feel abused and neglected or loved and secure, or at least that parent's care. Far too many so-called adults blunder into childbearing and family life, often hardly grown up them-selves. For these and other reasons I have sympathy with the idea that people should be encouraged not to have children until they have first become reasonably healthy, happy and stable human beings themselves, with at least a little understanding of the difficulties and responsibilities of bringing a child into the world. By the time I was twenty-one it was becoming clear to me that I didn't want to repeat the above pattern, and I freely admitted that I might need to spend much of life, just learning how to become a reasonably happy, healthy and consistent human being, and in many respects I'm still working at it. Thus I live the way I do, not because I eschew family life, but more because I believe that the full flowering of family life, needs certain conditions if it is to flourish. Within the F.W.B.O. some people live with their families, some on their own and others in communities. It's not a question of right or wrong.

***

It may be that society places too much emphasis on one model, like putting all its eggs into one basket, rather than cultivating a range of experience and ways of living. Just like plants in a garden, children and adults all have special needs. The residential spiritual community, which is just one of many models for living, it may be a single sex or mixed community, or a community of families. Some may be practicing chastity, while others may continue to have sexual relationships. What is important is that the people in the community are relating on a basis of shared aspirations and values, rather than out of just mutual dependence. If people care for each other, then they should encourage each other to flourish, we all have duties and responsibilities to try and make life better and not worse. Vajrakula where I live is just one of many F.W.B.O. communities. Yet we are all part of a larger community, called 'Humanity', though choosing to practice meditation, along with ritual and devotion, or yoga and whatever else helps. Even so we are not indifferent or closed to the needs of the world. People in residential communities are encouraged to go on occasional solitary retreats or 'holidays', since paradoxically learning to spend time by oneself, can help one to relate better to others. F.W.B.O. Buddhist communities also stress the importance of being in good communication with one's parents and to relate to the world in a positive, healthy and creative way. Buddhist philosophy, Hatha Yoga, The Arts, Festivals, and Celebrations, may all give expression to meaningful lives.

Involvement with a Spiritual tradition means that one starts to have roots within that tradition, which in the case of Buddhism goes back two and a half thousand years, which may give one a sense of stability and meaning, during life's constant changes, whether that change is in the residential community or the wider world.

The practice of meditation can help one to loosen one's grip on things or people and to dance just a little more lightly to the constant flow of change. In Buddhism the Three Characteristics of Conditioned Existence are: Impermanence (Anicca); Unsatisfactoriness (Dukkha), and Insubstantiality (Anatta). Having been at Vajrakula for seven years, I am aware Saddhaloka before long shall be leaving, having performed many years of dedicated service: Giving talks, running and organising classes, cleaning, visiting people in prison, administrating, conducting funerals, running courses, arranging celebrations, being a friend to many, as well as getting away on camping treks with his son and being a caring father to his three children.

* * *

Adult Learning

My endeavours while at Vajrakula also included attending basic maths classes at the nearby Notre Dame high school in evenings, with a view to doing a government training course in carpentry, but despite some progress it wasn't worth pursuing. Anyhow I contented myself with a more informal class where I learned a little carpentry and made a wooden case for my xylophone, which I gave to Ratnaketu, for Dhardo Rinpoche's school for Tibetan refugee children in India. Then I learned some basic 'word processing' at a community hub before they closed down. Later the office at Vajrakula obtained a word processor, which thanks to Sadhaloka I was able to use to commence this manuscript, late at nights and sometimes in the early mornings when it was mostly available. Also I started attending classes at Wensum Lodge adult education centre, housed in an eleventh century complex of buildings by the river Wensum and complete with its own impressive crypt. There I enjoyed courses including Western Philosophy, Art History, and Poetry workshops with John Waterfield a youngish 'Old Etonian' with whom I became friends. Then there was Life Drawing and Pottery, during which among other things I enjoyed making a large vase 'Leaves of Grass', which to my satisfaction was displayed in an exhibition. I also enjoyed occasionally playing badminton at Wensum Lodge, as well as swimming in various places.

Later I attended an Astronomy Course, as a result of which, I went on to obtain about a hundred colour slides of the planets, nebulas, and galaxies, along with slides of nature and classical art and others depicting Buddha Figures associated with the various directions of space. Then using Classical Music and Poetry, I put together a colourful and expansive 'Tour of the Cosmos' which as well as being appreciated by those that attended, also raised money for the Norwich Buddhist Centre, and further shows as far afield as Cromer and Ipswich as well as various informal showings. Subsequent to seeing my slide show 'Lokapala' sent me his reflections on it; this is an extract from the first part:

'THE COSMOS GOES FOR REFUGE'

"A friend showed me his cosmic slide show today. It is a collection of images of stars, galaxies and nebulae; set to music and poetry. The music was by Vivaldi, Bach, Mozart, Aled Jones (snowman), David Bowie, and Monty Python! The poetry was by Blake, Shelly, and from Diamond Sutra. Fantastic. The slideshow; the music; the poetry and my friend. Infinity: I remember when I was young that I used to think about being in a rocket. The rocket would go on and on and on and on. No end. No beginning. No sides, No me. I and a friend would try to imagine it. What if it didn't have an end at all, and just went on and on.............. It was like being really still and solid and happy and thrilled all at once and that was the best. It left you really quiet and calm afterwards. Full of wonder, like you had seen this huge answer you couldn't explain because there weren't words for it that could describe it. That was the best. The dizzy excitement was just something you made and did, like scaring yourself. This was more like a really real experience. It touched you and made you small and humble. I thought I may have met God. When I first heard that Blake thing, you know, "To see a world in a Grain of Sand, And a Heaven in a Wild Flower, Hold Infinity in the palm of your hand, And Eternity in an hour.

Blake understood! Vivaldi understood, and Mozart and Bach really understood. They all experienced this wonder and awe. You only have to listen to them…

Gratefully received from Lokapala: re: my 'Cosmic Slideshow'…

Later at Wensum Lodge I also went to singing classes and was amazed at the vocal scope of the fellow who was teaching, and as a result of simple exercises loosened up my tenor voice. It was perhaps partly as a result of this, that I later had the confidence to become involved with a Buddhist Choir, rehearsing a choral piece named 'Carpe Diem' which translates as 'Seize the Day', which was written by Bodhivajra. Then after much rehearsing, we later performed before a large and appreciative audience at an event held in Dulwich College in London. An extract of the piece even found its way on to Radio Four. To my amusement, I even got acknowledged on the programme as 'a tenor'. Last but not least, I also undertook a formal class at Wensum Lodge in English Language which ran for three terms under a hard working teacher named Mrs Ellis, which culminated in sitting my first GCSE exam for which I was pleased to get an A grade, though I still find writing a slow and challenging process, and still spend much time trying to figure out what does and doesn't look like acceptable punctuation.

* * *

Minor Excursion

I had been at Vajrakula about three years when Francis moved in. He was a likable and friendly fellow with whom I enjoyed playing snooker and also chess, he had been a schoolteacher but shortly was to start up a small building business called Albion. At about this time he or someone else told me about an exceptionally cheap car hire firm which rented out old Morris Minors. Thus I decided to hire a car for three days and to go south to Abbotsbury in Dorset, sleeping in the back of the car on the way since it was early summer. My plan was to call at various significant places of my childhood and perhaps thereby be more able to leave them behind. On the afternoon I set off the weather was atrocious and driving conditions were quite hazardous. Ten miles or so before Oxford, with some caution I picked up a hitchhiker who was not only very friendly but also invited me to his home about eight miles on, where I was restored with a vegetarian meal and hot tea. It was dark as I later drove past the silhouetted facades of Oxford and then sometime that night slept out close to Stonehenge which I visited in the morning after the sun had risen. It was an exquisite day and before long I was driving through delightful Dorset countryside with golden fields and rolling vistas before me.

***

To my surprise the village of Abbotsbury (near Weymouth) turned out to be just as beautiful as I had remembered it, despite my having had some difficult times there. Also I was also amazed to find thirty years later, when I was now thirty-seven, that Mrs 'Lexington' the keeper of the sweetshop close to Seaway Lane, where we had lived was still alive and well. I was taken to meet her and expected to find a doddery old lady and was further surprised that at eighty she was very much alive, sprightly and in good spirits. As we had tea and ate some of her Swiss roll, I confessed to how I had pinched a few of these from her shop when I was hungry as a kid, she laughed and seemed amused to meet me again and had clear memories which she volunteered about our spell in Abbotsbury.

Also, she informed me that Mrs Simmonds who was the headmistress was still alive, though in a wheelchair, but even if I hadn't been pressed for time, I wasn't sure it would be appropriate to visit, since my main recollection of her was that of being caned on frosty mornings for arriving late at school. Later I strolled down Seaway Lane, which was as leafy as ever, and as I started to approach the cottage a little boy of about seven ran out to play and, surprised to see a stranger, he glanced at me with friendly playful eyes before dancing on his way. I then climbed up the hill to St Catherine's Chapel where I meditated and did some singing exercises while a heavy shower passed over. The thick walls created an echo chamber, and outside I read about a particular ghost haunting the place.

Continuing on my way, I drove back along the coast stopping off in Brighton where I went swimming and later passed by where I had previously lived in George Street, and then bought some food before spending another night in the back of the Morris Minor up in the hills. The next day I visited the inside of Brighton Pavilion which I had never seen as a kid, then journeyed on through Sussex to Balcombe near Hayward's Heath where I called in at Highly Manor, with its still splendid grounds and vivid rhododendron bushes, to find that the place was now a rather exclusive country hotel. I explained that I had lived there as a child and was permitted to have a look around. After leaving I read one of their brochures and noticed it described Highly Manor as "a beautiful old English Mansion, with a history that can be traced back to 1326, and whose past owners include Queen Elizabeth 1st and Percy Bysshe Shelly" but of course it made no mention of the whole romantic world which I had experienced while living there for about a year or so, as a boy of about twelve.

From Sussex I continued on past Seven Oaks in Kent to Orpington on the outskirts of London, it was here that I had been at St Josephs, a school for homeless children, which at the time was supervised by catholic monks, at first I couldn't find the place but I asked a passing woman, at first she looked puzzled, but then she said 'oh you mean the old orphanage dear, that closed down some years ago' then she gave a sympathetic smile, and added that some of the buildings were still there and gave me directions. Though there was now a new church on part of the estate, enough of the school property was still there to have made my stop-off worthwhile including the playground, where I mused for a short while on the long and lonely times, as well as some of the ordeals and battles I had endured there. Then it was a matter of skirting around London and heading up to Cambridge which I hadn't been to before. I appreciated the architecture and meditated for a while in Kings College Chapel, before going swimming at the public baths and later had a cup of tea at Browns Cafe. Then I bought some groceries before driving on to just outside Ely, where I slept as usual in the back of the car. In the early morning I drove into Ely, parked near a lawn, and went jogging to warm myself up before meditating and some breakfast. Then I visited the cathedral. There was an entry fee and extensive renovations were going on, I talked with a part-time guide, a friendly student of about twenty-three who after giving me the standard tour, then showed me other parts of the cathedral which one wouldn't normally get to see. From Ely I continued back to Norwich in time to return the car within the three-day hire period, and felt that by and large I had had a pretty good run for my money and that the time had been well spent.

* * *

Changes at Padmaloka

By now Padmaloka Men's Retreat Centre, was going through changes and had a sort of 'perestroika and glasnost' process of its own, under the guidance of Subhuti, as a result of which the various prescribed retreats, known as Going For Refuge (G.F.R.) retreats, which make up part of the ordination training process, took on a new more creative approach and were becoming not just more effective but also more enjoyable to be on, or so I was to find out in the coming months. The first of these retreats which I attended was a G.F.R. on the theme of going for refuge itself and was based around a book which Sangharakshita had written on his own experience of Going for Refuge. In some ways this retreat felt like a turning point, in that I was to some extent required to look at the history of my own going for refuge. Then later giving a short talk on this subject in a group with Aloka, which I found to be quite revealing and helpful, and it was subsequent to that retreat that I decided that I really must get down to this completing writing this journal which I had been meaning to do.

***

Later came the Mythic Context Retreat with its 'touch of magic and poetry', aimed at bringing alive the whole realm of imagination with the help of ritual, devotion and symbolism. The basis for all these retreats is that one is well versed in practicing the ethical precepts expounded in Sangharakshita's book 'The Ten Pillars of Buddhism'. After this retreat that I started making small reproductions of the Amitabha Buddha Statue (Rupa), which like the original that I had visited at Kamakura in Japan has its own significance, in this case Infinite Love and Light. Symbolic objects may be likened to 'Fingers Pointing to the Moon of our innate potential, we need not to mistake the finger for the Moon', reminding us of our potential to develop compassion and insight in our lives. And thereby help to create a society which centres less on greed, hatred and delusion and more on qualities such as Goodness, Beauty and Truth.

Another such G.F.R. retreat was on the theme of spiritual friendship, on which Subhuti gave a series of talks during the retreat. What this encouraged us to cultivate good friendships, and not just leave them to happen. By and large we need to approach friendship as a creative endeavour, in which two or more people with shared values and aspirations, consciously work at getting to know one another, not just indulging each other's bad habits or flattering one another, but actually helping each other to acknowledge and deepen one's good qualities as well as working on changing shortcomings. Partly because of this retreat I became part of a 'Going for Refuge' group when I was back in Norwich. G.F.R. 'groups' are like fledgling Order meetings, and are made up of people who have reached the point of asking to be ordained and they may consist of about five or seven people who meet up on a regular basis.

Meanwhile in Norwich I was doing well with various activities, particularly an intermediate and satisfying Iyengar Hatha Yoga class, run by Brian Platts at the Centre's Queens Road Yoga Studio. My plan in this respect was to train to teach yoga. Also, I started attending occasional yoga day courses, one of which was run by Silva Mehta, who had taught me years before at her Baker Street Studio in London, and which was particularly excellent. But alas even the best-laid plans can be laid to ruin and I'm sorry to report that this plan of action was devastated by an unexpected turn of events.

***

Setback

In NZ I had accepted the opportunity go and give blood with Buddhadasa and continued too occasionally do so. Later in Norwich I much enjoyed raising money 'Swimming for Dolphins', with Sarvananda. Thus, when good friend and fellow community member Patrick Dye, asked if I would like to to attend a one-day event at Norwich City Hall, about Alleviating Poverty in the third world, I naturally accepted, and thought little of it. The day was going well, and we decided to return for a short lunch break back at Vajrakula Community, which is where the trouble began. At this time J/D, a relatively senior order member, who occasionally had drawn me, in a life drawing class, called at Vajrakula. Prior to then, I had experienced J/D as being a relaxed, friendly and positive person.

It seems some days earlier J/D had had a serious encounter with another order member, who had done something he had found very upsetting, and he came to Vajrakula in an angry state looking for that order member, thus he burst into the kitchen in an angry and indignant state looking for that person, and complained we had been slow to press the button to open the front door. Myself, I couldn't quite believe what was going on, and asked him gently whether he thought it was appropriate, for someone who wasn't part of the household, to storm into our kitchen in that sort of way. Then he went into a rage and physically assaulted me, by wrenching me violently to the ground causing serious damage to the vertebra in my upper spine. I was now on the floor and was out of my body for a few seconds, as I came to curled on the floor, I saw he was white with rage and Patrick Dye bravely intervened to stop his further approach. Apparently, J/D had a previous history within the order of such events.

Some minutes later he was in the next room in a state of despair and regretting what he had done, and then he demanded that I forgave him, which I did. Later he sent me a card sincerely apologising and acknowledging full responsibility for what had happened. I realised that he didn't really have any feelings either for or against me, and that because of his short fuse, had unduly lost his temper. In due course a panel of Order members was set up to resolve any feelings, and I did subsequently tell him that in future he would do better to vent any of his feelings on inanimate things rather than people.

Subsequently, he later intimidated another order member 'Sujvala'. Thus, Bruce resigned from the order. After being verbally 'set upon'. 'Bruce' later complained to me, that I should have spoken out more, and then he would have been fore warned. In fact, I had spoken out.

The day after the assault, I was further shocked and traumatised to find my upper spine was suffering the effects of 'whiplash', which even decades later has not fully healed. While the immediate effects were that for the following months, I was in intense pain and could no longer easily walk, or ride a bicycle since I couldn't turn my head, swimming was ended, and meditation posture was uncomfortable.

Then I realised my Iyengar Yoga Training Course was completely scuppered and ended. As a result of all this my general health deteriorated, soon it became clear that somehow during this episode one of my knees had sustained some sort of damage, and whereas formerly I much appreciated being able to meditate comfortably, sitting in the half lotus posture for sustained periods, and the full lotus for shorter periods, now physically I found it difficult to sit, except for short sessions. Basic cleaning tasks and carrying bags all impeded.

J/D paid for one of my numerous visits to an osteopath, and sent me a postcard saying he was sorry, beyond that he didn't really seem to understand that his actions had long-term debilitating consequences.

J/D is a very good artist, and usually a good, intelligent and thoughtful person and I still appreciate and feel for him. Though as a then muscular person, he should have known a lightweight person is easily damaged by such aggressive behaviour. In his card he stated:

"Dear Patrick, I have been thinking these last weeks about what has happened. I realise now that I was entirely to blame, for which I am deeply ashamed. I only hope that out of this disaster something positive may arise between us."

Looking at card it, must have been sent about 1992. I noticed there was also a subsequent letter sent, which seems to be dated 21-10-2017.

"Dear Dharmika I am sending you a letter I have sent to Lokeshvara, Bhante and other members of the Order. As the unfortunate witness to my past outbursts of uncontrolled anger, it is only right and proper that you should be made aware of its contents.

Please forgive me for my past behaviour towards you, for which there was and can be no justification whatsoever. It was and is totally incompatible with the principles of the Dharma, and is an aspect of myself that I now recognize it is imperative for me to deal with.

Once again please forgive me for my past behaviour towards you for which I am truly sorry. Best wishes, Yours Sincerely, J/D

In case you should read this J/D, even though in some respects I continue to suffer the consequences of what happened and cannot pretend otherwise. Even so I forgave you then and do so now!!!

I understand any of us, in certain circumstances can lose our temper and do drastic things, and then feel regret. As that expression goes "But for the grace of god, goes any of us". Anyhow I am glad you are changing for the better, and I hope you may continue to do so.

I recall seeing Bhante, and he asked how I was? Without complaining, I felt I needed to lightly touch upon my change of circumstances. Then I noticed Bhante cease up and close. Rather like Kashyapji's response when Bhante tried to unburden himself about an event, as recorded in his memoirs, and recently printed in June 2023 Shabda.*

(*A confidential journal for Order Members).

Anyhow worse things happen at sea, and with partial healing, the issue became less loaded, and we resumed a friendly disposition towards each other, at some point as an artist J/D asked me to 'life model' for him so I did. The 'whiplash' injury means I must avoid intense yoga, and only carry less, and try to be aware and kind…

* * *

New endeavours

The following couple of years were a difficult time. I realised I needed to engage positively and continued to support classes, as well as watering plants and making shrines for various festivals, I also started to organise and introduced video events and later overhauled the Dharma tape library. At about this time I also applied, and was accepted for an Enterprise Allowance Scheme, (funded by the government) my project was to write a small book/let on the subject of 'How to Stop Smoking' (and feel good about it), which with persistence was eventually completed. Mark (who became Mahasraddha), a friendly and kind fellow, was back in the community, working as a research scientist at the John Innes Institute. Other new incumbents included the deep and imponderable Vidyaraja who could be warm and sensitive. Later there was the no less mysterious Sarvananda, a playful playwright and witty bloke from Glasgow. John Woodhouse was a bright spark, who headed the English Department at Long Stratton High School; he also had an interest in political and social developments and had noticed my letters on various social issues appearing occasionally in his local paper The Evening News, as well as at times in The Observer and The Listener before it folded.

At about this time my connections with the press took a more down to earth turn, after Saddhaloka drew my attention to an advert for the free local paper The Mercury. Thus I started up a new career as a 'newspaper delivery boy'. Thus twice a week for a couple of hours I was obliged to deliver in any weather from a sweltering summer in shorts, to gloves and coat during a winter in thick snow. My paper rounds took me on a journey across a wide range of social categories, from large stately houses with coats of arms, to small council tenements with shabby cats. While I was friendly with an old lady and occasionally came across occupants, mostly they were out. I came to know places through their gardens, which I enjoyed especially in spring and summer. I also occasionally delivered the new Norwich Buddhist Centre programmes and when I concluded the job I also delivered to each house a copy of the Metta Sutta on Loving Kindness.

Another way I had of keeping in touch with wilder aspects of nature, was occasionally visiting my secret spot, which I had sought out and adopted. This was secluded patch in a grove of large old broken-down trees, near to Whitlingham Lane, a local beauty spot. It was here that in the summer I would go for the occasional hour or so with a flask of tea and bask nude in the sun, perhaps reading a book, or just enjoying the silence away from the noise of Norwich traffic. The following poem captures one such afternoon excursion...

Naked in a concealed glade,
Caressed by summer breeze,
Birds tweet, bee's buzz
My bottom feels the warmth of cosmic fire!
Contented I feel no desire.
This wild place, is an ancient spot,
Unsullied by coming and going,
Here time breathes softly!
Alone in quiet repose, I study English,
And attempt to compose.

One such afternoon there was noise from bulldozers and I found out that this was the start of a large scheme to extract minerals from under the ground on either side of Whitlingham Lane. Later the developers declared that they wanted to rip up Whitlingham Lane itself, which is a winding leafy and attractive place valued locally by walkers, cyclists, joggers and horse riders and replace it with a straight road more effective for conveying traffic. I found this incredible and there ensued a long battle, which I got involved with, to the extent of making a statement at the eventual public hearing, where I also took the opportunity to cross- examine the developer's witnesses. I also had a letter in the local paper drawing attention to the case, which gave the address to which people could lodge their concerns. I was impressed at this hearing, by the comprehensive presentations put forward by various dedicated people on such subjects as, effects on flora and fauna, as well as on the subject of landscape history and conservation. To this I can add a couple of years on, the case went in favour of protecting the environment.

This event was followed by questioning the community charge fiasco. While I considered the poll tax to be ill-conceived, I was prepared to pay my community charge, but I required a valid receipt. Though as a result of bureaucratic bungling, the post office was unable to offer me a proper receipt, I decided to let it go to court. On the morning that I arrived it emerged I would be the first to appear as soon as the magistrates were in court. When I enquired whether I should refer to the magistrate as Your Honour, he replied its 'Your Worship'. So, with that sorted, the case commenced and I explained I had already paid my community charge, though this had been delayed due to my requiring a proper receipt.

What was now in contention was whether I or the poll tax office should pay the court costs of twelve pounds. The magistrate had accepted what I had to say, especially after the legal clerk informed him that mine was an unusual case, and that he had the discretion to grant either way. Then after four or five minutes his two assistant magistrates seemed to advise him to be careful of setting a precedent, and so I was required to pay the small costs which I did that afternoon. Before leaving the court, I asked the magistrate if he or anyone in the court could translate for me the Latin motto placed in big letters above the court, his answer was that they couldn't or wouldn't, so the court's motto remained unknown. After tangling with that bit of red tape, I then got involved with some videotaping. As for some reason I had hired a video camera, and it happened I had use of the equipment for an extra twenty-four hours, and so made a spontaneous video recording of Vajrakula Community, and parts of Norwich which was engaging to make, and looked good, but unfortunately got lost. Sorry Amoghavamsa (who wanted a copy), also sorry that we both lost are good friend Patrick Dye, who after that event left and moved on.

***

Going for Refuge

The Mitra G.F.R. group I was in continued and at some stage we all gave short accounts of our life stories, which was a worthwhile exercise and clearly people benefited from doing. During one of our evenings, I found I had the opportunity to be a refuge to an unexpected refugee. This occurred as during the talking, there was a commotion in the garden when the cat caught a swift or swallow. There was an immediate attempt to rescue it but the cat was too quick, yet as we sat there talking I kept on hearing heart-rending cries from the bird and realized while not wanting to give offence to the people in the group who had tried, I felt I had to make my own response which I was glad I did, as fortunately I managed to trick the cat and got the swift from him. While the bird was traumatised and dug its claws into my hands, I was glad to notice the small creature wasn't actually damaged. After taking it home and looking after it, which included with the help of Sarvananda opening its tiny curved beak so as to give it some 'rescue remedy' (natural medicine), after which it began to perk up and that night I put it high up in a tree in a home-made nest and the following day the swift was out when I visited, or had flown to the beyond...

At about this time there was a need to restructure the G.F.R. groups since a number of people had been invited to go to Guhyaloka on an Ordination Retreat in Spain for a few months. So at this juncture I moved into a new G.F.R. group which consisted of Peter Womack, John Rousel, Derek Smith and myself and a bit later Jarp (from Holland). Some of us had recently seen the film 'The Dead Poet's Society', which itself harked back to decades before when a small group had met up in a cave to be inspired by poetry and friendship. In a way this served as an added metaphor for our G.F.R. meetings, which being based in the Dharma, mostly took place in a spirit of fun, friendship, and creative endeavour. By now Nick Taylor had moved into the community and was soon doing a full-time course in general art and design under the auspices of an employment training scheme (E.T.)

The course was created by the tutor Chrissie Chalmers who was employed by Broadland City Council. In due course I also applied to do this course and had a successful interview with Chrissie, though she pointed out that due to financial cutbacks the waiting list would be moving quite slowly. Meanwhile Nick had mentioned they were having difficulty with life models not turning up, and since I had finished my paper-round and wanted another job, I decided to give it a go. I had previously done some modelling in N.Z. at the 'Auckland Arts Society', I was in shorts and a top, there were two nuns in the class, I sat still on the chair, and they seemed pleased with me, after the class the tutor said to me next week they would have my kit off. I felt too shy to go back; my main anxiety was in case I got an erection, especially with the nuns there. After which I felt guilty and sorry about not having turned up. Anyhow here in UK, I phoned Chrissie and before long, became established as an experienced life model.

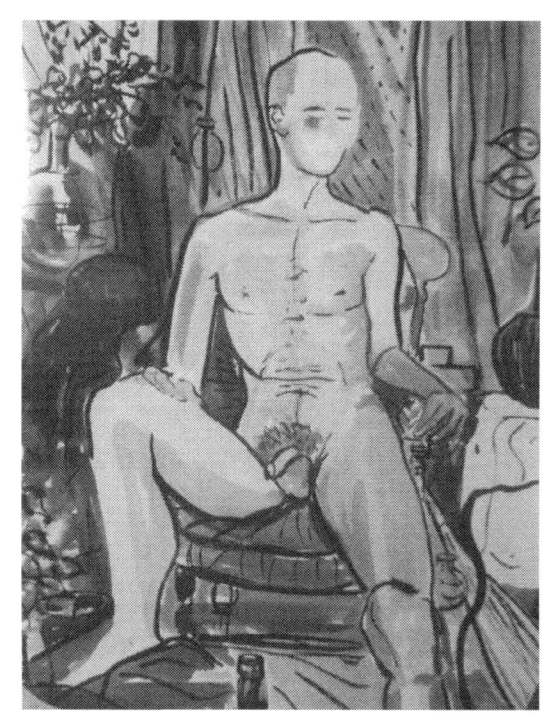

Initially I had been a little anxious and reticent at the thought of being naked before all sorts of people young and old, for sustained periods of time, but to my surprise, found my first and subsequent experiences of this to be in some respects quite liberating. I had talked with Saddhaloka and he had quipped something like either I would need to be completely spent or contained. I had thought the same way, and in any case, apart from one slip in the first month of moving in; I was chaste all the time I was at Vajrakula right through to now, thirty years on. Even so I formally chose that (brahmacharya) i.e. chastity was the basis on which I would do life modelling.

Soon I realised as long as paid attention to my thoughts and state of mind, it was usually easy enough to do. Also because of Yoga and Meditation, I was supple and could easily keep still, and thus I was requested to life-model by Dianna Lamb at Wensum Lodge (Ad-Ed), City College, Hewitt School and other Sixth-Form Colleges and various other establishments. Thus over a number of years I made up for letting those nuns down, and in a sense became a male 'nun' myself, inasmuch as I was now accustomed to chastity and was living in a spiritual community. As well as doing a day at Norwich Art School led by the then principal (Head), who was Glaswegian and named 'Mr Black'. I also modelled for Steve who had a Studio in Muspole Street. One hot summer he ran a summer school and lots of middle-class ladies came from London; there were also a couple of young girls who were preparing portfolios for art school applications. There was a swim-pool nearby where at lunchtimes I could cool down, or limber up and rejuvenate. Later I would stand, sit or lie on a large wooden box, with sun streaming through the skylight, and listen to the strains of a Maria Callas cassette and other pieces of music, wafting through the air, it felt like one was in ancient Greece or Italy, and I appreciated that one of the ladies gave me the Maria Callas tape as a memento.

On another occasion at a standard evening class 'Mark', a not so happy, ex-Order member was in attendance, and realizing I was a Mitra, in the tea break sought to dissuade me from my involvement with the F.W.B.O, I in turn quoted the Dhammapada verse: "Hatred is not ended by hatred, but by love, many do not realize that we are all heading for death, and those who do realize this, do not fight one another, but compose their quarrels". Anyhow I remained friendly, and wished him well. For the most part my life modelling has been done in a spirit of stillness simplicity and contentment.

Other activities in the following year or two included door to door collections for Oxfam which can be a challenging experience, a cycle excursion to Seaford and walking under and over the Seven Sisters cliffs; where I was once on a school camp, and back in Norwich to appreciate at a free performance of Handel's Messiah, which led up to an encounter with the B.B.C. about a week before Xmas '91. This came about after Sarvananda got call from Radio Norfolk asking if a Buddhist would be prepared to be interviewed live, on "what it's like to be a Buddhist at Xmas"? And he passed it on to me. I agreed to give it a go and turned up at the studio having done some preparation. Being aware that fools rush in where angels fear to tread, I decided not to let myself be rattled by anything, and that if I did get into any deep waters, I would just pull back and keep to 'damage limitation'.

In the event, though I was nervous to start with, and though the interviewer did try to push my buttons, I managed to do well for my first live interview on air. In response to various questions I pointed out that while at the heart of Christianity there is 'A Saviour' born on Xmas day, at the heart of Buddhism there is 'A Shower of The Way'. On the subject of Vegetarianism, I mentioned that while I wouldn't be eating any Turkeys, I did hope to take the opportunity to go out and feed the swans. While in relation to being asked whether Buddhism wasn't perhaps mostly suited to Guardian readers, I explained that there was nothing wrong with being a 'Guardian', in the sense of upholding real values and making them available in society. I also explained that the practices of friendliness and mindfulness taught at F.W.B.O. Centres are found helpful by people from all walks of life. After about fifteen minutes we concluded, and I agreed with his comment that the interview had gone well, in that it had been positive, friendly and informative.

* * *

Dave and Jersey

One of the practices which I sometimes did when life-modelling was to contemplate how all things are impermanent and the inevitability of death. This may sound morbid, but this Buddhist practice I would only enter into by first cultivating a sufficiently positive basis to start with. But anyhow the next episode is poignant for me to write on, as it's about the death of David Havers, Saddhaloka's good friend and helper, whom I referred to earlier on, and who I had come to appreciate and respect for his almost unfailing warmth and good humour. I along with others was much saddened when he became ill with what turned out to be cancer, which if not caused, certainly wasn't helped by his smoking, from which we had tried to encourage him to stop. After the illness had set in one could only do one's best to ease and help and in this respect, one day after taking Dave through some simple physical exercises, I ran him a bubble bath and put on a tape of South Seas music and then brought him a cold orange juice, all of which he enjoyed. But gradually his health declined and he went into hospital for a while, where I did whatever seems to need doing, but mostly I just sat by his side, occasionally holding his hand. On one occasion he had requested an extra cushion or two and when a nurse came to enquire how many he needed, he was only partly conscious, but answered in a loud clear voice that he wanted hundreds, bringing smiles to various faces including the nurse. Before he left hospital I spent a couple of days at Dave's home painting his bedroom ceiling, fixing his bookshelf near his bed and putting in a telephone extension.

***

As it was, Saddhaloka and I had previously arranged to go to Jersey for a weekend retreat, which he was running. Before going we sat with Dave who was now back at home and shared silence, as well as chanting the Buddhist refuges and precepts together, at that time Dave's condition was stable, even so I asked if he would like me to skip Jersey but he said to go. In Jersey I stayed with Saddhaloka at his parents' house and the weekend retreat went well. But then on March 17th at about 3am Dave appeared that night in my dreams very vividly, I responded to him as though he was still ill, but he seemed to be in a joyous state and he seemed to indicate that he was much better. Then next morning the news came by phone that he had died that night at about 1am. While upset I was not surprised, and the following night he appeared again (in my dream), I indicated to him not to be overwhelmed by his euphoria and just to be at ease, or something to that effect.

Later back in Norwich I sat with his body on a few occasions, just generating warm thoughts and wishing him well. Then in due course we had a positive and bright funeral service, which started at the Buddhist Centre where we rejoiced in Dave's merits which included friendliness, cheerfulness, readiness to help out as well as other good qualities, followed by a service at the crematorium. I daresay that by now almost a year on, he may well have already been reborn, hopefully into a good, happy and auspicious situation. With the passing of the months, I got on with various things which included taking on the caretaking and cleaning of the Buddhist Centre's Queen's Road Yoga Studio, one of the many voluntary tasks which Dave used to do.

A new activity for me which occurred later in the summer was accepting an opportunity to give a public talk, which was advertised to take place at the Norwich Assembly Rooms for the general public, under the auspices of the Theosophical society. This happened as the planned speaker wasn't going to be able to attend, and so I stepped in at a few days' notice, during which I wrote a short talk under the advertised title The Way of The Buddha. The talk was well received by the audience of about sixteen, and lasted about an hour after which there was questions and attempted answers, which continued for about another hour. This event put me on the spot, though I found it to be a worthwhile experience. The talk looked at the life of the Buddha, and at the Buddhist path in one of its simple formulations: The three-fold way of Ethics, Meditation, Insight and Compassion. Then we went on to consider their relevance and application for today's world.

Other activities in the coming months included taking the opportunity to give a short flute recital for a fund-raising event held at Padmaloka retreat centre and giving a ten-minute presentation of artwork at the Norwich centre, which was well received. I might add here that I did eventually start and complete the Employment Training course in General Art and Design which I had applied for. Though from my time of applying to actually entering the course, it had shrunk from ten months to be a ten-week course. But anyhow it went quite well, and I enjoyed cycling to the course on summer days via a quiet cycle track, which sometimes passed gypsy horses grazing on public land, and continued over a bridge similar to the one painted by Monet. Another event which I found quite stretching and fulfilling, was writing and reading a half-hour short story, for a 'Short Story Evening' at the Norwich Buddhist Centre a few weeks before Xmas, which seemed to be appreciated and enjoyed by those attending. Bodhiraja a bright and cheerful chap who was working school teaching, as well as studying Greek had joined the community a few months earlier, made a contribution by reading a reading a piece by E.M. Forster.

Around the end of January 1993 I received a letter inviting me to attend the forthcoming four-month ordination course at Guhyaloka, a Retreat Centre in Spain, in a mountain valley between Alicante and Valencia. While there was a large chance that I would be ordained during the course, there was no guarantee of this. Anyhow I accepted the invitation, and to offset some of the costs, I agreed to go out a month early. Before leaving I visited my mum who was now seventy-three and had just had to stop doing film work, because of having developed 'osteoporosis'. Over the past few years I had become accustomed to visiting my mother every so often, and as well as enjoying seeing her, had appreciated her kindness and hospitality, as well as the vegetarian meals which she cooked for me. And I am glad that in the last few years we have been gradually getting to see and know more of each other.

***

I vaguely remember Frederick Leboyer once published a short book promoting what he called 'Birth without Violence'. In NZ as a Mitra I wrote a short article after reading his book, this is a later reflection: "I only have myself to blame for being born, but I couldn't have done it without my mother. Recently I noticed one of my fingers was on my bellybutton, tummy-button or umbilical cord knot. I was about to pull my finger out, but instead I let awareness go into my lost cord. Then I recalled there was a time when it was not obstructed by a knot. At that time, like a popular café, it was wide open for business and tea; toast; and buttered scones, endlessly passed down the cord into the sleeping me, then one melodramatic moment, my little pond of dreams was shattered, as I was pushed; spilled and plonked into the wondrous world of Edinburgh, wearing no underpants and a small kilt."

Chapter Thirteen
Guhyaloka (43)

Invitation

Prior to being invited to the Guhyaloka course, I had just about come to the point of deciding that if I wasn't accepted that year, then I would let my request wind down and just continue with leading the 'good life' as best as I was able to. I had been involved with the F.W.B.O. since I was 24 and was now 43, and had first asked about ordination about fifteen years earlier. I had come to a point where I didn't want to go on projecting import into an endeavour which seemed to be so perpetually elusive. Even so I continued to stay in contact with the situation. I had started to adjust to the idea of dropping the pressure and becoming more freelance in my approach to Buddhism, when I received a letter telling me that the team at Padmaloka had decided to invite me to the ordination retreat at Guhyaloka, though they stressed there was no guarantee of my being ordained.

In New Zealand I had managed over ten years to scrape together about a thousand pounds, and so far had felt obliged to keep this available for the ordination course. Now I was thinking, I had never really had a holiday and I might go to Greece for a month or two and still have enough left over to replace my bicycle. But anyhow having come this far I decided I should be patient and see what I could make of the situation. The actual cost of the four-month retreat including return fare to Spain, had now risen to about two thousand pounds, but I decided I wasn't prepared to go into debt which I wouldn't be able to easily repay, and so I negotiated to pay fifty pounds a week which along with my plane ticket came to about the sum I had, and this was accepted on the basis that I was to go out and do a month's labouring at Guhyaloka, prior to the start of the retreat. I had already taken on to do a voluntary job painting the community hall, which was going to take up a couple of weeks and would consume both time and energy.

Then arriving in Spain for a month's labouring, before the four months intensive retreat, all seemed a bit daunting, but having made the decision, I just had to get on with it. In the event I enjoyed my two weeks decorating the entrance and stairways at Vajrakula, which after completion looked beautiful and quite transformed. My remaining two weeks preparing to leave for Spain, along with bringing this manuscript up to date and the visit to my mum in London, all kept me quite busy. Then before long it was time for me to bid farewell to Norwich and Vajrakula community, for the coming five months.

I continued to have heartfelt convictions in the Buddha Dharma and the worth of the Bodhisattva ideal, dedicated to the good of all beings, and was prepared to make the effort to try to contribute to our world, real values, a meaningful vision of existence, and practical ways to change, including clarifying our understanding with regards the various social ills in society. By the time I left for Spain I was in a bright; and alive state, and while I seemed to be heading into the unknown, was at the same time feeling quite engaged with what I was doing. My flight was due to be departing from Gatwick at about 5am (March 93), fortunately a friend who needed to go down to London was able to give me a lift.

It was close to full moon as we departed from Norwich, the drive through the night, on mostly traffic free roads bathed in moonlight, passed quickly and smoothly. Arriving in the small hours the airport seemed semi-deserted, after a quiet cup of hot chocolate with the then Derek (later Viprasanna), we bade farewell. Then I had forty winks, with my luggage stored in such a way that it couldn't be taken without my waking. Later the airport started to spring into life and I was able to check-in my bags, after which I sat by a water sculpture called 'Slipstream' and wondered, before eventually embarking. The cheap flight with Monarch airlines was enjoyable, especially as the sun started to rise and I was able to look out from my window seat across spectacular views of the snow-capped Pyrenees which seemed dazzlingly beautiful. I also reflected on my previous trip to Spain aged about eighteen, when I had hitch-hiked with Toby and walked through those mountains.

* * *

Guhyaloka

Coming through the terminal, it was a relief to see Sthiravajra's bright face, and that he had been able to come and pick me up, thereby cutting out all the hassle of carrying luggage, while trying to find the right bus connections, with only a few words of Spanish language. After driving through Alicante and along the coast for a while we came to Villajoyosa where we had some refreshing coffee, before driving on and up into the mountains. My last visit had been during the tail-end of Franco's reign, so the present period was politically a lot more relaxed. Despite the coffee being a stimulant, I too became more relaxed, and could hardly keep awake for the remainder of the journey, along steep winding tracks high up into mountains, well removed from the world. Guhyaloka (the Secret Realm) occupies a large rugged and secluded valley surrounded by mountains; the area was large enough to contain a number of related communities without these impinging on each other. At the entrance to the valley there was a support community (which consisted of Order Members and a Mitra or friend), who were in charge of the valley and shopping for the retreat centre. While to some degree I expected to have to 'hit the ground running', it soon became clear that I had been dropped into an awkward situation and had let myself in for all sorts of unexpected difficulties.

Since, while the environment was brilliant, it quickly transpired that due to various mishaps or misunderstandings the group working up at the main community where I was to lodge didn't at that stage include any order members, and were to some degree out of harmony with the support community, with the exception of Vic, a Mitra who behaved very decently. I found the situation very trying. Individually those involved did have good qualities, but had become disgruntled, the chemistry and general group dynamic wasn't pleasant, and when they realised I was there not just for the month's work, but also for the following four month ordination course, I became the butt of quite a lot of jibes and put-downs, which in some ways were quite amusing, for their blatant provocative nature. Anyhow while it was an unexpected ordeal, I decided I would just have to ride the situation and not take it too seriously. So I cooked occasional meals, got on with the work (which in my case initially consisted in driving the Landover and hauling large amounts of rocks). After a couple of weeks and with a new arrival things improved a little, meanwhile when not working I started to explore the environment and enjoyed some long walks.

To me Guhyaloka was indeed a wonderful place with its rugged scenery, delightful birdsong, enchanting wildflowers, clean air and lots of stars at night, along with hooting owls and other sounds. There was no electricity except for solar panels providing small lights in the huts, of which there were two main types, some made out of 'yeso' (plaster) and the others made of wood. The weather was still cold and keeping warm at night, I quickly learned, depended on having collected adequate dry pine needles and a stock of wood to fuel the pot-belly stove, which at full strength, would start to make puffing noises like a steam train, and before ebbing out would take away the dampness and create enough warmth to last till morning. I had brought three latex moulds with me, which I had made from a small Kamakura/Amitabha Buddha, and after some experiments found it was quite possible to make acceptable statues out of yeso/plaster and so began a practice of making about a couple of figures per day, in all I made about forty-nine which I gave away before and during the retreat. I continued to go on long walks looking for a particular cave, and on one excursion I made a point hiding a few cans of soft drink, with a view to rediscovering them at a later date, when out walking with anyone. Generally for the most part I got very drawn into the work, I was determined to do what I could to transform the wooden pallet huts. In fact I became quite a workaholic and most nights couldn't drag myself away from what I was doing, until it was starting to get dark. While this produced good results, the only drawback was that by the time the retreat started, and most people arrived fresh and ready to start, by that time I was feeling whacked and ready to collapse.

A few days before the retreat started, Andy Gilbert, Phil Travers and a little later Nick Wallis arrived, and it was really refreshing to have some reasonably happy and straightforward people actually resident in the main retreat community. Meanwhile I became the camps Solar 'Electrician' and was kept busy, trying to make sure that all the lights were working and that all the huts were clean and ready before the forthcoming influx of about another twenty-eight people, making a total of thirty-two: consisting of twenty-six mitras who had asked to be ordained and a team of six order members.

* * *

The team & preparation

Before long everyone had arrived and the retreat was under way, I noted that I knew hardly any of the other participants, apart from John Rousel and Derek Smith who were both based in Norwich, and it was with Derek that I shared a hut. There were contingents from London, Cambridge, Croydon, Glasgow and Wales. While others came from France, Germany, Holland, America, Canada, Australia, and New Zealand. My plan was that once people had had a few days to settle in, I would select a few people to try and spend regular time with. From the second day the structure of the retreat was quickly established: early morning Prostrations, Meditation Practice, breakfast, Group Study or other activity till 1pm. Then after lunch either read, walk or catch up on chores. At 4.30pm there was Meditation before supper and then talks or other activity before Puja and bed. Apart from being on a rota to cook or wash-up about every other day, there were also weekly Work Days digging ditches and that sort of thing. So people were kept quite busy, as there were various other ritual events and activities. After a few we days we had a Robing Ceremony (which was not compulsory), in which we exchanged our normal clothes for blue robes, once I had got used to them, I enjoyed being draped in loose robes, and felt less polarised, they seemed to have a symbolic and positive effect and I appreciated being out of trousers/shorts. We also in most cases had our heads shaved, symbolic of Renunciation and along with other Precepts, took the Precept of Chastity/Brahmacarya.

In due course it became clear that there were to be Three Main Phases to the retreat: Preparation; Ordination and Bodhicitta (or clarifying our purpose). 1/ Preparation was to consist of Purification with a corresponding Lotus-Ceremony. 2/ Determination was to consist of a corresponding Vajra-Diamond Ceremony, and 3/ Transformation with a corresponding Fire-Ceremony. Not long previously I had dipped into William Goldings 'Lord of the Flies', in which a group of youngsters are marooned on an island and degenerate into Rival Tribes. In our case we hoped not to end up eating one another, not just because we were more mature and vegetarian, but because we shared Common Spiritual Ideals, and as the months unfolded with the help of meaningful rituals, we did become integrated and harmonious. Even so there were aspects of the retreat which slightly reminded me of the pagan atmosphere and conch blowing, in Golding's Book, such as the very atmospheric Blowing of Conches and Tibetan Horns, in the ceremonies mentioned above, which were performed during the first month.

The first part of Preparation took place about a week into the retreat. Guhyaloka valley has near its centre a very large and rugged rock rising up into the sky which is called The Phoenix, further along there are other large and impressive rocks which include The Owl and The Dragons Back, while on one side is the vast Whale and on the other side, the no less large Goat's Pass and North Ridge. For the Lotus ceremony (and the others later) we were allocated a place around the valley, though we could choose whether we wanted a difficult, less difficult or easy place to get to. I choose the first category as I fancied going high up. To perform the Lotus ceremony we gathered in the shrine room not long before dusk and after some chanting and being given some instructions, we made our way to our various spots.

My climb up the North Ridge, I think led by Jayaraja, was a lot more demanding and challenging than I had anticipated, the rocks being very jagged and steep. At one point pulling my body over a ridge, my hand came within inches of a snub-nosed adder, which looked at me and fortunately drew away; later returning in the twilight was even more precarious. Even so the ceremony went well; and was very moving; especially at points where the Chanting of Mantras was relayed around the valley, punctuated with deep sounds from the Tibetan horn, by Suvajra who was up the Phoenix, in the central region where we could all hear him, from our respective places. The only minor drawback from this occasion was that when I got high up, it was Colder and Windier than I expected and I got very cold. In the next day or so I came down with a very severe sore throat, followed by an equally debilitating cold, and found the following couple of weeks difficult enough just to get by, and didn't have the energy or inclination to do anything except wash hankies and make flasks of lemon tea to take back to my hut.

Consequently by the time I was really functioning again, those people who needed to make new friends, had already formalised any new alliances. Meanwhile other aspects of the retreat started to take place including, sharing of Brief Life Stories which was followed by Confession Groups. In due course I grew to appreciate our study leader Jyotipala, but at that stage I didn't know him or anyone else in our Confession Group, and didn't really feel like being there, partly as I was still trying to get over my head cold. Anyhow despite the stubborn cold and accompanying tinnitus, I was very glad to be on retreat with an excellent and delightful team of order members, consisting of Suvajra, Surata, Ratnaguna, Yashodeva, Abhayakirti and Jyotipala, most of whom I knew in varying degrees. I also had occasional contact with Subhuti, who was intermittently resident at Bhante's place, engaged with writing.

* * *

Retreat and determination

Having just got over my cold, I decided I needed to regain the initiative, so I undertook to do the Prostration Practice, every morning for the following month. I did complete this; though it became increasingly difficult to do, as I had an on-going problem with tinnitus. This was because earlier in Norwich, just before giving a Public Talk, I deemed it necessary to go swimming, in an effort to clear a slight head cold. Swimming with a head-cold was a Mistake, and led to the Tinnitus. Thus often I was lucky if I had had three or four hours sleep. This continued for much of the retreat, and did undermine my efforts, since some of the time I felt not entirely with it, from having had little sleep. I think if I had been enjoying basic good health, I could have meditated more effectively and generally being more on top of the situation. I decided I would have to take the initiative and follow a more organic and less fixed programme, and to focus on those things that I actually found relevant and helpful. So I listened to taped lectures when I couldn't sleep, or took my sleeping bag and camped somewhere under the stars, so that I could just reflect on the vastness of the heavens.

At other times I slept on top of the Phoenix, or in the cave up in the amphitheatre. In the mornings I went running while it was still cool, sometimes coming across the Shepherd moving his herd of goats with their tinkling bells. Then sometimes I would climb a mountainside and paint water-colours of sweeping vistas while the morning was still fresh. I continued to engage with as much of the retreat as I could, and though I was only half awake in some of the meditations, I stayed engaged with most of the scheduled events. Some of the many Pujas were very moving, and almost as alive and inspiring as my first Sevenfold Puja which I had encountered at Pundarika (Archway) in my first days of involvement with the movement. Later on in the retreat I enjoyed being in the study group led by Yashodeva, I also appreciated Suvajra's kindness, Ratnaguna's good humour, Surata's yoga and brightness and also Abhayakirti's warm-heartedness.

Occasionally I tried to write notes, such as the following which alludes to the varied wildlife including the lizards which at times could be coaxed into nibbling bits of pear from one's hand.

> Valley sounds
> *Calling cuckoos*
> *Hooting owls*
> *Singing birds*
> *Silent lizard*

Sliding snake
Splashing frog
Beating sunrays
Brewing storms
Misty clouds
Bells echo
Feet on the path
Friendly eyes
Leaving the past
Accepting the present
Opening in silence....
Ant hills
Mountain peaks
Rising moon

In the afternoons there were excursions with friends, or walks to the bathing area to shower and wash clothes. While at other times I went to a secluded place I had found, where I could throw my clothes off, and for a short while absorb myself in reading Sangharakshita's 'Facing Mount Kanchenjunga', or whatever studying I needed to do, with occasional breaks for lemon tea from my flask. At other times I just relaxed and appreciated the natural environment, which included many beautiful wildflowers. Sometimes on the way back I would pick small sprigs of wild herbs such as the thyme, the fragrance of which was delightfully refreshing. The Retreat continued to proceed from the

Lotus ceremony & purification, to the
    Vajra ceremony & determination, and then
        to the Fire ceremony & transformation.

It was during the Vajra ceremony, high up in the mountains on my own, that I read a slip of paper which informed me, quite to my surprise, that I would be ordained during the retreat…

* * *

Ordination and Re-entry

(I admit, sometimes I can't always get my head around all the sections)

With the section on preparation now well underway, we started to move into the ordination section of the retreat and the start of a period of on-going Silence which would last for about twenty-eight days. So far we had had a series of talks on 'The Precepts', a series of talks on 'The Human Condition', as well as a talk on 'Myth and Ritual' and now one on the 'Six Element Practice'. This is a form of Meditation on Impermanence, which we were to practice in the mornings during the next few weeks, while the Private Ordinations were conducted (individually) in the Stupa which had been constructed especially for this purpose. This was all to culminate in the Public Ordinations in the main shrine room when we would learn each other's new names.

Suvajra (who was leading the retreat) needed four people to carve Purbhas (ritual implements) to be used during a ceremony around the stupa and asked me if I would like to do one. Initially I made one out of pine wood but then found out they were supposed to be made of almond wood. This was quite good as it obliged me to go for an early morning walk down to the Almond Grove which I much enjoyed. In the next few days of doing wood carving (in a basic fashion), I was interested to notice how almond wood is on the one hand so very hard, and yet on the other so fine and unique with its milky texture.

The Ordination Initiation would include receiving a Visualisation Practice and the corresponding Mantra of a Bodhisattva Figure (a sort of Archetypal Angel-Bodhisattva Image). As well as Chanting the Refuges and Ten Precepts and being given a New Name.

I found myself in three camps as I felt a strong connection with Padmasambhava on account of the Bardo Thodol and its Root Verses which I had committed to heart, and I had a strong affinity for both Amitabha and Vajrasattva. In the event, after a short discussion with Subhuti, I decided that since I was obliged to 'formalise' one of these, Then I would opt for Vajrasattva, as he symbolises Primordial Purity and absolute truth which underpins and doesn't exclude the other two.

I did not feel I could make a clear decision, and wanted an approach which would be open and all-inclusive.

With silence established and the Stupa consecrated, the twenty-six ordinations commenced, one each evening. In a playful way, the person to be ordained was dubbed 'King of the Day' and would be afforded preferential treatment through the day, such as being given a sweet and not having to wash up. Before dinner commenced everyone would look out for his arrival and clapped. Having taken the King's seat, he would then be crowned with laurel leaves. Then in the evening there would be a special puja, and the person to be ordained would have the chance to make an 'obituary speech' before departing to be initiated and Spiritually Reborn. They would also be given cards and presents, myself I would bring petals or bubbles to throw or blow, as well as one of the Amitabha figures (which I had made earlier) for that night's recipient. On the evening of my private ordination, for my 'obituary speech' I gave a brief account of the various events and experiences which had brought me to the present point, expressed appreciation for various people who had helped me along the way, and recited some verses I had written on the six elements (the last two being space & consciousness).

The Elements:

Naked birth on revolving earth
Offers no permanence.
Whatever our worth
Gushing, rushing, torrential rain
Seven seas
Within our brain
Dancing flames fade away
Clammy cold
We cannot stay
Clad in snowdrops
Shrouded in stars
Heart heaves
As breath leaves
Sinking, twirling
Swimming, swirling
We vacate our space
In the human race
Elements flown
Mind blown
Consciousness meets
What it has sown.

(Dharmika Guhyaloka 1993)

Then I concluded with a short flute recital, explaining that any rough notes could ward off unwanted influences, while the better parts could express my aspirations and invoke higher influences. The short recital went well, and it was on a high note, that I slowly and mindfully made my way along the Secret Path to the Stupa, where Subhuti would be waiting to ordain me. I had been told that once in the stupa, I should take my time to just arrive and get my breath back. In the event Subhuti seemed keen to commence proceedings immediately, which threw me a little, anyhow I didn't want things to get more confused; and so I just responded to the pace of the given situation, so that the ceremony passed straightforwardly. Significant and effective as the event was, I did afterwards feel that it was also underpinning the strong and positive experiences I had had with Subhuti years earlier at Pundarika, when he and Chintamani had introduced me to the Three Refuges and Five Precepts.

While Subhuti wasn't on the present retreat; he was resident in the valley, so as to be able to get on with his writing. Although very engaged with his work, he did manage to make time to see me and others on a number of occasions. At some time I had expressed that I hoped I got a name which was simple, uncomplicated and easy to say. So when he gave me the name Dharmika (which means one who lives by the truth) it easily fulfilled those criteria, and while it took me a while to grow into the name, I was soon able to relate to and feel inspired by its meaning and connotations. The period which I spent in and about the Stupa, was spent reflecting, meditating and absorbing the event, after which I looked at the various cards and things which I had been given, and thus enjoyed my spell in the Stupa. Before long the day came for the Public Ordinations, which was a light and bright occasion performed in the main shrine room. It was during this day that we learned the new names of all the people who had received their private ordinations in the previous weeks of silence.

Bodhicitta

Shortly afterwards we moved into the third and final section of the retreat. I was in a group led by Yashodeva, during which we studied Shantideva's classic text 'The Bodhicharyavatara' plus a chapter of the Ratnagunasamcayagatha, also we studied Subhuti's inspiring 'Visualisation Workshop' of which Subhuti kindly gave me a copy. In the coming weeks we all had the opportunity to give a talk, (many of which were very good) and also led Pujas. Then the retreat was rounded off with a series of talks on 'The Order and The World', before coming to a closing ceremony and a couple of work days. During these last two days, retreatants were permitted to go on longer excursions to help prepare for being back in the world. For my excursion on the penultimate day of the retreat, I didn't fancy going to the coast, but I thought it would be helpful to start relating to the outer world. So I decided to walk the few miles down to Sella ,the local small town. Ironically, after my sometimes-precarious activities at Guhyaloka, while running down the road to catch up a couple of friends who had gone on ahead, I managed to twist my ankle in one of the hidden jeep tracks. Anyhow I sort of over-rode what had happened, and went on to have a very lovely day in Sella, quietly wandering about observing people and the small old streets and general architecture. This culminated in a steep walk uphill to an abandoned church overlooking Sella. The church had a bell tower with stairs leading up to it, and from there I was able to look out on Sella, which seemed like a small and quaint reflection of the world at large. The bell had had its gong removed, even so before leaving I gently tapped the bell a few times, and chanted the Vajrasattva Mantra, while sending out goodwill towards all beings.

A couple of days later, at about ten at night, Silaratna kindly drove me to the airport. As we made our way through Alicante Town, there was a Fiesta of some sort starting up and it all seemed a little surreal as we passed people with masks and painted faces, and drove through the bright lights into the night. Having bid farewell to Silaratna and checked in my baggage, I went and sat outside the airport in the warm air of the Spanish night, by a white flowering bush. Back in UK I followed the suggestions that I had made in a short talk on 'Guarding the Doors of the Senses', and my arrival back was quite straightforward. Even so, after the mountains and retreat atmosphere things seemed small, constricted and a bit empty. While I made some efforts, I noticed after a few days that I was feeling emotionally quite vulnerable, in part due to feeling wrenched from where I had been and plonked into the middle of a noisy city.

Then after about ten days, came the Western Buddhist Order's 1993 convention, which I wouldn't have got to but for the generosity of people on the Guhyaloka Course. In a way it wasn't really what I needed, but despite my twisted ankle, which was taking quite a while to heal, tinnitus keeping me awake at night and picking up a cold, I did appreciate the friendliness of people and also seeing Bhante, and was glad that I got there, even though I wasn't as engaged as I would like to have been. Back in Norwich re-engaging with daily life was a slow process. At first I just wanted to pretend the world didn't exist, partly due to having a slight flu. After a while I started doing flute practice again, and also some general reading, including books on positive thinking as well as various Buddhist texts. I decided for the moment to let my health improve and to assimilate and consolidate the previous few months. Meanwhile I was starting to feel more emotionally robust, and writing this helped to clarify things. Fortunately, in due course my ankle improved, which meant I could sit to meditate more easily, and before long I was walking, swimming and feeling much better.

We had an open day at the Centre, and I enjoyed helping with that. After a while I started to be involved with Meditation and basic Dharma classes, which I found to be both worthwhile and satisfying to do. Later I started doing life-modelling again, as well as attending a G.C.S.E. Art Class at Norwich City College, which I enjoyed doing. And was suitably pleased to learn that I had achieved an 'A*' grade.

This chapter concludes this account of 'Bridge Over Turbulent Waters', which roughly details how I got from 0-43 and also how P. Burleigh became Dharmika.

Meanwhile, as Tsongkhapa so eloquently puts it:

"This life we should know
as the tiny splash of a raindrop,
a thing of beauty which disappears
even as it comes into being,
therefore set your goal,
and make use of each day and night
to achieve it".

* * * * * * * * * * * * * * * * * * *

May All Beings be Happy.

CHAPTER FOURTEEN
Bridge Over Turbulent Waters (43-73)

30 years later...

Chapters 1 to 13 of this memoir were written when I was about forty-three. Now at age seventy-three I am producing this fourteenth chapter, which briefly covers various pivotal events in that period.

Dissolving of Community

Eventually Vajrakula started to reduce in numbers, until gradually I was the only community member left. It felt like I was on a lifeboat, which was sinking, and one by one the occupants noticed new opportunities and jumped ship. Now I was alone, and someone from the F.W.B.O council, who rented the property from Norwich City Council, came and asked, would I mind if they turned the community from a men's to a women's community. I reflected and felt it would be ungraceful to stick my heels in, and so consented, and accepted a few weeks' notice, after all the work I had done on the place, I hoped they would make good use of the place, but it only lasted a few years, so the property went back into the hands of the Norwich City Council, and was sold and turned into exclusive flats. Deep in the basement is a small cellar, which I used as a darkroom, and where I made small Amitabha Figures (Rupas), and behind an old wall, I hid and plastered in, a paper copy of this manuscript along with a floppy disc, which is probably still there, waiting to be discovered in the distant future. Incidentally the first draft of this manuscript was written in the community office, on Amstrad floppy discs, and it was only Thanks to Shantavira that I was able to retrieve the material on to current discs.

Solitary Community

Eventually, having viewed a variety of bedsits, I was fortunate enough to obtain a council flat, a few hundred yards from the city rubbish dump and recycling centre and close to Andersons Meadow, where the 'gipsy, travellers or Romany's' graze their ponies. On various occasions when I have been en-route to do life modelling, I enjoy feeding, and, when needed, disentangling the ponies tether ropes. On one occasion I had a letter in the local paper, when the local council were trying to ban the ponies. My own lifestyle is fairly uncomplicated, I have continued with chastity and taken the Anagarika vow at Padmaloka conducted by Suvajra, and that has been my normal way of life, pretty much since I joined Vajrakula Community aged about thirty-seven. So even though I was doing lots of life modelling in various establishments, it was simply platonic with minimal sexual element, and thus being naked at work became normal, like relaxing on a naturist beach.

My council estate has many mature trees with hooting owls and occasional woodpeckers, as these grounds used to house a private or 'up market' mental asylum, and the grove opposite mine is named Watson Grove. The author of Sherlock Holmes Conan Doyle was a medical doctor, and a good friend of his, who was also a doctor, was crippled after a hansom cab accident, and thus he came to Norwich and created a mental asylum here, at Heigham Hall, which about a hundred years later, was demolished and in 1960s turned into council flats about three stories high. I often see small deer in the grounds, as Anderson's Meadow across the road, connects to Marriott's Way, an old steam-train railway track, which is now a cycle and walking track which goes deep into rural Norfolk, emerging at Aylsham, and nearby is Blickling Hall, which for me has associations with Ann Boleyn. Below my ceiling, between two doors I have a wooden framed canoe salvaged from Padmaloka (Lesingham House), it was originally built by Mark D, though I needed to cut off the rotten end, and refashioned it to fit where it does. For its maiden voyage, on nearby River Wensum and River Yare, I paddled for about three hours, to arrive in time for an event at Padmaloka. Finding it now sits low in the water, I now do shorter journeys. The canoe is named 'Satyakaya' (body of truth).

My mother's and other deaths

My mother Vivian died about twenty years ago and did quite well. Looking through bits of paper, I notice my name is on the funeral service, and I gave quite a heartfelt eulogy, and concluded with the Poem by an Unknown Soldier (2nd World War) "Do not stand at my grave and weep I am not there I do not sleep, / I am a thousand winds that blow, I am the diamond glints on snow, I am the sunlight on ripened grain, I am the gentle autumn rain, / When you awaken in the mornings hush, I am the soft uplifting rush of quiet birds in circled flight / I am the soft stars that shine at night, / Do not stand at my grave and cry, I am not there I did not die".

Later, as well as an oil painting of my mother by my father, who died about 1966 when I was sixteen, also I received a handwritten letter from Vivian "My dear beloved Patrick, when you receive this I should have departed from this earth to join 'the light', this is just a word of love, and to ask you to be happy for me. --- I am so grateful for the calm, and I think fulfilling way you lead your life. --- Look after yourself, God bless, my love will always be with you…"

I also did a eulogy for my older brother Toby, who died about fifteen years ago, partly related to alcohol effects on his body. Odd as it sounds, he left behind a son Christoph who is Austrian and a 'psychiatrist'. My younger sister Mary-Honey sadly died from a cocaine mishap, she was married to Richard a charming and wealthy American, whom I understand became the owner of a book, signed from Clementine Churchill (also American) to my mum. Vivian had been a paid companion to Lady Churchill in later life, when with failing sight she needed more help, and my mother used to read to her. Mary and Richard had a large estate, Ash House in (Iddesleigh) Devon, complete with his collection of classic Porsches, and then they moved to Santa Fe in New Mexico. Mary appeared in various films, and in her memory some of her things were donated to Brighton Museum. Mary-honey had a golden quality, though sadly, when I was on a 'Buddha-Field' camping retreat, perchance not far from where she had lived, she appeared, into my dreams, in a disturbed state, somehow intuitively I imbued her with a degree of kindness and calmness, and less disturbed she drifted away.

Despite the whiplash: injury incurred at Vajrakula, I decided to become a swim-pool lifeguard, and with a degree of effort, against the odds I completed and passed the course. The training was from a female teacher using a swim-pool at Heathersett Girl's School, I didn't initially get through, though she intervened, and the male examiner agreed to re-examine me a week later at Barnham Broom Golf Club which also has a swimming-pool, where I passed the physical and verbal elements to his satisfaction. In the event I only used the qualification once, and that was at nearby Wymondham College, at a Buddhist Convention, when they needed a lifeguard. Subsequent to this I did a two-year course with The British Wheel of Yoga.

Training as a yoga teacher: The British Wheel of Yoga are physically less strenuous than the BKS Iyengar system, though they make up for it in other ways, thus I was obliged to study and write about twenty essays. Patanjali a prominent teacher about eighty years after The Buddha, chose to systematise Yoga Teachings into an eight-fold system, approximately: 1/ Yama (in relation to outside world): Non-violence, Non-exploitation, Brahmacharya/Chastity, Truthfulness and Non-covetousness, 2/ Niyama (in relation to oneself): Purity, Gratitude, Discipline, Study and Worship. 3/ Asana (posture) Helped by Hatha Yoga (and disciplines such as Tai Chi, or Chi Kung). 4/ Pranayama (modest breathing exercises) taught by a qualified teacher, so as to practice carefully, and at an appropriate level. 5/ Pratyahara (with-drawing and turning inwards). 6/ Dharana (concentration). 7/ Dhyana (absorption) and 8/ Samadhi… Thankfully previously, this was all put into a wider and deeper context or perspective, by Urgyen Sangharakshita's lucid Lectures on 'The Buddha's Noble Eightfold Path', as well as 'Evolution Lower and Higher', along with fascinating teachings on The Wheel, The Spiral and The Mandala. Available via <Free Buddhist audio.com>

My own practice of yoga (as well as becoming vegetarian and mostly vegan, and stopping smoking) was instigated by an LSD trip, and also influenced first by Selvarajan Yesudian and Elisabeth Haich's simple book 'Yoga and Health', and later B.K.S. Iyengar's 'Light on Yoga', both published by Unwin Books. I was also very much influenced by W.Y. Evans-Wentz Oxford edition of 'The Tibetan Book of the Dead', as well as Timothy Leary, Ralph Metzner & Richard Alpert's simplified version: 'The Psychedelic Experience' (Penguin Modern classics). Now all that's left is to use each day meaningfully and despite failures; aches and pains, still endeavour to live and die consciously with faith, and awareness…

***

Sangharakshita Died on 30th October 2018.

Even so his insight and teaching are alive and well in his Triratna Community and in his enigmatic and heartfelt array of poetry, as well as extensive recorded talks and books. Bhante's kindness and poetry have been just as important to me as have his lucid teachings, thus I wrote elsewhere: 'Dear Urgyen Bhante, I am sad and sorry at your departure, but also happy and joyful for you. May your transition; awakening or whatever, be refreshing and fulfilling Thank-You for giving so much, in so many ways…

Many Were the Friends…

(Verses I and II of III). By Sangharakshita

1/ Many were the friends who sought with eager hands to lay hold of me as I passed along the way; / But I have shaken them all off and come with lonely longing to the door of my friend. / Many were the flowers that blossomed around me in the garden where I strayed; / But I have sought out the White Rose while it was still bright with morning dew./ Many were the instruments I heard playing in the symphony of life; / But I have cared to listen only to the melancholy sweetness of Thy flute beneath the stars.

2/ When the dawn wings like a great bird from the East, / In the cool of early morning, beside the pine trees, I wait for the…/ When the sun hangs poised like a red flamingo in the heavens, / In the quivering heat of noon, wrapped in the mauve-blue mist of the jacaranda, I wait for the… / When the pale moon breasts the sky like a silver swan on a blue lake, / In the lone garden of my dreams, beneath the wide-spreading branches of the tree of life, I wait for the… / While youth comes and goes, while manhood waxes and wanes as the moon, / In the midst of the worlds tumult, and in the deep silence of my heart, / Through life and through death, through the birth and dissolution of millions of universes, eternally I wait for the …..

***

When I first encountered the Buddha's Noble Eight-Fold Path, it didn't mean much to me; it seemed dry cold and lifeless. Then when I listened to Sangharakshita's taped lecture on this topic at Pundarika, I realised it wasn't about the words, but about one's whole attitude to life. Whether you precede the eight limbs with: Noble, Holy, Right or Perfect, depends on what translation you find helpful, as well as what speaks to you. The eight limbs consist of three sections: 1/ Right Speech, Right Behaviour and Right Livelihood, which equate with Ethics or Morality, 2/ Right Effort, Right Mindfulness, and Right Communion, which equate with Meditation. Then 3/ Right Vision, and

Right Emotion, which equate with Wisdom. So you can see the Eightfold Path can be simplified into Ethics (thus enjoying a good conscience), Meditation (watering and cultivating one's inner garden) and Wisdom (which includes compassion and insight into how things really are). Buddha-Dharma teaches all phenomena are ultimately: Impermanent, Unsatisfactory and Insubstantial.

Conversely we learn in another 'formula' that instead of being bound by the 'Wheel of Life' which can seem like a vicious circle, and is driven by Ignorance, Greed and Hatred, alternately we could choose to cultivate a spiral path which consists of developing qualities, each of which are augmented by the previous ones thus cultivating: Faith> Joy> Rapture> or Ecstasy, Calm> Bliss> Concentration> or> Samadhi and thereby opening to Knowledge and Vision of things as they really are, and ultimately crossing the stream or river of ignorance, greed and hatred and going to the 'further shore', and thereby be more able to help both oneself and others. Sangharakshita, around the time men landed on the moon, in one of his talks equates Ethics with the Launching-Pad, Meditation with the Fuelled Rocket, and Wisdom the Satellite, which has gone beyond the gravitational pull. Sangharakshita in one of his Aphorisms states 'approximately': "You may forget it, but it doesn't forget you, and at the same time you are it".

***

In his poem **'Secret Wings'** Sangharakshita writes:

"We cry that we are weak although/ We will not stir our secret wings; / The world is dark – because we are / Blind to the starriness of things. / We pluck our rainbow-tinted plumes/ And with their heaven-born beauty try/ To fledge nocturnal shafts, and then/ Complain 'Alas! We cannot fly!'/ We mutter 'All is dust' or else/ With mocking words accost the wise: / 'Show us the Sun which shines beyond/ The Veil' – and then we close our eyes. / To powers above and powers beneath /In quest of Truth men sue for aid, / Who stand athwart the Light and fear/ The shadow that themselves have made. / O cry no more that you are weak/ but stir and spread your secret wings, / And say 'The world is bright, because/ We glimpse the starriness of things'. / Soar with your rainbow plumes and reach/ That near-far land/ where all are one, / Where Beauty's face is aye unveiled/ And every star shall be a sun. (Sangharakshita, Complete Poems, 1941/1994. Windhorse).

The point is there is more to life than food. Sex and Sleep. Each of us in our own or shared way, may choose to cultivate a relationship with 'God' or 'Reality', or 'Buddha-Nature', myself I don't care or mind if we call it Christ, Krishna or Buddha or Spiritual Awakening.

As human beings on this wonderous planet, we may freely choose 'To Awaken from The Great Dream' and to spiritualy develop, regardless of caste, colour or creed. This attitude was exemplified by the heroic Dr Ambedkar, whom in India inspired by The Buddha's respect for all forms of life, converted from Hinduism to Buddhism, therefore so called 'untouchables' could be liberated from the indignity of the caste system, and enjoy full human rights. Such as being free to delight in 'Nirmanakaya' or the historical realm and human goodness, 'Sambhogakaya' or the spiritual/ mythical/ or archetypal realms, and Dharmakaya or the transcendental realm of Supreme Enlightenment.

***

Thoughts, speech, and actions: affect all aspects of our lives. The Buddhist precepts are not commandments, but Training Principles, and if I had learned about these as a youngster I would have benefited, even just from trying to adhere to them. The Five precepts for Beginners, and the Ten Precepts for Order Members, are practical guidelines, and are helpful, despite upsets and occasional failings.

1/ with deeds of loving kindness, I purify my body.

2/ with open-handed generosity, I purify my body.

3/ with stillness simplicity, and contentment, I purify my body.

4/ with truthful communication, I purify my speech.

5/ with mindfulness clear and radiant, I purify my mind.

NB Order Members continue after 4/ as listed below.

5/ with words kindly and gracious' I purify my speech.

6&7/ with utterances helpful and harmonious purify my speech.

8/ abandoning covetousness for tranquillity, I purify my mind.

9/ changing hatred into compassion, I purify my mind.

10/ transforming ignorance into wisdom, I purify my mind.

***

Chapter and setbacks

Shortly after returning to Vajrakula Community, I had being in a Chapter with about five others, and I was the Chapter Convenor. About a year or so later, one of my Chapter members had asked me to help him with his elderly mother's needs. Thus, one frosty morning waiting for his mum to answer front door, he then decided to lead me to the back-door, unfortunately the slanting concrete path was iced over, I put my arm out to break my fall, but sustained a strong shock to my cervical vertebra, which ruptured the eighteen months of healing, so the injury inflicted by J/D at Vajrakula, was back to square one. So for now I was semi incapacitated, and was obliged to take time out from the Chapter, due to a mixture of acute and chronic pain. After about two or three months, I was given an ultimatum to return to the Chapter within about a week, or to cease being a member of the Chapter. Instead of a group decision, it may have helped more if some had contacted me individually and realised how I really was.

***

Trauma

Anyhow feeling abandoned and let down, I accepted an offer of minding a cottage for a week near Eastbourne, and use of an unfamiliar bicycle. Not helped by my recurred injury, the handlebars suddenly swung backwards, I came off the bicycle on a main road. I lost a tooth, had long term damage to my right hand, later involving an operation. Meanwhile in the ambulance I felt traumatised but vaguely ok, but then at the hospital I realised my left arm had swollen to about twice its normal size. And the x-ray revealed the elbow was fully broken in three places. I was in a pair of shorts and had a top on, and tried to go and make a phone call, but was obliged to stay on the stretcher/bed.

Later they informed me in three days they would put a metal plate in my arm and that I may regain about 75 per cent of arm mobility. About seven hours later with my arm in an open cast and sling. Needing a cup of tea, I talked with the team and thanked them very much for their dedication and kindness and added that I was going to return to the cottage about ten miles away, and next day take a coach back to Norwich, and eventually to the hospital there. Unconventional as it was, they decided I had the right to do that, and shortly supplied me with medical notes and a copy of x-rays. Eventually back at the cottage I somehow made a cup of tea and had peace and silence, though I noticed my body was trembling and I was still traumatised.

***

Medical Brilliance

The next day on coach to Norwich, I realised it was end of term, and as a yoga tutor for the Adult Education Department, I became aware that there were various yoga classes I needed to complete (just teaching verbally due to arm injury), and then to return the registers. When I eventually presented at the Norwich and Norfolk Hospital, they quite rightly told me off, for the delay. They then went on to do a brilliant job on me. Instead of a metal plate, they used a 'figure of eight'method, by which they secured all the broken bits in place with a piece of wire. Then about a month later, they agreed with me that the wire was too tight and needed to come out, thus after about eighteen months my left arm was fully healed and with almost 100 per cent movement. Thank-You international medical team very much!!!

***

Check-Mate

At least for time being, above events spelled an end to teaching yoga classes, and I stopped doing life modelling. Even so in due course I was teaching meditation and some dharma classes at the Buddhist Centre. Elsewhere my generic adult education teaching certificate, allowed me to take on a position to teach chess at an adult education class at Downham Market, known as 'Chelsea by the Sea'. The class consisted of about a dozen astute and elderly ladies. I had a Renault 19 GTX with a sliding roof, which I had bought for Three hundred pounds. My route took me past Lord Nelson's childhood home, and invariably I would blow him a kiss as I drove past. As a boy my father had taught me to play chess, though I had to do some revision at the public library, and re-learn the 'en-passe' move. The ladies were more challenging than Nelson, and they did eventually beat me, though by then they had accepted me as the class moderator, even though I am only a basic player, sometimes I was required to play a number of games on the go, which was like trying to have three conversations going one after the other. Unlike chess life is not black and white and has many colours.

***

HMS Prison

Was a somewhat more challenging set of conversations. Over a period of time I had been asked by Sarvananda two or three times, if I would like to take over from him as part-time Buddhist Chaplain at Norwich Prison thus eventually I succumbed. In the discussions I was sort of reticent, but I also mooted the idea that if I was going to engage with the slightly daunting world of Prisons, then I would also be interested in taking on his other role as 'schools officer' which was becoming vacant, since in past I had already done a few school visits with him, and had found the children, both at the Buddhist Centre and in schools, to be bright, friendly and straight-forwards to deal with, and I also got on fine with the teachers. In some ways I may have benefited from my year as a school caretaker at Parnell High School, and a period working at Selwyn College in New Zealand. Later when Sarvananda was showing me around the prison, I was following him down some stairs, when in a stair-well he looked back to see my head stuck between two bars, and asked what I was doing? To which I retorted 'trying to escape', not surprisingly he looked concerned.

***

Prison Notes

I seem to recall I had to sign something akin to 'the official secrets act' So I shan't be too specific, the big-hearted Rev Judith over-seeing the multi faith team was friendly and helpful as were the admin team, by and large the inmates seemed respectful, in what is not an easy situation. The prison officers mostly did their best in quite trying circumstances. As well as regular meditation teaching, usually followed by a large flask of tea and biscuits. Occasionally I would be requested by Rev Judith, to attend to difficult individual situations, such as a person involved in a mishap or accident involving several deaths. He was highly disturbed, though slowly I got him to sit down, and then to make eye contact, I asked him if he would like me to do a Buddhist mantra associated with purification, which he appreciated and later thanked me. On another occasion I was asked to see a person in the sex-offenders wing, in response to how he led the conversation, I felt obliged to stress that actions have consequences and regardless of his own feelings one has to draw a clear line, and respect the rights of others not to be interfered with or taken advantage of. On another occasion I had an encounter with an impressive; strong and domineering character, he insisted on telling me all sorts of things he had done. Generally in the prison one had to be constantly aware of what was going on around one, and to be alive to each situation, and to listen carefully and be mindful of one's own speech.

***

As well as being closely vetted before I was accepted for the above position, I also had to drive my unreliable car all the way to a Forest Hermitage near Sherbourne in Warwickshire, to meet Ven Ajahn Khemadhammo OBE, who had started 'Angulimala' the organisation which started making Buddhist Chaplains available in UK Prisons. Anyhow we had a relaxed and friendly, conversation, and if I remember correctly, when I mentioned a particular incident, and how at that time I had in a small way, been working on a TV series 'Special Branch', he mentioned how long ago, as an actor he had worked on the same series. Of course we covered lots of other stuff, and he was happy for me to accept the role. I would also add that looking at issue Number 5 of the Forest Hermitage Newsletter / 2003. He mentioned how as a Buddhist monks or bhikkhus are strictly forbidden from any direct physical contact with a woman. And how both a friend (Lord Avebury) and then himself contacted the Palace and the official they spoke with turned out to be wonderfully understanding, and very courteously said that he would see to it that Her Majesty was briefed not to try to shake hands, and they went on to be very helpful in other ways. Here I am reminded that when I was on a retreat with the Burmese Buddhist Teacher Sri Goenka-ji, one of the guiding principles for the intense ten day retreat, was not only 'not to give offence' but also 'not to take offence', and one doesn't have to blow things out of proportion, or make mountains out of mole hills, though one may at an appropriate time, question and resolve things in a friendly and civil way. Earlier in the article Ven Ajahn Khemadhammo states 'I've nearly always found that if you're confident and take the trouble to speak up for yourself and explain, people will respect your position, and do their best to accommodate you whether they agree with you or not'.

***

Prison Escape

After about six months, by which time I had encountered various situations, and had my own keys to move through different parts the prison, I was informed there was now a two-night residential course for training chaplains and that I would be the first Buddhist Chaplain to attend. I don't recall the location perhaps eighty miles from Norwich, in an old stately home with its own boathouse and a small gym. In short, I appreciated the grounds, used the gym, meditated in my room and sat through and engaged with the course, which was friendly and not complicated, and probably have a certificate of some sort, to show I was there. At some point, I attended an event of some sort at HMP Waylands Prison and Rev Judith had offered me extra work in other Prisons, and with regards HMP Norwich, asked if I would like to start doing Yoga Classes there. I felt I had to acknowledge the cervical vertebra and arm injury, made me feel reticent about taking on Yoga Classes at that stage, much as I would have liked to. Also, an experience on the M25 when my car cut out, on my way to mind Court Lodge a family property for Subhuti, had forewarned me that I couldn't rely on car to fulfil regular schedules further a-field, whereas in Norwich I could always use my bicycle. After I had completed about a year, in a written notice I thanked Rev Judith and others for their kindness and helpfulness, and told her I had checked with Sarvananda, (previous Buddhist chaplain), and had been given the name of someone whom I was sure would make a very good new Buddhist chaplain. In our talks about replacement, I explained there were a couple of small 'glitches', but that she and the admin should overlook that and meet him, and that I felt sure she would quickly find Viryashalin an excellent asset to her multi faith team, and in the event, it turned out to be helpful for him and her and worked out well.

***

Back to School

Alongside the above, my first year 'doing' schools seemed almost always to be relaxed, friendly, appreciative, and worthwhile, the children from six- to sixteen-year-olds and the teachers, generally seemed to be a delight to work with, and on various occasions I was invited back. On one occasion a school forewarned me to expect some difficult and challenging behaviour, but in practice even they turned out to be no trouble. My self perhaps being a bit of a simpleton, I had come to feel, that whether dealing with the elderly at a chess class, inmates within a prison, participants in a yoga studio, or a class of school children, 1/ I needed to arrive prepared and in good time. 2/ As well as being aware of my own state, I needed to take stock and be fully aware of the participants in as far as I could, and 3/ whatever the class content, I needed to be prepared to modify it to meet the needs of each situation. Generally with school classes, I would introduce myself, and why I was there, along with a few words about the small shrine and my kesa (abbreviated 'robe').

Thereafter I would give a concise version of the life of the Buddha, along with question and answers. Then I would explain that the next section was a brief introduction to mediation practice. Importantly, after I had explained the basics of the mediation practice, including about posture. I would then invite them all to stand up and lead them through a few minutes of exercise to wake them up, clear their heads and just enliven and rejuvenate their energies, this always seemed to be enjoyed, often with lots of laughter. Then we would establish a good posture, whether cross-legged, kneeling or sitting in a chair, then having allowed time to settle down, the mediation would either be centred on developing calm; clarity and concentration through the mindfulness of breathing, or cultivating positive emotions towards oneself and all forms of life.

Usually, some element of both practices would be included, followed, by questions and answers. A lasting memory was a primary or middle school on the Norfolk coast, when after a class the teacher asked if I had time, as there was some one she wanted to introduce me to, then took me to a secluded part of the grounds, where by a small compound she called a name, then out of his/her accommodation, a floppy long eared rabbit or hare, much larger than normal came down the walkway, and fully engaged my attention by just looking at me with large and beautiful eyes. Anyhow I continued with schools for another year or so, and in due course it felt time to hand on. There were changes at Norwich Buddhist Centre, and when I handed on a new team of two were ready to take on the school's role, I felt pleased with the work I had done, and happy to hand that responsibility to others.

***

Maurice and Friendship

While at Padmaloka on a retreat for about a week, I encountered Maurice in my dormitory, he was shimmering and bright, apparently, he could read invisible forces and told me I had a vivid blue aura. Much as I liked him, I later excused myself, as I had to move to a dormitory with less central heating. That may have been the retreat where he became a Mitra i.e. having a more specific friendship, with The Friends of the Western Order. Later the F.W.B.O became The Triratna Community. Tri = Three/ Ratna = Jewels/ 'Buddha, Dharma and Sangha'. I think it was on that retreat that I painted Maurice a small watercolour of a mythical Wind-Horse carrying the Three Jewels on his back and galloping across the Universe. Later Maurice told me he lived in a large thatched barn opposite what was his family home, where he was born in an air raid shelter during a raid in 1941, situated about four miles from Lesingham House (Padmaloka).

***

Maurice is very discrete, and it is certainly not his idea, for me to be writing about him. When we met Maurice was about fifty-two and myself about forty-four. He also mentioned he was quite well off; this was before a subsequent UK financial crash. My internal response was, 'well I hope you may enjoy it, and I am not going to interfere in your life, partly as I have my own complications to deal with. Some weeks or months later, Maurice turned up at my flat with some flowers or fruit and saying he had heard I was unwell, and I assured him I wasn't too bad. Consequently I arranged to pay him a visit; he already knew that I was an anagarika practicing chastity or brahmacharya. At Maurice's place I was sensitive to the atmosphere, and it soon became clear to me that Maurice actually needed an affectionate and practical friend, who could respond to some of his needs, and not let him down. I was also aware Maurice already had many good friends both within 'Triratna' and in the wider world.

It was clear Maurice needed his own space just as I needed mine, though as our friendship developed, I would spend one or two nights a week at the barn. On the first night I slept there, I told Maurice two or three horses had come to me in the night and been friendly towards me. Thus I learned the kitchen below had been a stable where his much-loved horses had lived, Ptolemy, Mulberry and others. From about age five, horses especially, were the love of his life, as well as a few human companions along the way, though his family did not much approve of his having male friends.

***

As well as my helping in practical ways, my visits were often co-ordinated, so that I could walk out with Maurice when he was exercising horses for his friends (June and John). Also at other times Maurice would invite me to go with him, when he was judging at Horse Shows, some of which were a bit up market and required me to dress up a bit; of course Maurice was always turned out properly, to suit the occasion. As time went on, at some point Maurice told me he would like to be ordained, so I made clear to him that 'The F.W.B.O/ Triratna' is not always perfect, and also that Bhante for all his accomplishments has never claimed to be 'perfect', and that in reality most people and organisations have short-comings and failings, or areas where they have made mistakes or get things wrong. So I emphasised one must not expect too much, either from preceptors or chapters or communities. In short I made clear if he wanted to be ordained, it is an individual affair and he shouldn't over idealise others and should have his eyes open. Anyhow on reflection he was clear that he wanted to be ordained. Thus I focussed on a few possible kindred spirits, and after a while found Ashvajit was open to possibly being his private preceptor, thus in due course Maurice was ordained at Padmaloka, and became Danashura (generous and courageous).

***

Danashura first set eyes on Bhante while riding past Lesingham-House which had become Padmaloka, though formerly was the home of Danashura's altruistic great grandfather Richard-Wright, who one summer had the teenage artist Edward Seago, (later a successful Norfolk artist), come to stay at Lesingham House for a whole summer while he recuperated from an illness. Subsequently Danashura had various meetings with Bhante at Padmaloka, Bhante was interested in Danashura and the history of Lesingham House, the meetings often ended with a warm hug.

Danashura has loved horses since a small boy (especially Ptolemy and Mulberry). He is more akin to a horse whisperer than a horse person. In fact he went on to have a conscientious and mainly voluntary role in the horse-world. For many years he was involved with The South Norfolk Pony Club and was their President for about twenty-five years. Also for about sixteen years he gave a lot of time and energy in facilitating 'Riding for disabled children'. Danashura attended and suffered at the King Edward the Sixth Grammar School, and subsequently obtained a degree from Norwich Art-School, where he enjoyed a happier period.

Then after his father's accident, he was obliged to support his mother and run the families general store and gas-supplying out-let in Claxton. Thus he became a Corgi-Gas engineer, and supplied gas cylinders as well as much kindness to many needy folk through-out Norfolk, I am also aware one of his customers was the Nun; Art Lover and 'T.V. Art Critic' Wendy Becket, who had a solitary caravan, in the grounds of a convent. After his rounds, he then needed to try and meet the needs of his elderly, ailing and sometimes difficult mother, and deal with ongoing business complexities and technology changes.

***

In due course Danashura (to be) was asked to supply Calor Gas to Padmaloka, where he was known to Subhuti and others as 'The Gasman'. Danashura also had a connection with a different 'Corgi world'. Per chance at some sort of equestrian event, he was handed the somewhat daunting responsibility of adjudicating the late Prince Philip, in his (horse) carriage driving skills. On other occasions, through his skills as a horse-show rider (dressage to music/haut-ecole), and as an experienced horse-judge, there was one occasion when he had tea with the late Queen's Mother at a Peterborough Horse Show, and on a second occasion he had lunch with her at Birkhall (Scotland). In other years there had been working visits by Princess Anne, in relation to his work with 'Riding-for-Disabled-Children' or his work as President of the South Norfolk Pony-Club.

Also further afield he once had tea with Princess-Grace (of Monaco), the connection was one Henri Palacci, who lived next door to Princess Grace at Chateau-Perigore. Back in the UK this chap had a collection of pure-bred Arab horses. Danashura (later to be) then aged about 33, was required to select five horses to be presented at The Paris International Horse-Show (1974ish), one of these Danashura trained, then subsequently in Paris he presented three horses 'in hand', and two 'under saddle'. There is a beautiful photograph (which appeared in the Paris Evening Paper) of Danashura seated on 'a winning horse' with the owner standing alongside, Danashura looks as if he is in spontaneous meditative state, with a subtle 'Mona Lisa' smile.

***

As a child Danashura attended dancing classes, and has natural rhythm and a wide knowledge of classical music, and often danced with his close friends first Norman (who had been a bursar at a

Cambridge college), and then after Norman died, some years later with his good friend Harry whom he first met working at a hospital, and had kindly come to his aid, when he needed help. I would just add another love of his life, was the family home help Merle, who from birth looked after him, and nurtured him in various ways, and did most of the home cooking. His father was an engineer and endlessly working running the garage and store, while his mother was once leader of the Girl Guides, and often doing all sorts of voluntary social work. Danashura has a lively sister Daphne who was a company secretary and a musician, and a rather charming brother Graham now deceased, who had been an officer in the royal horse artillery, they were both about several years older than him. About fifteen years ago Danashura had major bowel-surgery, after which his good friend and dedicated surgeon, advised him to get back on his horse, thus Danashura has enjoyed another decade of riding, simultaneously helping out a friend, who needed her horses exercised and also giving support and friendship to her now deceased husband John, who was also a good friend to Danashura. After that long and complex operation, I took whatever food or home-made soup was required to the hospital, each of those dark and cold November nights. Then later back at the barn, I improvised a foam cushion with the centre cut out, so Danashura could sit more comfortably and gradually regained health, and confidence.

***

Sometimes at meetings Bhante would say to Danashura 'I can't see you very well, but I recognize your voice', in fact Danashura does have a fine voice, and prior to covid19, he was part of a choir, which gave expression to his voice and positive emotions, and he regularly enjoyed lots of bright and multifaceted songs. Up until covid19, for many years Danashura was very active in keeping the Surlingham Meditation Group not just going, but also alive and well. Also, for a number of years I used to very much enjoy accompanying Danashura by foot while he exercised various horses. At a steady pace I could just about keep up with him, these days we both go by foot, and I invariably benefit from his wide botanical knowledge. It was Danashura who taught me 'Why did the bullrush? Because he saw the cowslip'! Another of Danashura's little jokes is: "Have you read 'Fifty-Years in the Saddle' (by Major Bumsore) 'Horse-Shoe-Press'. Anyhow after seventy-three years in the saddle, Danashura has gracefully concluded horse-riding, though he may still occasionally help with horses, from a dismounted position.

Currently we continue to attend Danashura's village art-class, (which perhaps helped me, per chance to win the 2022 N.B.C Art 'Competition', and thereby I received a beautiful 'singing bowl'; and as stated, they used the artwork for promotional purposes). As well as painting fine watercolours, and enjoying singing, reading and walking, Danashura continues regularly to ride on his meditation-cushion, and to engage with the Lotus-Born Padmasambhava, who communicates the Dharma to queens, kings and all beings. Thank You Danashura!!! For completion I shall just add, until a few years ago I was companion to Danashura on various excursions, such as to Monet's beautiful Garden near Paris, and elsewhere to some fascinating and ancient parts of Germany, and to Prague, these were often by coach. Though the Norway trip, where we visited Grieg's house, was by ship, while the Switzerland trip was by plane where among other things, we scaled The North Face of Mont Eiger (with the help of a Cog-Railway-System), at which point, I did 'Tadasana' (Mountain pose), right on the edge of oblivion. Also, fascinating and beautiful was going into the extensive Ice-Tunnels, I was wearing long shorts, with shoes and a warm jacket, but still I was younger then, and seemed to amuse a few people. To conclude, I was fortunate to be companion to Danashura on a very enjoyable and interesting Saga Mediterranean Cruise, which I briefly chronicled, and you are invited to make a cup of tea, relax and come join us, at least in imagination, as I shall include the outline here:

***

Mediterranean Voyage

Foreword:

I shall be away on a sojourn/voyage April 19th to May 3rd, 2006. Should anyone need to contact me during that period, you may send your thoughts via telepathy or via my email address, as the ships library includes access to computers. I shall try to be receptive. Though should we happen to cross Mediterranean equivalent, of the 'Bermuda Triangle', or any other such event, then further communication may be deferred to another life heart/mind…

My good friend Maurice (who later became Danashura) whose 'companion' I shall be, is unassuming and likes to lead a simple life – including getting to bed my 9.30pm- and thus has opted for an available cabin on the bridge deck, mainly as it should be quiet. Later per chance, I noticed the cabin came not just with room service, but also as the literature puts it "with the benefits from a butler service".

After my mum's death in February, I brought several of her books back to my flat and created a mini 'memorial library'. I recall a moment when I was about seven, my mother told me 'That I should count my blessings' and that one day 'my ship would come in'. Currently I am reading her copy of P.G.Wodehouse's 'Very good Jeeves!' and thus shall be interested to have the chance to observe a butler in action. Other authors and titles yet to be enjoyed include: C.P.Snow's 'Last Things'; Shakespeare's sonnets, Sir Arthur Conan Doyle's 'Sherlock Holms', Graham Greene; and Agatha Christie, as well as some Yoga books and the Observer's 'Book of Wild Flowers', one of many subjects Maurice is well versed in.

My main objectives on this sojourn are: To abide in mindfulness, kindness and awareness, which includes having to work/play with whatever happens. For Maurice to have a good and rejuvenating two weeks. For us both to arrive back safely and not too exhausted.

It occurs to me; it may be a bit of an anti-climax arriving back at my council estate. So, I was thinking if anyone would like to volunteer (just for a week or so), to be a part-time butler, to help facilitate my transition, then perhaps we could come to some sort of arrangement.

I hope to interact with events, through eyes of both: 'pilgrim' and as a Buddhist. May 'Bodhichitta' arise even 'quicker' than sea-levels and may we all be well, and continue to serve the universe with kindness.

A Saga Mediterranean Cruise: 19th April to 3rd of May 2006. Visiting: Cyprus; Egypt; Lebanon; Syria; Turkey; Greece and Crete.

Tues 18th April: National Express coach was an hour late. A highlight of that leg of journey was meeting and talking with Ramin (and his 8year old son), from Iran, and very much a 'peace-nic' and to whom I gave a copy of the Metta Sutta and details of FWBO. Later at Gatwick, Maurice was early to bed, I unwound in foyer of Renaissance Hotel, perusing a newspaper, and was interested to read and see a photo of one of the world's newest and largest cruise ships 'The Freedom of the Seas'. The aforesaid ship has 18 decks and carries 4370 passengers. Fortunately, the ship we later embarked at Cyprus, 'The Spirit of Adventure' was an elegant fifties style (recently refurbished) modest cruiser with approx. 7 decks and carries about 370 passengers. Putting down the paper, I then reflected on the forthcoming voyage.

Weds 19th: 4am rise went well. We noticed two order members (Gambhiravajra and Shantivarman) in Gatwick airport and later on the plane. Good flight despite a slightly bumpy landing, oddly the flight to Cyprus was less onerous than the Norwich to Gatwick coach. Particularly appreciated was seeing the snow-covered Italian Alps 'Dolomites'. A lady told us about a female mountaineer, who along with several others was blown off the side of K2 Mountain. Later we had whirlwind coach tour of parts of Cyprus with an enthusiastic leader; the overview was quite varied and included a stop to see 'Aphrodite's Rock'. Then eventually we embarked the ship and had a full lifeboat drill, before afternoon tea.

Thurs 20th: Woken by 'butler' (Noel) with tea. Peeped through blinds and was looking a bit cloudy outside. After quiet chanting and meditation with Maurice, we then enjoyed a secluded veranda breakfast, looking out over an unusually blue sea. At 9.45am with Maurice we attended a well delivered talk 'Essential background to today's Middle East in 45minites', given by former British ambassador Sir Michael Burton, who along with his wife Henrietta, was serious and easy to talk with. Then after a leg-stretch around some of the decks and a spot of table tennis with Maurice, we then returned for a further talk given by Dr Ann Birchall, on Ancient Egypt. Followed by alfresco lunch and resting, later in afternoon a refreshing plunge in the open-air swim-pool. We skipped early evening cocktails with the amiable Captain Alistair Mclundie, though subsequently I booked for us to do a bridge tour later. At 7.30pm we dressed 'formally', as on a few other occasions (i.e., jacket and tie) and had a friendly dinner with a couple of other voyagers, inadvertently brought to our table.

Fri 21st: Beyond normal engine and air conditioning noise, there was also erratic and loud creaking, so Maurice and I had to 'adjust' to not having much proper sleep. It was overcast as we slipped into the port of Alexandria, and after a quick cup of tea, I had to be ready to disembark and board a 7am coach, for a twelve-hour excursion to Cairo. Maurice was going to be visiting nearby Alexandria. On the desert road to Cairo, I listened to an enthusiastic guide explain how 85 per cent of Egyptians are relaxed Sunnis and the other 15 per cent are Coptic Christians who believe Christ was entirely divine. The fellow beside me wanted to be with his wife, so I relinquished my window seat, only to find my new aisle seat was next to Bill, an 86-year-old Scottish ex-naval navigation officer. As it turned out we had some good exchanges, and he thanked me for a time we both enjoyed. We had an armed police escort both at 'bow' and 'stern' of the coaches, as well as an armed plain clothed officer on board. (Later that day about twenty people died and many were injured, in three bomb blasts about a hundred miles 'East of Cairo). Cairo was hot and hazy.

The National Archaeological Museum was busy due to a public holiday. Yet, despite that, for me a highlight was standing alone in front of Tutankhamen's blue and gold Mask. Sadly, the museum seemed a bit dilapidated, perhaps due to a lack of funding. After lunch, we then finally arrived at The Pyramids. Soon I went off on my own and should have paid more attention to Maurice's remark about avoiding camels. In the event I was gullible, when by charming incremental steps I was induced to sit on a camel (first the camel rider, asked me to take photo of him, then added he would take a photo of me on his camel), then he immediately commanded his camel to rise, and a cohort on a camel appeared and whisked me away, then out of sight, in some sort of dark area/alley, and in the shadow of a pyramid.

He kept look-out, I was in long shorts and a shirt, and he told me not to scream like a girl, though I hadn't made a sound. It happened I hadn't managed to access cash that day. I felt close to being 'mugged'. My camera was taken, and the film removed, and he implied with his hand movement that he had a weapon. Just then about a hundred yards away, I saw a couple wander past a gap. So, I swung my legs and slipped to the ground. He returned the empty camera, and offered his hand, so I reciprocated, and they let me go. The look-out was cross; when he learned I had not left any money with his cohorts'. As I made my escape, I recalled, coach passenger Bill had said to me: "Soft replies, may turn away wrath". And I was glad to have survived. Also, earlier that day a lone uniformed policeman gently enticed me to sit on a pyramid while he took a photo, and fortunately I was able to appease him with half a packet of Murray Mints, after explaining bank had been closed.

Sat 22nd: Tour of Port Said: military museum, cemetery, Coptic Church (short meditation). Also appreciated the lovely ceiling, then later took chance to give to a man, as well as to a boy with a horse and buggy, and enjoyed walking with Maurice, who had survived Alexandria, also along the way photographed canal buildings and a Mosque. Later we sat on deck, and watched as the ship pulled away from Egypt, while I folded a copy of the Metta Sutra (of loving kindness), into the form of a Peace Plane, which I gently floated down to the port area, and imagined love, compassion, joy and peace, arising through-out Egypt and beyond. The weather was muggy and overcast. We then had tea and were impressed by the shipping lane in the distance; with hazy outline of about eighteen large ships. That evening we had a next port talk re Beirut and Lebanon, and later after a shower, I relaxed in the ship's rather beautiful, spacious and peaceful library.

Sun 23rd: Intermittent sleep thus a bit tired. Enjoyed table tennis with Maurice and later a plunge in pool before lunch. Our tour into Beirut was overseen by Sir Michael Burton (currently on pc opposite me) and his wife, as well as a softly spoken local girl, who was our main guide. In the morning coming into Beirut, I happened to photo a ship named 'Angel Protector'. We were first taken about fifteen miles left along coast to Byblos (possible origin of the bible's name) to an ancient and charming area and the old town and origin of Beirut. With hill fort, quaint harbour, and beautiful view of bay and residential Beirut in the high hills. After a dreamy and delightful time, we returned past the main harbour to the business area of Beirut, where we saw a large area of Roman ruins and visited a church.

Also, we learned that the late Prime Minister 'Harare' had laboured in Israel, then became a schoolteacher in Saudi Arabia before going into construction and became one of the world's richest men. He was philanthropic and did everything to reconstruct Beirut, but (despite all high-tech efforts) was assassinated with a large bomb by extremists about a year ago. Sadly, we saw the remaining carnage. He was almost an Islamic 'Bill Clinton' or 'Ambedkar' (of sorts) to his people. Per chance, visiting his place of burial was both impressive and moving, as also is the beautiful (Sunni) blue turquoise mosque that is a memorial to his life and endeavours. As our Lebanese guide put it: they have everything, yet without peace they have nothing. I think the poet Kahlil Gibran was from Beirut. As elsewhere here too I symbolically launched a copy of the Metta Sutta in form of a 'Peace Plane' which glided towards each port at time of leaving.

Mon 24th: At 6am woke reasonably well so went for a run around decks to warm up, and then for a much-enjoyed swim in pool below decks which was warmer than outdoor pool. We were then processed onto coach, which took us about 27k inland to 'Krak des Chevaliers' (Castle of the Knights), which Maurice was particularly keen to see, and he knew all about its history. Krak des Chevaliers was acquired and extensively rebuilt by the Knights Hospitaller in 1144ce and considered virtually impregnable; it was the largest Crusader Castle in the Middle East.

Syria seems to be very green and lush (and it also just happened to be overcast and raining. Our tour guide was a quietly spoken Syrian; he started by giving us some fine Syrian biscuits and water. We rose high up into the hills through winding roads to a plateau, with a large impressive medieval castle about 11th century. We plumbed its depths and rose to its height via spiral stairs of various types as well as tunnels and arches. At one stage the castle was lost in clouds, as if the gods were defending it from possible attack, so I declared our peaceful purpose. Later enjoyed table tennis with Maurice, and then enjoyed watching the tugs pull the ship away from the harbour and launched another 'Peace Initiative'. Later we attended a classical concert: Vivaldi, Brahms, and Mozart, which was appreciated. The subsequent half of voyage includes three ports in Turkey, and then Rhodes, Delos, Mykonos, Crete and Piraeus for direct coach to Athens's airport.

Tue 25th: At 6am I enjoyed a run around the decks and swim, before meditation and breakfast with Maurice. Later we were taken 25k to a smaller but charming castle, with a most peaceful atmosphere; there were high walls and eight towers with access via precarious steps. This 'old' complex included a pretty Mosque with a lovely courtyard, including a 1000-year-old olive tree, as well as a defunct Turkish Baths and 'Mall'. Also, we later enjoyed an orange grove with lovely blossom and rich scents. Back on ship 'The Spirit of Adventure', after tea, we later enjoyed table tennis, which Maurice played well. Subsequently there was a talk by Dr Andrew Goody (from British Museum), on antiques, art and restoration.

Wed 26th: Alanya is a beautiful place, a sort of 'Turkish Riviera'; at 1pm our tour bus took us way up to a large sprawling hilltop fort, which had a good atmosphere and spectacular views of bays to either side. After taking pictures, we descended into the more modern town area, where Maurice kindly bought me some sunglasses, as well as a cashmere shawl for Karunachitta, then we walked back to the ship, in what was an easy and un-hassled atmosphere. After some tea we borrowed a bicycle, then ran and cycled to a nearby beach, where I was able to spend twenty minutes swimming out to sea and back.

Thur 27th: Enticed Maurice to come for a stretch and swim, followed by meditation and breakfast. Then at 11am we attended a talk by Dr Ann Birchall on Seven Wonders of the World. Subsequently at 2.30pm we had a tour of the bridge and were fortunate to have the captain: Alistair McIundie. He values the old, as well as the new ways. Many of the bridge functions have fallback and manual systems, I did mention they could borrow my compass if need be. He was very friendly, with a straightforward manner and a mild Scottish accent. If anyone falls overboard, they do a 'Williamson Turn' and hope to reach the person within five minutes. NB Starboard on the right is denoted by green, while Portside in the left is denoted by red.

Then after a short spell in the sun, at 3.45pm there was Sir Michael Burton's multifaceted talk and presentation on the crusades. Then at 6.30pm Maurice and myself enjoyed meeting up with Gambhiravajra and Shantivarman, first we went to their cabin 417 which was light and bright, with old-fashioned portholes and very quiet. Back at cabin 11 we enjoyed a relaxed cup of tea, before making our way to the main restaurant, where we enjoyed a pleasant meal together. It seems they were both geography students at the University of London. There is more to Geography than maps and dry data. Now when I reflect on my experience of an environment, I am aware it may be sub-divided into: Elemental> Social> Economic and Political factors. Later that evening in the Library I logged into one of the personal computers available, to type in material, then enjoyed perusing some of the tangible books.

Fri 28th: 8am Tender (ship to shore boat) to the 'Turquoise Coast' and Bodrum Castle, with lots of old pots, fine ancient glassware and lovely songbirds. Lunch and table-tennis with Maurice, then while he had a head and shoulders massage, I went to lower pool and enjoyed a swim and sauna. Watched tender been winched out of water, and then a talk by Dr A Oddy: 'Unmasking forged Antiquities'. Later while enjoying table-tennis with Maurice, I came across a little Green-Finch under a chair (deceased), and so I stroked it and wished it well, and then one of the staff spotted it and probably gave it a sea burial. In the evening I had a walking meditation with some chanting on the upper, outside deck.

Sat 29th: At 7am we docked into Rhodes, alongside some very large liners. After meditation, at 8am we were taken by a sophisticated tour leader, for a spin around parts of Rhodes, before rising up into hills and a longer journey to 'Linnos', a pretty and traditional Greek Community, then from the Square/ Piazza we slowly walked up to the Acropolis area and wonderful views, also charming were the quaint little lanes, then on way down, we sat and meditated in a 'Byzantine Church'. Also, en-route back I was mesmerised by the skill of a good-looking Greek potter (apparently only nine are left on the island). Later after enjoying lunch with Maurice, we went for a cycle along the coast, and Maurice found the 'grandmasters residence', and then we returned into the old town.

Sun 30th: 8am to Delos by 'tender'. Which for unknown reasons reminded me a little of 'Waiheke' Island off Auckland NZ, where friends Purna and Malini live. Though the weather today at Delos was just ok, it gradually improved, but was too cold to hang about, so we wandered about at our own pace. Saw many enchanting sights including a temple to Apollo, as well as ancient dwellings, also scaled to highest point and had 360-degree panoramic views. I was the only passenger on the last tender back, my name was checked out on the ships P.A. system, but I had let them know that I was returning on the last boat. After lunch on ship the afternoon was spent in Mykonos. We were told about the islands rise from rags to riches in the sixties due to the influence of Onnassis family and others. We had a spin around the Island and visited a small Greek Orthodox Monastery, then later appreciated a wander back to ship via 'Little Venice'. In evening after swim, I had dinner with Maurice and Iris White (a friend).

Mon 1st May: 12.45 Crete tour: ancient civilisation, mountainous countryside. Overview of Island, lovely in parts, lots of high hills. From Heraklion to Kristos (about an hour). Lots of rain visited an unusual cemetery, also took photo of a donkey with an elderly man, both being driven by a rather strong-willed old lady, also saw some 14th cent church frescoes. We had been due to visit the 'Palace of Knossos, but this was closed due to the May 1st holiday. Later there was a ships staff 'variety'show.

Tues 2nd: Day at sea, 9.45 am talk 'Early Christianity' with slides by Sir Michael Burton. 11.15am 'Athens and the glory that was Greece' Dr Ann Birchall. Later she also gave commentary, after we sailed into the inner circle of an ancient massive earthquake 'Santorini' (also known as Thera). Had good views from halfway up the navigational ladder. Then had a relaxed lunch with Maurice, and later enjoyed a quick swim. At 3.30pm Sir Michael Burton presented a short talk about Iraq with Q&A. Later there was packing to be done in preparation for disembarkation tomorrow.

Wed 3rd: 6am swim and meditation. 8am vacate and breakfast. 9.30am disembarked and boarded a plush Mercedes Benz coach; later en-route passed a view of a fleeting, misty and mythical silhouette, of a distant Acropolis as we sped along motorway from Piraeus to Athens Airport departure lounge. Did walking and some stretching till eventual 1.45pm departure. Left a copy of 'The Metta Sutta' in the transit area. After some peculiar airline food, which was compensated for by a very good cup of tea, then took photos of snow-covered Alps.

It seemed we would miss our coach connection at Gatwick. Though on landing, after obtaining our luggage and whipping through customs, I gently rushed Maurice and myself, and made the coach by a whisker. Then five hours through lush UK spring countryside via main airports and then continued to the fine ancient city of Norwich, where I was in time to, the next day, vote Green in the local elections. Gratitude !!!

***

The nature of life and death:

I only have myself to blame for being born, but I couldn't have done it without my mother. Recently I noticed one of my fingers was on my bellybutton, tummy-button or umbilical cord knot. I was about to pull my finger out, but instead I let awareness go into my lost cord. Then I recalled there was a time when it was not obstructed by a knot. At that time, like a popular café, it was wide open for business, such as tea; toast; and buttered scones, endlessly passed down the chord into the sleeping me, then one melo-dramatic moment, my little pond of dreams was shattered, as I was pushed; spilled and plonked into the wondrous world of Edinburgh.

Traditionally the nature of death should only be reflected upon, based on first cultivating a happy, healthy and positive state. Any such reflections are not meant in any way to engender negative, morbid or unhappy states of mind. As the Buddhist teacher Tsongkhapa states: "This life we should know, as the tiny splash of a raindrop. A thing of beauty which disappears even as it comes into being, therefore set your goal, and make good use of each day and night to achieve it". The Buddhist path aims to cultivate Punya (good conscience), Samadhi (Meditation) and Prajna (Wisdom/Compassion), or Human goodness, Spiritual Beauty and Divine Truth. Please also first see and appreciate the Metta Sutta on Loving-Kindness, in the appendix at back.

***

Facing Death:

Speaking as a human being not far from entering the last quarter of one hundred years, I realise at some point, 'Ready or Not' I shall die. Death may occur in all sorts of ways, whether slow or sudden, one way or another that moment is approaching. Throughout my life, I have through the 'news', and in other ways, been exposed to and affected by knowledge or experience of: Accidents, Assaults, Catastrophes, Sickness and Deaths. This objective knowledge may gradually or suddenly become my own subjective experience. I may experience trauma, shock, disbelief ('if only'), and if I am lucky, come gradually to an element of acceptance, equanimity and or peace.

According to 'The Tibetan book of the Dead', and later simplified in the adapted version in The Penguin Classics book 'The Psychedelic Experience'. Various Signs of dying have been reported and recorded by Tibetan Lamas. Approximately these are: 1/ Intense bodily pressure (Earth sinking into water). 2/ Clammy coldness then feverish heat (Water sinking into fire). 3/ Having a sense of the psychophysical organism being blown into atoms (Fire sinking into air). 4/ Intense pressure in head and behind ears and eyes, (Rocket launching into space). 5/Tingling in extremities of body. 6/ Feeling of body melting as if a wave of dissolving wax. 7/ Nausea. 8/ Trembling or shaking, beginning in pelvic regions and spreading up torso. 'These physical experiences of whatever nature should be recognized as signs heralding transcendence. Avoid treating them as symptoms of illness, accept them, merge with them, in faith or joy just relax and let go…

Psychologically, three of the Seven Root Verses from the Tibetan Book of the Dead (Oxford University Press) state:

4/ O now when the Bardo (moment) of death upon me is dawning! Abandoning attraction and craving, and weakness for all [worldly things], May I be undistracted in the space of the bright enlightening Dharma/ teachings, may I [be able to] transfuse my self into the heavenly space of the unborn: When the hour has come to part with this body composed of flesh and blood; May I know the body to be impermanent and illusory.

5/ O now when the Bardo of Reality upon me is dawning, Abandoning all awe, fear, and terror of all [phenomena], May I recognize whatever appears as my own thought-forms, May I know them to be Apparitions in the Intermediate state, [It has been said] 'There arrives a time when the chief turning point is reached; Fear not the bands of the Peaceful and Wrathful, who are your own thought forms'.

6/ O now when the Bardo of [taking] rebirth upon me is dawning! One pointedly holding fast to a single wish, [May I be able to] continue in the course of good deeds through repeated efforts; May the womb-door be closed, and the revulsion recollected: The hour has come when energy and pure love are needed; [may I] cast of jealousy and meditate upon the Guru, the Father-Mother. (See appendix for complete list).

***

In a hospital or care-home situation, rigor-mortis or intense stiffness may occur, subsequently followed by cold storage, cremation or burial. While in a more natural setting after rigour-mortis and stiffness fades away, then in due course varying degrees of discolouration, blotation, infestation, disintegration and dust…

***

Philosophically: Death is a normal and natural occurrence.

D-E-A-T-H, for some may have connotations of: Divine-Enlightening,-Angelic-Transcendental-Holiness, or of reaping the results of having enjoyed a life of: Human goodness, Spiritual Beauty, Divine Truth… Or however we happen to relate to 'it'…

The Elements Is a poem which I wrote in 1993 on what was for me, a five-month retreat at Guhyaloka in Spain:

The Elements: (Earth; Water; Fire; Air; Space; …)
    Naked birth on revolving earth
      Offers no permanence
        Whatever our worth/

    Gushing, rushing, torrential rain
      Seven seas,
        Within our brain/

    Dancing flames fade away
      Clammy cold
        We cannot stay/

    Clad in snowdrops
      Shrouded in stars
        Heart heaves
        As breathe leaves/

    Sinking, twirling
      Swimming, swirling
        We vacate our space
          In the human race/

    Elements flown
      Mind blown
        Consciousness meets
          What it has sown/.

Bridge over Turbulent Waters

***

There are numerous teachings on the nature of life, death, the universe and beyond, such as Ram Dass's Book Be Here Now…

Many years ago, on a two-week retreat at Vajraloka Retreat Centre in North Wales, I learned these verses which from Tejananda. They are simple and, and comment on the nature of all phenomena…

"All these forms appearance emptiness, like a rainbow with its shining glow, in the reaches of appearance emptiness, just let go and go where no mind goes/

Every sound is sound and emptiness, like the sound of an echoes roll, in the reaches of sound and emptiness, just let go, and go where no mind goes. /

Every feeling is bliss and emptiness, way beyond what words can show, in the reaches of bliss and emptiness, just let go and go where no mind goes/

All awareness, awareness emptiness, way beyond what thoughts can know, in the reaches of awareness emptiness, just let go and go where no mind goes".

These verses are attributed to one of the teachers of Lama Shenpen Hookham, she is the author of a very readable and short book entitled 'there's more to dying than death' a Buddhist perspective.
(Windhorse Publications).

***

One thing we may learn by going on a retreat, is that we are not alone in wanting to understand our place in the universe, and to fathom the nature of our mind, heart, spirit or soul. Meditation may be an individual and shared practice which can help us 'Stop and Realize', or to actualise our human potential for spiritual and transcendental awakening. Traditionally Buddhist 'Samatha' Meditation starts with training in mindfulness of breathing to develop calm, clarity, and focus, and Loving Kindness Meditation to develop friendliness, warmth and positive emotions, towards oneself and all sentient beings, and then brings in 'Vipassana' Meditation for cultivating insight and appreciation of how things really are. For instance, all worldly phenomena are impermanent, unsatisfactory and insubstantial. This doesn't mean we have to be in depression, on the contrary, despite the fleeting nature of existence, we can learn to appreciate the beauty and wonder of life, and to have insight and appreciation of our true potential, with help of the Three Jewels: Buddha Dharma and Sangha.

***

NB About ten times a year, over the last thirty years (1993-2023), I have 'reported in', i.e., written in personal reports to 'Shabda', which is a confidential journal for Order Members. Some but not all, of content below, is short extracts of just a two or three of those reports:

Reflections on a recent two-month 'Tong Len' Retreat:

Here I briefly reflect upon being on a retreat with Vessantara and Vijayamala about a year ago: During which, they created a relaxing, harmonious and insightful retreat situation, with a variety of friendly participants Whether one calls it: Mahamudra, Dzogchen, or 'it', makes little difference to my 'beginners' level'. Focussing on less conceptual practice was time well spent Though I shall probably in daily life, return to a balance of what are referred to by Subhuti, as the imminent, imaginal and developmental modes, which I roughly equate with: 'Reality', 'Myth or Archetypal', and 'Historical' modes, or Dharmakaya, Sambhogakaya and Nirmanakaya. On the retreat I much appreciated regular meditation reviews with Vessantara.

We were situated: in an old hunting-lodge, except in this case the 'hunting' was aimed at discovering and entering the true nature of 'mind', or to glimpse with our heart/mind the 'perfection of wisdom/compassion'. This was an enquiry, that may have been well suited to Agatha-Christie, and who knows, 'she' may have been on the retreat, having re-become in a new life. Eventually I discovered the rambling and intriguing property had its own library, though I don't recall seeing any deceased bodies in there. Occasionally I would feel like I was on or in an old Edwardian Cruise-Liner, such as the Queen-Mary. My own cabin was single and (like most) en-suite. My meditation practice and understanding are pretty basic if that. Anyhow with regards a practice called 'Tong-Len'; giving and receiving or vice-versa, I like the theory, though I am not very good at it. One way it is taught, is to start by visualising a 'Refuge Tree' above our head. From a scale of 1-100, my visualisation ability is about 1-8; also, I am not particularly visual. Even so I can try to feel and imagine.

Thus, I imagine Nirmanakaya, Sambhogakaya and Dharmakaya (three increasingly refined states or images) above my head, a bit like historical saints, spiritual angel/bodhisattvas and pure reality above my head. So now being in complete submission to the three jewels or three refuges. I then do something a bit peculiar, as I then imagine all the stuff out there in the world, defilements, sins, bad behaviour or whatever; I imagine it as dark matter or smoke and draw it into my self as I breath in (just natural breath), and as I do so, by virtue of my submission to higher forces it is immediately turned into innate purity, which is then breathed back out to all of humanity, as moon beams of compassion, so ultimately we come to feel that the world and beyond has become a pure-land, and in reality at the deepest level we are all pure beings, in a pure land filled with pure beings, though we still have to deal with all of life's worldly difficulties, and it doesn't mean we have to become spiritual door-mats.

***

Environment

Gower is beautiful, and I loved the 'Vultures-Peak' high up on a rocky ridge, where I sang Milarepa verses, and gazed up into the blue sky, or looked down to the long and beautifully curved (Oxbridge) beach. At other times I enjoyed descending through Nicholaston Woods and walking back barefoot in the lapping water. While at other times high up, I appreciated encounters with groups of wild Welsh ponies. Opposite a small church there was a bench with a notice: "Please Remember Brinn and Alice Griffiths, 1880-1967". Elsewhere from nearby Notts-Hill, I could sit under an old tree, and look down to Three-Cliffs-Bay, where nearby one can encounter rock formations approximately 340 million years old, during which time I guess about a hundred billion people, and trillions of other forms of life have lived and loved and died. Perhaps we would all like to be remembered. But really the thing that's most important, is to remember, that we have a 'true nature' above and beyond our little selves, something which is wondrous and beautiful, which we can aspire towards, over one or many lives. I also enjoyed visiting elsewhere, some beautiful woods and nearby an ancient burial ground; and once inhabited caves. May all beings be fulfilled and find supreme liberation…

***

Gratitude

All human beings have faults; failings and shortcomings, and most have some accomplishments, in this respect, Ven Urgyen Bhante-Sangharakshita is no exception. By the time I came in contact with the F.W.B.O at Pundarika Centre (1974). What I needed was a 'High-Lama' combined with an English-Master, who was prepared to come down of his perch, and be a real human being, and Bhante was certainly that. In due course sitting in half- lotus; as our engaging Subhuti played the tapes, I was won over and mesmerised by Bhante's endless eloquence; wit and sonorous discourses. Once I came down the stairs, to find just Subhuti and Bhante alone, on introduction I was embarrassed; as I couldn't recall the name of the lecture just listened to, simultaneously I was surprised as Bhante's body sort of shimmered and I seemed to see within him a radiant youthful figure, even though Bhante then was about forty-eight and myself about twentyfour. Subsequently about five years later, a rather different me; ran up some stairs in a New Zealand community (Suvarnaketu) and to my surprise Bhante and Purna were there, on this occasion it was crystal clear, when a very beautiful figure/emanation projected out of Bhante and just stopped me in my tracks.

Then next day Purna said to me something to the effect of 'don't think I didn't see what happened'. Also in NZ I appreciated a meeting with Bhante in the Gipsy-Caravan, and on another occasion his looking at and consenting to a particular Buddhist practice, I had years previously come across at Swiss Cottage Library. While looking after Bhante at the community; I regret when called into the bathroom, that while I performed whatever task was needed, I wish I had been less shy and should have offered to wash his back, but one can't think of everything. I felt both bereft and a slight sense of freedom when Bhante and Ratnaketu went to India, I remember the stillness and silence making them tea at about 4am before journey to Auckland-Airport, I guess we are all constantly in transit…

Also Thank-You for various other meetings and the two spells of cooking for you at Madhyamaloka. I notice I still have a few much-appreciated hand-written cards from Bhante, including this one dated 18-3-81 which travelled from Padmaloka to N.Z. The picture-card is of L'Absinthe by Edgar Degas and in beautiful neat writing runs:

"Dear Patrick, Thanks for your letter, which was waiting for me when I returned from Crete a few days ago, (Slightly bronzed). Glad to hear you are more optimistic; and gradually turning to face the light. Tomorrow I head south for London, Purley and Brighton, just visiting the centres and meeting people. Weather at present is dull and rainy. Love, Sangharakshita"

***

Bhante's kindness and poetry have been just as important to me as have his lucid teachings, thus I wrote elsewhere: 'Dear Urgyen Bhante, I am sad and sorry at your departure, but also happy and joyful for you too. May your transition; awakening or whatever, be refreshing and fulfilling…

Many Were the Friends… by Sangharakshita

(First two of three verses).

Many were the friends who sought with eager hands to lay hold of me as I passed along the way; / But I have shaken them all off and come with lonely longing to the door of my friend. / Many were the flowers that blossomed around me in the garden where I strayed; / But I have sought out the White Rose while it was still bright with morning dew./ Many were the instruments I heard playing in the symphony of life; / But I have cared to listen only to the melancholy sweetness of Thy flute beneath the stars.

When the dawn wings like a great bird from the East, / In the cool of early morning, beside the pine trees, I wait for the…/ When the sun hangs poised like a red flamingo in the heavens, / In the quivering heat of noon, wrapped in the mauve-blue mist of the jacaranda, I wait for the… / When the pale moon breasts the sky like a silver swan on a blue lake, / In the lone garden of my dreams, beneath the wide-spreading branches of the tree of life, I wait for the… / While youth comes and goes, while manhood waxes and wanes as the moon, / In the midst of the worlds tumult, and in the deep silence of my heart, / Through life and through death, through the birth and dissolution of millions of universes, eternally I wait for the …..

***

The last meeting with Bhante

At an Anagarika event, I was posting a request, when Ashvajit was passing and took it, then minutes later, called me to say "Dharmika, Bhante will see you now". In the event I asked Bhante if there was anything I had or hadn't done, which he had any concerns about, and he said he wasn't aware of anything. Then I was aware just how serene Bhante was, and gently told him so. All too soon the short spell came to completion. In the last few days, I walked up to Oyster Hill, where I climbed up on to the 'triangulator' and chanted some mantras and reflected on the poet PB Shelleys words; "Peace peace, he is not dead; he doth not sleep; he has Awakened from the Dream of Life".

* * *

PS: There is an expression 'S/he who loves life, also loves death' … This is not morbid, it is natural, to come to terms, with both life and death. In this respect I would just add, Thank-You to Vidyadevi, for compiling, 'Urgyen Sangharakshita '108 ways Of Looking at death'.

About a month after Bhante died, I had an 'experience' within a dream, which to me felt like a visitation from Bhante, in which I was given a fulsome hug, which I enjoyed, and then he dissolved away. So far I have only occasionally dipped into said book, I notice the 108th way of looking at death, is a four-line Haiku…. Perhaps it's best to peruse the book before appreciating its last verse.

* * *

Instead I shall just approximately, quote William Blake: "He who clings to a joy, does the winged life destroy, but he who kisses the joy as it flies, lives in eternity's sunrise"…. More correctly it should read

"He who binds to himself a joy/ Doth the winged life destroy/ But he who kisses the joy as it flies/ Lives in Eternity's sun rise".

William Blake.

(Courtesy of 'Blakes Poems. Selected by David & Virginia Erdman.)

Appendices

1/ The Metta Sutta of Loving Kindness
2/ Hakuin's Song of Meditation
3/ The Bardo Thodol Root Verses
4/ Six Elements Poem
5/ The Heart Sutra
6/ Tsongkapa: This Life
7/ Tips on how to stop Smoking.

***

This Life

"This life we should know as the tiny splash of a raindrop, a thing of beauty which disappears even as it comes into being, therefore set your goal, and make use of each day and night to achieve it"…

Tsongkapa

***

The Metta Sutta of Loving Kindness.

Whoever seeks his welfare to improve
Desiring vision of the perfect peace,
He should live nobly, gentle in his speech,
Obliging, honest, humble in his deeds.

Living contented, satisfied and free
Because his choice is for simplicity:
Tranquil his sense, thoughtful and aware,
Mild and not covetous in need and deed.

So, he must refrain from any action
That gives the wiser reason to condemn:
May every being live a life secure
And may they always dwell in happiness.

May all the living beings that there are,
Those that are stationary and those that move,
The long, the great, the medium and the short:
All creatures that are weak or otherwise.

Beings visible and invisible,
Dwelling so near and those that dwell so far,
All that are born and those which wait for birth,
For always may they dwell in happiness.

There is no place where one may cheat another,
Nor hold another being in contempt:
Let none to wrath or anger ever yield,
Nor ever suffering wish to anyone.
As her only child, a mother protects,
If need be, at the cost of her own life,

So should we develop a boundless love,
To each and every being that exists.
Develop thus the mind in boundless love,
Tranquil and free from hate and enmity,

Projecting love to all and each that lives,
Extending it above, below, around.

Whenever one walks stands sits or lies:
Alert with zeal and mindfulness controlled;
He shall be known to all the wise and called
The one who has attained the highest state.

When virtue and clear vision are supreme,
And wrong and evil views brought to an end,
Attachment to the senses will have passed,
And rebirth in the womb is known no more.

***

Hakuin's Song of Meditation

Sentient beings are primarily all Buddhas, it is like water and ice, apart from water no ice can exist, outside sentient beings where do we find the Buddhas. Not knowing how near the truth is people seek it far away. What a pity, it is like him who in the midst of water cries so imploringly, it is like the son of a rich man who wandered away among the poor.

The reason why we transmigrate through the six worlds, is because we become lost in the darkness of ignorance, going astray further in the darkness, when are we able to get away from birth and death.

As regards the meditation practiced in the Mahayana, we have no words to praise it fully. The virtues of perfection such as charity, morality etc The invocation of the Buddhas name, confession and ascetic discipline and many other good deeds of merit, all these issue forth from the practice of mediation, even those who have practiced it just for one sitting, shall see all their evil karma wiped clean, and nowhere will they find the evil paths. But the pure land shall be near at hand. Let them to this Truth listen even for once, and surely, they will be blessed most infinitely. For such as reflecting within themselves, testify to the truth of self-nature, that self-nature is no nature.

They have really gone beyond the ken of sophistry, for them opens the gate of the oneness of course and effect, and straight runs the path of non-duality and non-trinity. Whether coming or going they remain for ever unmoved. Taking hold of the not thought which lies in thoughts, in every act of theirs they hear the voice of Truth.

How boundless the sky of Samadhi unfettered, how transparent the perfect moonlight of the four-fold wisdom, at that moment what do they lack as the truth eternally calm reveals itself to them. This very Earth is the lotus land of purity, and this Body the body of the Buddha...

The Root Verses of the Six Bardos

(These reflections should be preceded by a period of Metta Bhavana)

1/ O now, when the Bardo of Life upon me is dawning, abandoning idleness, there being no idleness in a devotee's life. Entering into the reality undistractedly, listening, reflecting, and meditating. Carrying on to the path knowledge of the true nature of appearances and of mind, may the Tri-kaya be realised. May there be no time or opportunity in which to idle it away.

2/ O now, when the Dream Bardo upon me is dawning, abandoning the inordinate corpse-like sleeping of the sleep of stupidity. May the consciousness undistractedly be kept in its natural state; grasping the true nature of dreams, may I train myself in the Clear light of Miraculous Transformation: Acting not like the brutes in slothfulness, may the blending of the practicing of the sleep state and actual waking experience be highly valued by me.

3/ O now, when the Dhyana Bardo upon me is dawning, abandoning the whole mass of distractions and illusions, may the mind be kept in the mood of endless undistracted Samadhi, may firmness both in the Visualising and perfected stage be obtained. At this time when meditating one-pointedly, with all other actions put aside, may I not fall under the power of mis-leading, stupefying passions.

4/ O now, when the Bardo of the moment of Death upon me is dawning, abandoning attraction, craving and weakness for all worldly things, may I be undistracted in the space of the bright enlivening Dharma (teachings).

May I be able to transfuse myself into the heavenly space of the unborn. When the hour has come to part with this body composed of flesh and blood, may I know the body to be impermanent and illusory.

5/ O now when the Bardo of Reality upon me is dawning, abandoning all awe, fear, and terror of all phenomena. May I recognize whatever appears, to be my own thought-forms. May I know I know them to be apparitions of the intermediate state. It has been said there arrives a time when the chief turning point is reached, fear not the bands of the peaceful and wrathful, who are your own thought forms.

6/ O now, when the Bardo of re-becoming upon me is dawning, one-pointedly holding fast to a single wish. May I be able to continue the course of good deeds through repeated efforts. May the womb door be closed and revulsion recollected. The hour has come when energy and pure love are needed, may I cast of jealousy and meditate upon the Guru, the Father-Mother.

7/ O procrastinating one, who thinks not of the coming of death, devoting yourself to the useless doings of this life, improvident are you in dissipating your great opportunity; mistaken indeed, will your purpose be now if you return (spiritually) empty-handed from this life: Since the Holy Dharma is known to be your true need, will you not devote yourself to the Holy Dharma, even now.

The Heart Sutra

The Bodhisattva of Compassion,
When he meditated deeply,
Saw the emptiness of all five skandhas
And sundered the bonds that caused him suffering.

Here then, Form is no other than emptiness, Emptiness no other than form. Form is only emptiness, Emptiness only form.
Feeling, thought, and choice, Consciousness itself,
Are the same as this.

All things are by nature void They are not born or destroyed
Nor are they stained or pure Nor do they wax or wane
So, in emptiness, no form,
No feeling, thought, or choice,
Nor is there consciousness.

No eye, ear, nose, tongue, body, mind;
No colour, sound, smell, taste, touch,
Or what the mind takes hold of,
Nor even act of sensing.
No ignorance or end of it,

Nor all that comes of ignorance; No withering, no death,
No end of them.
Nor is there pain, or cause of pain,
Or cease in pain, or noble path
To lead from pain;
Not even wisdom to attain! Attainment too is emptiness.
So know that the Bodhisattva Holding to nothing whatever,
But dwelling in Prajna wisdom, is freed of delusive hindrance,
Rid of the fear bred by it,
And reaches clearest Nirvana.

All Buddhas of past and present, Buddhas of future time,
Using this Prajna wisdom, come to full and perfect vision.
Hear then the great dharani, The radiant peerless mantra, The Prajnaparamita whose words allay all pain; Hear and believe its truth!
    Gate Gate Paragate Parasamgate Bodhi Svaha

***

Practical Tips on Stopping Smoking:

The prospect of my stopping smoking was almost unimaginable, since my very existence (age13-21) almost totally revolved around smoking. But I wasn't deterred and decided that if need be then I would just have to change the nature of my existence. Despite a relatively deprived childhood I didn't learn to smoke until I was thirteen and now having learned, I could see no reason why I couldn't just 'unlearn' the habit, by cutting back and persistently weaning myself off nicotine addiction.

The smoker's predicament is a puzzle, in that we would like to stop, but don't really want to. So it does help to carefully create a comprehensive plan of consistent action, as with persistence the results do follow. The smokers predicament can also be likened to the well-frog which wants to head for the ocean, but each time he tries to climb the wall of his slippery well, he just keeps slipping back, and instead of noticing that all around him are the implements for building a ladder, he or she just decides not to bother and instead adopts a face of bravado or complacency.

So if you want to stop, it can help to be clear, not so much how you became stuck, but just of the fact that one is stuck, caught in a web of addiction, and to climb out of that web, like any other addiction, it requires not just a methodical approach, but also the conviction that it is worth doing. Not that after you have stopped smoking that; you shall be in heaven all the time, or that the process is totally painless. What I am saying is that, if you can first create a reasonably happy, healthy and supportive basis to work from, then stopping smoking is possible for you to achieve and it is worth the effort.

Even though the first week of stopping may be a bit hard, and the first month a bit trying, by the second and third month you may well find yourself free of nicotine addiction, without any need for a smokescreen cushioning your experience and draining resources. Of course you may at times experience some un-satisfactoriness. Though this 'healthy' dissatisfaction can be a creative tension which may entice you to act in faith and to take refuge in that which can actually help you to grow and develop, such as friendship, yoga, tai-chi, swimming, walking, meditation, the arts, helping others etc. While smoking may have helped some people 'get by' in the short term, most smokers no longer really need to smoke. Often the pain, emptiness or peer pressure which may have led one to start, has long since passed. Continuing to smoke is like carrying redundant baggage which relates to the past and has become a habitual addiction, but which with the appropriate approach, one can be liberated from.

Giving up smoking, is helped by kindness towards oneself and gradually working more completely and truly with the nature of one's own existence! Although the going may not always be easy, you may well find the results of stopping smoking as invigorating as breathing in fresh air, after having years in a musty dungeon. Of course, even a dungeon becomes 'home' after a while, and it's quite natural that you should feel some trepidation and even homesickness at the prospect of leaving smoking behind, but you shouldn't worry. Giving up smoking is basically about 'taking up' a better way of life, and the initial inconvenience and discomfort soon passes. Yet at times you may have mixed feelings, when you notice people about you drawing those toxic fumes into their lungs. But don't be misled, if you look closer into their faces, then you'll see that smoking is one of life's small diseases, with large scale consequences.

The reason why I am treating such a small issue with seriousness; is because the tobacco industry does not have your best short- or long-term interests at heart. Perhaps I am influenced because my father died of lung cancer when I was sixteen; and also because a friend of mine, who died of cancer, expressed to me at the hospital when close to dying, how he felt the tobacco companies had sucked him in? Also I recall one of my schoolteachers went out to get a pack of cigarettes and got killed by a lorry. In my own case between ages thirteen and twenty-one I was totally addicted and exploited by tobacco companies. Thus I feel wary when I see human beings, young or older caught in the same trap. I think smokers and non-smokers alike need to be clear about the nature of smoking, and how it affects various aspects of ones being. Hopefully you shan't be in a hurry to start, but if you already have and now want to stop smoking, then really you just need to do three things:

1/ Convince yourself that you really do want to stop. Take whatever time is needed; to completely change and re-programme your whole attitude to smoking.

2/ Work out a reasonable course of action. Learn to roll your own cigarettes (then make them thinner and thinner, then add filters). Keep your tobacco in an unattractive container. Start to cut back both the amount, and times at which you allow yourself to smoke, i.e. none before breakfast; then none before lunch. Then don't allow yourself to smoke indoors, until eventually the addiction becomes more bother than its worth, and sooner or later....

3/ Take the plunge, and have your last cigarette. Having first cultivated various supportive practices; which can keep you occupied: psychologically, physically, and emotionally, especially for the first month, such as swimming; running, walking; dancing; singing; yoga, meditation and supportive friends. In this respect you may need to be your own best friend, and insist to yourself that you don't backslide, and if you do then stick to 'damage limitation' and maintain your course of action.

Try not to be pulled down. If you have bouts of anxiety, just muddle through one day at a time and very soon the worse passes. Set your 'quit date' at a carefully planned time, when you know you can be occupied, but not under too much stress. And when actually stopping, make use of supports available such as, nicotine gum, or patches, or whatever might be of help. Keep a sense of humour and enjoy your endeavours. The Rothmans (tobacco) empire wasn't built in a day. When a train is going fast in one direction, if there's not to be a derailment, first one needs to gently and firmly apply the brakes and then in due course you can build momentum in a new direction.

***

"Thus shall we look/think upon all this fleeting world: As a star at dawn, a bubble in a stream; A flash of lightening in a summer cloud, A flickering lamp, a phantom and a dream."

The Diamond Sutra
Clear Light Series Shambhala Berkeley 1969

***

Printed in Great Britain
by Amazon